PRINCIPAL
PHOTOGRAPHY

PRINCIPAL
PHOTOGRAPHY

Interviews with
Feature Film Cinematographers

Vincent LoBrutto

Westport, Connecticut
London

Library of Congress Cataloging-in-Publication Data

LoBrutto, Vincent.
  Principal photography : interviews with feature film
cinematographers / Vincent LoBrutto.
      p.   cm.
  Includes bibliographical references and index.
  ISBN 0–275–94954–0 (alk. paper).—ISBN 0–275–94955–9 (pbk. :
  alk. paper)
  1. Cinematographers—United States—Interviews.
2. Cinematography.   I. Title.
  TR849.A1L63   1999
  778.5'3'0922—dc21   98–46797

British Library Cataloguing in Publication Data is available.

Library of Congress Catalog Card Number: 98–46797
ISBN: 0–275–94954–0
      0–275–94955–9 (pbk.)

First published in 1999

Praeger Publishers, 88 Post Road West, Westport, CT 06881
An imprint of Greenwood Publishing Group, Inc.
www.praeger.com
Printed in the United States of America

The paper used in this book complies with the
Permanent Paper Standard issued by the National
Information Standards Organization (Z39.48–1984).

10 9 8 7 6 5 4 3 2 1

*To my uncle, Gino Damiani,
and my father, Anthony LoBrutto,
for sharing Kodachrome dreams
and to Phil Scandura, who taught me that
passion for the arts is contagious.*

Contents

Acknowledgments

Thanks to my parents, Rose and Anthony LoBrutto, for their support and for allowing me to borrow the family standard 8mm movie camera to discover my passion for filmmaking. From overseas and cross-country, my children, Rebecca and Alex Morrison, continue to inspire and motivate me with their own flights of discovery. I thank them for their unconditional support. My wife, Harriet Morrison, aided in research, tracked down subjects, chauffeured, acted as consigliere, and, as always, lent her fine hand to the manuscript. My respect and thanks also to Dr. Manhinderjit Singh for his wisdom.

I express my appreciation to the American Society of Cinematographers (ASC) for their assistance, especially Victor J. Kemper, former president, and Karin Sciaratta. *American Cinematographer Magazine* made an essential contribution to this project. I thank Stephen Pizzello, executive editor, David E. Williams, associate editor, Christopher Probst, technical editor, and George E. Turner, ASC's history maven, for their kindnesses and professionalism. My gratitude to the International Photographers Guild, Local 600, IATSE, particularly George Spiro Dibie, national president.

Thanks to Barbara Halperin of The Gersh Agency, Wayne Fitterman of United Talent Agency, Smith/Gosnell/Nicholson & Associates, and to Everett Aison for help in contacting interview subjects.

My appreciation to Sam Gill of The Margaret Herrick Library in Los Angeles, Kathy Bowles-Ruediger of the Steadicam Operators Association, the New York University Library, and the School of Visual Arts Library for research materials. I also thank Saal and Deborah Lesser for special support and use of their office facilities.

My heartfelt thanks to everyone at the School of Visual Arts, especially Reeves Lehmann, chairman of the Department of Film, Video, and Animation, and Sal Petrosino, director of operations, for their unconditional support and friendship. Thanks to all my colleagues and students for inspiration and encouragement. My appreciation to instructor and cinematographer Igor Sunara, who told me as I was about to embark on this project, "Everyone says, 'cinematography is about light.' Cinematography is not just about light. Cinematography is about *movement* and light."

Sincere thanks to the entire staff at Le Montrose Hotel in West Hollywood for their hospitality, especially John C. Douponce, general manager, and to John Sawyer for driving skills second only to Kerouac's Dean Moriarty.

I am most indebted to the thirteen cinematographers who took time out of their busy working and personal lives to allow me to learn firsthand about the art and craft of cinematography. This book would not exist without their knowledge and commitment.

I respectfully recognize the passing of Stanley Cortez, ASC, and Linwood G. Dunn, who were not able to share their extensive knowledge and experience about cinematography with me.

My sincere thanks to Michael Ballhaus, Ralf Bode, Fred Murphy, and Robert Richardson, who, by spending many hours sharing with me their passion, knowledge, and experience about cinematography, enriched my understanding and respect for this craft. Time, logistics, and space did not allow me to talk to cinematographer Philippe Rousselot; I thank him for his interest in this project.

I want to thank everyone at Praeger Publishers for their continued support and the care and attention they provide. Particular thanks go to this book's original editor, Nina Pearlstein, and to Elisabetta Linton, who faithfully saw the project to conclusion. The manuscript was given expert care by the production editor, Heidi Straight, and the copyeditor, Frances Lyon. My thanks to John Bailey for reviewing the glossary and for his expert comments.

Filmmaking is a collaborative process, as is a book of interviews; again my thanks to all who have contributed to this project.

Introduction

The purpose of this book is to allow cinematographers to speak in their own words about the art and craft of cinematography.

On the surface, cinematography is not hidden in the mysteries that surround the crafts of editing, production design, and film sound. The photography of a film is there for all to see. Audiences have been educated in interpreting photographic beauty and drama and in understanding that images come from light and shadow, but the layers of narrative and the atmospheric and psychological impact imparted by the camera suggest and demand a deeper understanding. This deeper awareness is informed by the role of the cinematographer—this most important cinematic collaborator.

Without light there would be no image, without movement there would be no motion pictures. Cinematography visually presents points of view and the verisimilitude and artificiality of movement for a narrative or psychological purpose. The camera records the force and subtleties of the actor's performance and places it in context within the physical environment of a scene. Cinematographers interpret a written screenplay in visual images. On the set, they translate the director's vision to a series of shots, long and short and in a catalogue of compositions, angles, and lens sizes so that these pieces can later come together as cinematic storytelling presented in images and sound.

The cinematographer reports to the director and, with the production designer, is a member of the triad who create the visual style or look of a film. The director of photography is the head of a department including the assistant cameramen, camera operator, electrician, gaffer, and grip.

During the studio system, cinematographers primarily worked in black-and-white and created the rules for Hollywood filmmaking that lasted until the mid-sixties. Conventions such as back light, which added pictorial beauty; diffusion, which eliminated flaws in the face; low angles, which created size and importance; and eyeline-matches, which linked the composition of one actor to another became the cinematic language filmmakers embraced to present their narratives.

The cinematographers in this volume helped rewrite the cinematic language used to make movies. During the sixties and seventies, cinematographers began utilizing natural light and more portable equipment to create contemporary images. Handheld camerawork, desaturated color, flares, the zoom lens, and the invention of the Steadicam transformed the formal aspects of the craft as filmmakers began creating a new kind of cinema which reflected our rapidly changing times and technology.

These interviews, conducted over a five-year period, represent a wide spectrum of artistic and technical accomplishments which embody cinematography in commercial and independent filmmaking. They are presented in an order that attempts to give a historical, developmental scope and to assist the reader in seeing the many connections among these diverse individuals and their work. Individual selected filmographies contain the majority of the subjects' feature film credits. They do not include uncredited work, additional photography, television, music video, and commercial credits. Cinematographers apply their craft in a multitude of ways. The discussions here on the art and craft of the feature film embrace the elements which face the cinematographer on all moving-image projects.

From the landmark single-shot films of the Lumiere brothers to the digital imagery of a cinema entering its second century, the camera has captivated our gift of vision. The true magic of cinematography is a synthesis of chemistry, science, and art that in combination bring images to the screen. Now, let us listen to the men and women who are both alchemists and artists—they make movies.

1

Conrad Hall

Conrad Hall, ASC, the son of James Norman Hall, coauthor of *Mutiny on the Bounty*, was born in idyllic Papeete, Tahiti. Inspired by the tradition of his literary father, Hall was first interested in becoming a writer, but while attending University of Southern California (USC) he switched from the journalism program to the cinema school. There he encountered Slavko Vorkapich, a pioneer in the use of montages during the Hollywood studio system, who headed the department and became Hall's principal mentor.

After graduating in 1949, Hall formed Canyon Films, a production company, with two colleagues from USC. When Canyon produced the feature film *Running Target*, the three partners drew lots to determine the producer, director, and cameraman—Hall cast his fate and became a cinematographer. The experience allowed him to enter the International Photographers Guild. Once in the union, Hall began to work as an assistant cameraman for many outstanding directors of photography, including Ted McCord, Lee Garmes, Burnett Guffey, Ernest Haller, Robert Surtees, and Floyd Crosby. After stepping up to camera operator on the TV series *Stoney Burke*, Conrad Hall became a director of photography, inaugurating a career that has influenced a generation of cinematographers.

Conrad Hall's distinctive photography on *The Professionals*, *In Cold Blood*, *Butch Cassidy and the Sundance Kid*, and *The Day of the Locust*, broke from the tradition of his Hollywood roots and helped to create a contemporary photographic aesthetic for a new kind of American movie forged in the sixties. Hall experimented with desaturated color, lens flares, overexposure, and many ground-breaking techniques to bring a pictorial realism to the stories he loved to tell with his camera. His work on John Huston's *Fat City* remains a landmark in cinematography, capturing the dim glint of a barroom glass and the glare of an oppressively hot afternoon which envelops the fate of a down-and-out boxer.

Conrad Hall has worked with many fine directors, including Richard Brooks, John Huston, John Boorman, Bob Rafelson, Michael Ritchie, and John Schlesinger. He has been nominated for an Academy Award eight times and won the Oscar for cinematography on *Butch Cassidy and the Sundance Kid*. In 1992, he received the ASC Lifetime Achievement Award. In 1995, Conrad Hall received the Lifetime Achievement Award at Camer-Image '95, the International Festival of Cinematography.

SELECTED FILMOGRAPHY

1958   *Edge of Fury* co-photography

1965   *The Wild Seed*
       *Morituri**

1966   *Incubus*
       Harper
       *The Professionals**

1967   *Divorce American Style*
       Cool Hand Luke
       *In Cold Blood**

1968   *Hell in the Pacific*

1969   *Butch Cassidy and the Sundance Kid***
       The Happy Ending
       Tell Them Willie Boy Is Here

1972   *Fat City*

1973   *Electra Glide in Blue*

1974   *Catch My Soul*

1975   *Smile*
       *The Day of the Locust**

1976   *Marathon Man*

1987   *Black Widow*

1988   *Tequila Sunrise**

1991   *Class Action*

1992   *Jennifer 8*

1993   *Searching for Bobby Fischer**

1994   *Love Affair*

1998   *Without Limits*
       *A Civil Action**

*Academy Award nomination for best achievement in cinematography.
**Academy Award for best achievement in cinematography.

Q: Storytelling has always been important to you as a filmmaker. Your father, James Norman Hall, was the coauthor of *Mutiny on the Bounty*. What influence did he have on you as an artist?

A: I inherited that sense of being a storyteller from my father. He used to tell me stories when I was a kid. I was fascinated. I'd be sitting on his lap and he read me "The Rime of the Ancient Mariner," all the way through. So I had a great respect for how I felt when he told me stories. I tried literature, but it's not my language. I realized there was another language; all you had to do was learn how to use it and you could be as fine a storyteller as my father was. I've just been spending my time learning how to use that language. I'm not an academic soul. I am a storyteller, and whether you use music, pictures, drawings, or literature to tell your story, we're all the same kind of people. We have to communicate. We have this sense of urgency to tell somebody a story that will make them feel one way or another. I had some good beginnings. I had Slavko Vorkapich and all those wonderful teachers at USC—people who gave us the principles with which to speak in this new cinematic language.

Q: When did you discover your medium was the camera and film?

A: It was the minute I shot film. In film school we had to shoot and edit a little story out of one hundred feet of 16mm film. I had a concept. I shot it, put it together, and looked at it on the screen coming at me bigger than life. It was very heady to feel that power so early on.

Q: You have been a major influence on a generation of contemporary cinematographers. Beginning in the sixties with films like *The Professionals, Cool Hand Luke, In Cold Blood, Butch Cassidy and the Sundance Kid* and in the seventies with *Fat City, The Day of the Locust,* and *Marathon Man*, your work helped to pioneer a new kind of cinematography employing desaturated color, natural light, and a sense of artistic realism in American filmmaking. What was your training and what motivated you to break the rules to discover your naturalistic and expressive approach to cinematography?

A: I studied with all the great cinematographers: Ted McCord, Ernie Haller, Robert Surtees, Lee Garmes, and dozens of others. They were the inventors of film. I started studying film at USC in 1947 and graduated in 1949. That's half a century from the beginning of film. So I was working with the first line after the inventors of cinema. They established rules and regulations that were awesome. They were also demanding. You had to conform to a rigorous standard. People weren't breaking many rules, they were all trying to make it look super-nice and not necessarily very real. I got my first chance at a union job from Leslie Stevens on the TV series *Stoney Burke* with Jack Lord, but he was having a hard time selling me as a cinematographer. So he made me a cameraman for the second unit and I hired Bill Fraker to be my operator. I made a deal with Ted McCord that he would shoot the first six episodes and then move on. Ted didn't want to do television, he did it for me.

If Ted didn't like the light when we were outside and dealing with close-ups, he would take all of the light off. Then he would bring in arcs and other lights and relight it to his satisfaction, which was totally unreal to me. One day he had an angina attack and they said, "Conrad, you've got to do it today." I thought, "What's wrong with the sun? Is there no way to make the sun acceptable other than take it away and make it what you want it to be?" So I just used the sun. I learned whether I liked or didn't like something from watching other filmmakers, but basically I learned from watching light and detail about life. Wherever I went, I was making mental notes. I have a computer right between my ears and it paid attention all the time.

You develop a visual language. I soon learned I could take flares and out-of-focus shots, which used to be called mistakes, and use them creatively to appropriately enhance and beautify the story. I observed naturalistic and realistic sensibilities and bit by bit I became more adept at breaking the rules and still telling the story well. When I'm into a story, I'm just pulling out from my experience. It doesn't mean that I don't love Gauguin, Rubens, Hopper, and all of the great artists, but I've never made a study of any kind. The story influences you more than the individuals you work with. The story is what takes the director to a different place.

The language of film is still not developed, it's only a hundred years old. We're still learning to speak. I've been paying good attention to it using the rules people before us discovered to be true. I learned them at USC from all the wonderful professors I had, but they didn't tell you how to tell a story—they just told you what would happen when you used these rules. They left them up to us to use them.

Q: Did you have to fight a lot of battles with producers and studio executives over your experiments in low-light photography and desaturated color?

A: You do get a lot of harassment from producers and studio heads who don't understand. On *Fat City* they said, "The photography is too dark, we can't see anything. What will the drive-ins do?" On *Tell Them Willie Boy Is Here*, I had to face the black suits at Universal who said, "It's too dark, we can't see Redford properly." So you have to sit there and suffer through the ignorance of their assessments. You know when it gets to the final print it will be wonderful. You have to tell them that. It causes a lot of strain, but I became strong as an operator working for Ted McCord. He didn't like to go to the dailies. He sent me to watch them on a Sam Goldwyn Jr. picture, *Huckleberry Finn.* The director, Michael Curtiz, would lay into Ted's work: "This photography stinks! We have to do this all over again." I thought, "Wow, it's wonderful!" I would have to fight with Michael Curtiz to defend Ted McCord. I developed a strength which I later used in my own work. Often, directors say the photography is wrong when really it's the acting. I was brave enough to tell them it was the acting, not the photography. We'd have shoot-outs, but I got it said, and more often than not we didn't reshoot. When you try to change the norm, you run into all kinds of people who have no sense of growth.

Q: Fat City visually captures the world of a down-and-out boxer played by Stacy Keach, with bleached out, overexposed exteriors which create the atmosphere of a hot, oppressive environment in contrast to the underlit bar interiors that allow the denizens to survive, lit by the dim glint off glasses and bottles of alcohol. Those sequences really capture the way people see in bars and create an ambience for the actors to reveal the psychological depths of their characters. How were they photographed?

A: What you have observed in bars is what I have observed in a bar. I tried to portray what occurred between Stacy Keach, the fighter, and those people in the bar. It was glaringly bright outside. The camera follows him through the bar door until he stops to adjust his vision to the darkness within—only the *sound* of voices and clinking glasses penetrate the frame beyond him. This was achieved by not lighting the interior. As the scene progresses, I wanted to elevate the visibility so it would be, in fact, what everybody experiences in a bar when they come from a bright outside. It's dark when you enter, blown out when you leave.

Q: Did you overexpose the exterior shots outside the bar?

A: Three stops. I worked right at the edge where the color would shift, but I didn't care if the color shifted—it might be interesting.

Q: How did you work with Director John Huston on *Fat City*?

A: Before the picture started, John Huston asked the production designer, Dick Sylbert (*Chinatown, Reds*), and myself what we thought the film was about. I said one thing and it wasn't that, Dick Sylbert said another thing and it wasn't that; Huston said, "It's about your life running down the sink without being able to put the plug in to stop it." Is there anything more visual than that? Huston established a way of approaching the story, which was to take all of the scenes and photograph them in one take from beginning to end, cut off the slates, hook them all together, and you'd have a movie. He suggested a few cutaways in order to shorten dialogue if the film was too long. So you'd do a great scene in one shot, telling the story visually as well as you could by approaching the actors with camera movement, choreography, and blocking and then you'd be done. Huston's idea was to make a film following real life without the use of cinematic technique.

Q: How did that concept affect the way you lit the film?

A: I lit it realistically, because I had to shoot in every direction. A room was lit with no lights inside, so I could point the camera in any direction and have it lit. I lit it from on top, through windows, and with the actual bulbs you saw burning in lamps. When we would go to work, John Huston would rehearse and block with the actors and then go play cards, backgammon, or shoot pool. I would get on the camera and try and figure out how to cover the scene in one shot—to be close on people when I felt it was important to be close on them, panning if there were three people talking. We didn't have video. Huston trusted me. He would then come in to see what I had done and used or altered it as he saw fit to do.

John Huston was a great filmmaker. He was one of the greatest storytellers. The only way you can stay alive in film is to be a contemporary soul, because it's a mass medium—it's about contemporary life. You're not talking to eighty-year-old people, your audience is young for the most part. You've got to learn if you put a baby on your lap and you tell it a story, and you put a ten-year-old on your lap and you tell it a story, you're going to do it differently. When John Huston was on *Fat City*, he stayed contemporary. John Huston stayed contemporary to his last dying breath. He was at the forefront of those who went on and succeeded, time, after time, after time.

Q: Morituri, produced in 1965, still has a very contemporary looking photographic style. What was the genesis of the visualization of the film?

A: I was working with Bernhard Wicki, a director who was a strong visualist. He had done books of still photography in Germany and a film called *The Bridge*. He was used to working in a documentary style. He loved the zoom lens. I learned from him how to use it so you didn't know it was a zoom lens. If you had been in a wide angle and somebody was coming toward you, you'd pan with their body as they got near you and zoom into their body—you didn't really notice the zoom because the body was filling the frame. Then, when that body clears the frame, you're at 100mm instead of 25mm and you don't know you've changed lenses. Techniques like that are very useful to help tell a story quickly without cutting.

I use the zoom lens quite a bit. I thought I used it fairly effectively in *Butch Cassidy and the Sundance Kid* to take it out of old-time Westerns and create new, modern visuals.

Q: The shots of the posse stalking Butch and Sundance were very effective in creating the visual impression that the posse was omnipresent. How were those shots accomplished?

A: I used telephoto lenses to frame long shots on the posse shots to create the feeling of being very close, and at the same time very far from them. It was a metaphor to contemporize the story of joblessness due to technological advancements—bank robbers being put out of business by modern-day superposses and invincible banks. The night scenes were shot day-for-night and then darkened in the lab. The actors playing the posse were carrying sun guns, which are very powerful lights. I said, "No matter which way your horse is going—left, right, or straight ahead—you always know where the camera is, so you just aim that light straight at me." It looked like they were carrying lanterns. It's quite effective. Any kind of lighting is problem solving—how to create the emotion to fit the story. Who are those guys? Where are they? So it was my language that visualized Bill Goldman's words. He was very generous in recognizing my language. It was a terrific script and he's a wonderful writer.

Q: The sequence with Paul Newman and Katherine Ross riding a bike to the song "Raindrops Keep Falling On My Head" is an early example of a music video. How did this come about?

A: It was kind of obligatory with studios at that time because the "Windows of Your Mind" sequence in *The Thomas Crown Affair*, which Haskell Wexler shot, had done very well. The scene in *Butch Cassidy and the Sundance Kid* was just a montage. We didn't know what kind of music, or song, or narration was going to go to it. The director, George Roy Hill, just said, "Here's Katherine Ross, here's Paul Newman and turned me and my camera loose with a long lens. We went out when the light was just beautiful and set up a visual involvement that quickly develops the nature of their romantic involvement. Then they came up with "Raindrops Keep Falling On My Head." Burt Bacharach won an Oscar for the song and one for the score.

Q: The shot which is photographed through a fence is particularly effective. The light is streaming in and you are not acutely aware the camera is moving past the slats of the fence.

A: Yes, that is pretty magical. When the lens is close to the fence, you have the illusion of not having the fence there at all. It's so good that they cut in the same shot twice. You don't realize it; you think it's a continuation. That's definitely a piece of visual eloquence.

Q: The color in *Butch Cassidy and the Sundance Kid* continued the experiments you conducted during the sixties. Did your work in this area grow out of a reaction to the use of overly saturated color during the studio era?

A: Yes, it grew out of the first early color processes like WarnerColor, which were very saturated. When color first came out, people wanted to see it colorful. I personally found the excess strength of color revolting. When I look out in the world, the colors with back light atmosphere and everything are all washed out. Desaturation was basically what I saw color to be. I strived for it and learned how to do it by overexposing. Then you could print it back to recoup the amount of color and hue you wanted.

It had to do with observing color beauty such as Sven Nykvist would produce in Ingmar Bergman films—this incredible light. We are making films here in California and we also have incredible light, but it's harsh light. We're in a desert. The fact that we made a garden of it doesn't mean the light has changed. We take that harsh light and use it appropriately. If you have to do a romantic story in Los Angeles, how do you do it? There's the idea of softening the light by overexposing it to the extent that it would affect the sharpness of the image. I sometimes overexpose it, 2, 2½, 3 stops and that would destroy some of the sharpness, so the edges between contrast would be softer. You learn how to make beauty out of harshness.

Q: You photographed *The Professionals*, *In Cold Blood*, and *The Happy Ending* for Director Richard Brooks. How did you first come to work with him?

A: There's a man I love—and I learned more about film from him than anyone that I've worked with. He was a great storyteller—not a contemporary storyteller, he was still stuck back in the forties and fifties. He was stuck in a good way. *The Professionals* was my first film with him. Tommy Shaw (assistant director and producer) and I had done *The Wild Seed* together. He worked with Huston and Brooks a lot and he brought me to Richard's attention. We had a shoot-out right to begin with. I put too much dust in a scene and you couldn't see anything. Richard was yelling and screaming at me. I thought to myself, "I don't really need this, I'll just take a walk on this one." I waited until we reshot it. Then I thought, "How are you ever going to learn anything if you give up before you have a chance to prove to him that you're worthy of being listened to?" So I decided to stay, and it was the best move of my life. He had a lot to offer filmically. We disagreed a lot, but you did what Richard wanted you to do. He was an auteur. You didn't help Richard as much as you would have liked. So whatever I got done, he could take a lot of credit for—like all of those amazing transitions in *In Cold Blood* that are so wonderful. That's all Richard.

Q: At the end of *In Cold Blood*, before the Robert Blake character is to be executed, he talks to a priest about his father. It is raining outside and it begins to look like tears are running down his face as he continues to tell the story rather dispassionately. How did this powerful cinematic effect come about?

A: Robert Blake rehearsed the whole scene in an empty set; it wasn't lit. When I was lighting the scene, I had a stand-in where Bobby rehearsed the scene. I wanted it dark inside. I kept the light pooled where the chaplin was sitting because he was reading from the Bible. We needed that light, but I kept it very localized; I didn't use it to light up the room. I had been to a real prison where I saw these strong lights outside in the prison yard—they're on all night long because they don't want anybody climbing walls. So I used a strong light from outside the window to come through. We had rain coming down as I was lighting. I had a little wind machine on, and it was taking some of the spray and creating a mist on the window. As the mist became heavier and heavier, it became heavy enough to form a drop which started running on the window. Instead of the drop running quickly, it moved slowly through the rest of the mist which hadn't formed droplets yet. It created these avenues for the bright light outside to come in. I saw the stand-in looking out the window and I said, "Richard, come and look at this," and he knew immediately what we had. I said, "Make sure Robert Blake stands there and doesn't move an inch." Richard told him to just take his place against the wall and say his lines. Robert Blake was very flat—all the emotion was in the visuals—but that counterpoint, that irony of remembering the father, is a very powerful moment of cinema. It was an accident I saw, and used, and capitalized on the moment. That's what I like to do. Often times the gaffer will turn on a light and I'll say, "Stop! Don't do anything else!" Did I put it on and point it in a certain direction?—not at all. It happened to hit, and I saw it. It's the same way when I'm making mental notes visualizing how light effects me emotionally. I make a note of it and then use it. I do it when I'm in the situation of lighting. Vittorio Storaro and Gordon Willis are real artists. They're people who plan. They're conceptualizers. I don't conceptualize, I extrapolate from other people's conceptual input—the actors, the production designer, the director, the writer, for sure—and all of that flows through my veins like blood. I pick out those things that are happening and then I throw in my own bit of invention, but it wasn't thought of a week before. I read the script the first time to get broad conceptual strokes, but I work out of the moment. I've got to wait for the actors to do something. They're too important to those characters to tell them where to stand or how to do something. I couldn't do that. I need to watch them, then maybe I can suggest. I'd rather watch them interpret the story, then I can quickly come up with ten different ways to see it—do it all in one shot, break it up in ten shots, close, far away, moving, nonmoving—all those things are happening organically with me and the story, the characters, the place, the light, the time of day, and everything else that's in motion. Everything is so interdependent. If you plan ahead, you're eliminating the possibility of finding the accident and using it. Actors capitalize on things all of the time: "Let me try it this way, c'mon let me try it that way." I seat myself in the story and the emotion of the characters. The rest of it is space you've got to fill up.

You have to make choices—hopefully good ones—because there are dozens of different ways of telling the story. There are a lot of rules that help govern that. When you do comedy, it's nice to have two people together so you can watch their interaction without having to cut from one person to the other. I look at a scene and say, "We don't want to break this up. We want to watch them do it," or, "This deserves studying each character and observing how they react to one another more specifically than maybe a two shot would." When I'm visualizing, I don't always think about the camera doing something other than watching actors behave and observing thoughtfully. That's a perfectly legitimate and an important thing for the camera to be doing—not showing itself off in any way by moving this, that, and the other way. All the decisions you have to make about when to move, how close, should you be emotional or should you be very quiet are instinctive with me. I just know when to move the camera and when not to move the camera.

Q: Electra Glide in Blue had a very striking visual style. The film was directed by James William Guerico, who at the time was the producer of the rock group Chicago. How did you work with this first-time director?

A: James Guerico grew up in Chicago, Illinois. His father was a projectionist. When James came out of school he would go to the theater, look at whatever was playing, and fall asleep in the back row until his father finished work. So this guy had seen an exorbitant amount of movies and knew a lot about movies. He liked detail, so we learned how to extrapolate the scene by picking up the elements of it and not going to the heart of the matter to begin with. It was shot anamorphic—it gave you a huge proscenium presence.

Q: The film is structured in a montage style. Were the shot units written into the film or were the scenes broken down on the set during the shooting?

A: Some of it was scripted, like: "He puts on his cuffs," "He puts on his shirt." The rest of the time it was choosing shots.

Q: What was your concept of the use of color in *Electra Glide in Blue*?

A: I don't try to stylize a film too much. *Electra Glide in Blue* is the strongest example of stylization because I was trying to sell James Guerico on pastels and he wanted rich color. I shot some tests. I was overexposing two or three stops. This was after *Butch Cassidy* and I was going in that direction more and more. I thought, "Oh boy, out here in the desert it would be wonderful." The tests came back, and you never saw a longer, sadder look on a director's face in your life. He didn't say anything. We said we'd meet for dinner. I got a telephone call from the production manager and he asked if I would stop by James Guerico's room before we met for dinner. He had put up a whole bunch of postcards on a bulletin board and said, "You know Conrad, I don't know about losing all of this beautiful color. This is what I like." Here were these shots with donkeys and cactus with blue skies so blue that you wanted to throw up. I said, "Why didn't you get Bill Clothier (*The Horse Soldiers, Cheyenne Autumn*)? He's the guy that does this kind of rich, beautiful, colorful, and sharp kind of photography. I like to interpret light, shadow, and sharpness to create different moods. I consider this false because this is not the way I see the desert." So we shot some more tests and I didn't overexpose too much. He got happier as soon as he saw some color come back in. I started the picture with a saturated look and then I weaned him away from that look by sneaking the colors into more of a pastel, desaturated sense which I felt the story belonged in. By the time we were in our second week, I was doing exactly what I wanted to do and he was liking it. But the film is much more saturated than I normally would have made it, because he liked it that way. So what could you do—I went with the director.

Q: The last scene in *Electra Glide in Blue* is a long take of the Robert Blake character after he is shot on the road. The camera, positioned on the back of a vehicle, pulls away from him in slow motion and seems to track back endlessly until the environment of the desert overwhelms the frame. How was this shot achieved?

A: That was a thousand feet. We started in slow motion at ninety-six frames a second. We had Bobby Blake falling and rolling after he was shot. He starts to sit up and then the camera pulls away to leave him sitting in the middle of the road. We drove back very fast shooting at ninety-six frames. The driver was in low gear and *whoosh* we were up to sixty miles an hour in seconds. We changed the film speed without changing the exposure. We were going faster and faster and it would get lighter, lighter, lighter, more surreal, mystical, and spiritual. Then a black crow flew across, and James William Guerico couldn't bear not to freeze frame, which I thought was very moving. It meant something to him. Crows are a very spiritually meaningful bird in Indian lore.

Q: The climax of *The Day of the Locust* takes place in the 1930s at a big nighttime Hollywood premiere. A riot breaks out and the expressionistic paintings of the central character, who is an art director, come to life. The contorted images and the presence of engulfing flames create the metaphor that the evils of Hollywood are bringing on the end of the world. How was this emotional and visually intense sequence created?

A: It took a couple of weeks to shoot. We started with 750 extras for quite a number of days, then we dropped to 500, to 250, to 125, then to practically nobody at the end. A lot of that sequence was storyboarded so the director, John Schlesinger, could visualize it. The idea of bringing the painting to life was thought up by John and the production designer, Richard MacDonald (*The Servant, Exorcist II: The Heretic, Altered States*). They got an acting company, built these masks, and got them to work together in a dance of horror. So all of that was planned, choreographed, and rehearsed. I put it in the context of shooting through heat waves. I put a lot of flames between. I made my own special effects, but it's all collaborative.

Q: The giant Klieg lights used during that period to advertise a movie premiere and bring awesome glamour to the event were a central image in the scene. How did you create this lighting effect?

A: We used real Klieg lights, which are huge arc lights six feet in diameter, on a trolley. When we first turned them on with a little smoke to pick up the beam, I couldn't do any lighting because they were so powerful. They would hit the ceiling, which was made of beautiful two by twelve and twenty by twenty wood and canvas, and it would bounce back and practically give me daylight. So poor Richard MacDonald had to paint all that beautiful wood black on top on all three stages so the black would not reflect back down again and ruin the lighting. That was quite an involved endeavor.

Q: You achieved many striking effects with those Klieg lights. At one point, the out-of-control mob carries the Donald Sutherland character past a blazing arc creating the symbolism of a crucifixion. The seminal image of the film is a shot of the crowd running past the scorching light pouring into the camera lens. How did these images come about?

A: I came up with the idea of carrying the man in front of the light and people running by. You get this strobelike effect of the shutter going by. Chaos is central to the story at that point. People are not moving like people move. The people running by and the body going up into the light is certainly the strongest metaphor of that chaos.

Q: What attracted you to photograph *Searching for Bobby Fischer*?

A: Searching for Bobby Fischer is a story that interests me. It is about a young genius. It's a wonderful, literate story. It's about competition and what coaches and parents do about it and the conflicts they're in. It's more about the game than being number one. It was a terribly important film in a world that is becoming nothing but competition.

At first I thought, "We want to be careful we don't do *Leave It to Beaver* here. We have to find a way not to end up being maudlin TV, and that's what made me go into magic naturalism. It's magical. Sometimes the light created is so strong the person doesn't seem to be walking on the floor—they seem to be floating on the floor because their legs are burnt out.

Q: The light and color in the boy's room created the magical fantasy relationship children share with their rooms.

A: Yes, it was a beautiful room. It was a real room. We didn't pull out walls. The camera had to be inside or shooting through the door or shooting through a window. There are contrapuntal visual ideas going on that create a sense of awe about him. I never would have gotten into any of this if it wasn't for the kid, Max Pomeranc, those eyes, and the way he behaved. He's a very special child.

Q: His eyes were extraordinary. Did you use eye lights to enhance the sense of wonder in his eyes?

A: No, there are no eye lights at all—he just has the light. He's got this intelligence. The director, Steve Zaillian, cast him because he actually could play chess. So how do you get the intelligence of a chess move in a person's eyes? On certain shots I would watch this kid looking around the board and you'd get the sense that he was just about to discover a move. Rather than wait to see that happen, I'd leave him with the camera. I tried to pick the moment when he was just about to do it. Then I would start slowly to get off of him, so you're leading the viewer to a different idea—a thought process he's having of what to do. Then, there's a flash of a hand coming through to the chess piece. As soon as this hand is flashing through, the camera is now whipping and probably not hitting exactly where the piece is—then catching up to it when he is banging it down. Then it stops in midair, looking at nothing, but slowly drifting back, arriving back at the eyes, again which is to give the idea the thought is developing again.

Q: Did you understand the significance of the moves? Do you play chess?

A: Not at all. I would say, "Which piece is he going to go for?" so I would get a focus, because I work very wide open. The lenses are 1.9 and everything is shot at 1.9. The focus on that is extraordinary.

Q: How did you communicate these complex visual ideas to the camera operator?

A: I operated myself. I'm pretty good, not mechanically as good as my operator, but he's watching on the video and he sees what I'm doing. Then he does it and it turns out even more wonderful, but it turns out the way I wanted it. None of it is rehearsed or choreographed, it's all photographing real life. Basically, the kid is playing chess and we're doing whatever we want to do with the camera. I take one character, my operator takes another character. I'll go sit on his camera and he'll sit on my camera and we'll pan back and forth as we want. If the director would like something different, he comes and communicates it to us, but basically it's just us playing with the camera.

I tried to make *Searching for Bobby Fischer* interesting the same way that basketball is interesting—it's fast break, slam dunk. I'm finding out more and more that the stories I choose have got to engage me on several levels. It's got to get to me on an emotional, and intellectual, and spiritual level. I've got to see something in the story I want to help communicate. So I'm careful about choosing stories now. Unless my heart, mind, and soul are engaged, I don't want to be involved. It's hard work to tell a story. It's not work at all once you have a wonderful story to tell. I call it play—I mean that in a very serious way. You can't wait to get to work. You can't wait to tell the story. You can't wait to see how it's received, because it's all about communicating and it's not just to tell yourself a story—it's to communicate what the writer put down into cinema.

Q: What legacy do you feel you and your work have left for other filmmakers?

A: Originality. A freedom of expression. The legacy I would like to be remembered by is the passion I gave to that endeavor, the joyous passion of being allowed to tell stories, being infused with the desire to communicate, and to make movies be more fun to do than anything else in life.

2

Gordon Willis

Gordon Willis, ASC, is the son of a make-up artist who worked at the East Coast studios of Warner Bros. during the depression. As a child, Willis took a turn at acting and experimented with stagecraft and still photography. During the Korean War, Willis enlisted in the air force and was assigned to the motion picture unit where he spent his four-year hitch making documentaries. In the mid–1950s, Gordon Willis began to work in the New York advertising industry as an assistant motion picture cameraman. He made the transition to cameraman, photographing documentaries and commercials, and took the leap into feature films in 1970 when he shot *End of the Road*, based on the John Barth novel and directed by New York film editor Aram Avakian.

Gordon Willis has a cinematic vision of the world and a photographic aesthetic that is rigorous. He has had an association with a series of directors with diverse personal styles, including Francis Ford Coppola, Robert Benton, James Bridges, Alan Pakula, Woody Allen, Richard Benjamin, and Herbert Ross, on projects as divergent as *The Godfather* and *Annie Hall*, but his imprint is indelible in each frame of the almost forty films he has presided over as director of photography.

Conrad Hall lovingly calls Willis "The Prince of Darkness," and he is on the top of every contemporary cinematographer's list of influential cameramen. A fiercely independent East Coast man, Gordon Willis fits the description of an auteur. His work on *The Godfather* trilogy and eight films for Woody Allen is legend. Gordon Willis has been nominated for two Academy Awards for *Zelig* and *The Godfather, Part III*. In 1995, he received the Lifetime Achievement Award from the American Society of Cinematography.

SELECTED FILMOGRAPHY

1970 *End of the Road*
      Loving
      The Landlord
      The People Next Door

1971 *Little Murders*
      Klute

1972 *Up the Sandbox*
      Bad Company
      The Godfather

1973 *The Paper Chase*

1974 *The Drowning Pool*
      The Parallax View

1975 *The Godfather, Part II*

1976 *All the President's Men*

1977 *Annie Hall*

1978 *9–30–55*
      Interiors
      Comes a Horseman

1979 *Manhattan*
      Windows

1980 *Stardust Memories*

1981 *Pennies From Heaven*

1982 *A Midsummer Night's Sex Comedy*

1983 *Zelig**

1984 *Broadway Danny Rose*

1985 *The Purple Rose of Cairo*
      Perfect!

1986 *The Money Pit*

1987 *The Pick-Up Artist*

1988 *Bright Lights, Big City*

1990 *The Godfather, Part III**
      Presumed Innocent

1993 *Malice*

1997 *The Devil's Own*

* Academy Award nomination for best achievement in cinematography.

Q: Over the course of your long career which covers many different directors and film genres, several visual characteristics become apparent. You often capture entire scenes in a single shot. Many times your camera shoots directly into a bright light source in the background and the characters in the foreground are dramatically modeled in shadow. You are known to work with extremely low light levels, and frequently position your camera directly in front of your subject as opposed to employing angles. Why do you apply this philosophy of cinematography so consistently to your work?

A: It essentially comes out of the way one sees and thinks. The trick is to take a sophisticated idea and reduce it to the simplest possible terms so it's accessible, not only visually but philosophically, which I think is the most beautiful. But what happens is people usually take a *simple* idea, blow it up to a very sophisticated form, and get it all bent out of shape because they feel compelled to *do* something. Something within the frame has to hold an audience glued to the screen. If that's not happening, you can turn everything upside down, sideways—it's not going to work. So I just approach films that way and most of the directors I've worked for feel the same way.

Q: So, rather than use a montage shooting style to move images editorially, you like the eye to move things around within the frame.

A: Actors move cameras. So you're watching the drama as opposed to watching the camera. I've always felt you couldn't really shoot well unless you know how to cut. A lot of people don't know how to cut, they overcover. They shoot a lot of film and end up with fifty pounds of ho hum that has to go into a five-pound bag. That lacks point of view. The editor makes the movie—maybe.

Q: Do editors tend to like your cinemagraphic style?

A: If I have any kind of rapport with the director, it cuts together when I shoot something. Editors tend to appreciate this. Whether they like the way it cuts together is something else, but it does cut together—not only mechanically and lightwise, but structurally. I have worked with directors who feel compelled to shoot everything ten ways. It tires the actors out, it tires everybody out—there are too many options.

Q: Your compositions are so carefully designed. You don't continue to move the camera over a couple of degrees and cover the same scene again and again.

A: I don't. If I have my way with a director, I won't do it. I'm very open to doing exactly what he or she wants to do. If the director's open, we'll discuss its pros and cons. Out of that comes a certain style of shooting, but it's how you apply it. I take one color of paint and apply it in a lot of different shades for a lot of different movies. Many times it's what you don't do that's more important than what you do.

Q: In your compositions, you make especially strong use of what classically has been called negative space, the area in between and around the focal point of a shot. Do you tend to think of this space as negative?

A: While I'm doing it, I don't perceive it as negative or positive, I just like it. One of my favorite things, especially in an anamorphic presentation, is to take advantage of the graphics like using small people in large spaces or taking a huge close-up and stuffing it way over to the right of the screen leaving all this space way over to the left. It doesn't matter whether it's a little intimate drama or a huge Western. Wide-screen photography is not applied simply because you're doing a big movie. It can be intimate. The negative and positive space aspect is not used enough. It's watching somebody come down a staircase way over to the right of the screen and crossing a lot of empty space to go make a cup of coffee over on the left side. That's fascinating to me because it places a person in an environment. Depending on the size you pick, it places somebody in a cozy environment or it places them in an environment which is hostile. There are many ways of dealing with it, depending on the frame size you pick and the lighting you choose, and also what the actors are saying or not saying. You can shoot it another way and pan the guy down the steps, and take him over to get a cup of coffee, and do inserts of all the cups. That doesn't really lead to anything, except many directors are so fearful of getting caught and not being able to cut out of, into, or around it. There are certain scenes where I will tell a director, "I don't think you have covered this enough because this scene runs too long." Well, it doesn't run too long in his mind at that moment, but I'll say, "Six months from now when you're cutting this together you're going to want to get out of here." I find myself talking certain directors into more coverage, not less, but at times it's the other way around. How it finally comes out on the screen refers to the form of shooting: how it's lit, the coverage, the size of the framing, whether it's close or not close, whether it's a long shot, or whether it's a moving shot that takes you around a room for ten minutes. It's what you choose that changes the structure of the movie—selectivity.

Q: How do you get so much clarity of detail in your full shots? The viewer doesn't feel the need to get any closer to the actor.

A: In some instances you can't see the actor well, but the emotional structure of the scene is working—there's great clarity in that. To perceive exactly what is happening without getting any closer—that's the trick. The director will say, "We can't shoot this one shot with him standing in the room with his back to us—I need coverage here!" We shoot it, and then we do all this coverage of him crying and retching. You see it in the screening room and the strongest cut is when you don't see this man's face at all. You just see him standing there and you know what's going on. It's emotionally more gratifying to watch it that way than to go in and undo everything with all these cuts. It's like watching somebody die in a movie. It's devastating to see this little figure fall down in a large field—it's relativity. I'm a great believer in big and small, light and dark. It's how you cut those images together. When people in a movie are talking to each other and the dialogue is good, it may be an interesting movie, but it may not move you to certain places you ought to go.

Q: What is the concept behind your tendency to have the camera shoot directly into a light source?

A: A window or a doorway is very good—there's a certain power in not actually completely seeing for a moment. In *Klute* with Jane Fonda there was a scene where she was up against a window. It was more interesting to play it that way and then at a given moment you go around and see her, rather than looking at her all the time. You can see into the image a little bit there; you've got to be careful of a dead silhouette because then it becomes a cutout—although I've done that and I like it. When you finally see her, what you want is a revelation.

Q: That scene is riveting. It allowed the viewer to witness the absolute fear of the Bree Daniels character as she is confronted with the killer. How did Jane Fonda feel about the low light approach you used?

A: When she first saw it in the screening room, she said, "You can't see it!" I said, "No, wait a minute." She was great, she realized we had done this in a certain way and we would get around to the other side. Emotionally it's very effective on the screen. Jane was wonderful in it.

Q: She was, and I don't think she ever looked better on-screen. There are no beauty shots in *Klute*, no eye lights, hair lights—all of those Hollywood star glamour techniques which had been used for decades were stripped away. How did you achieve your results?

A: It depends on where you put the key light. A key light is a primary light source, the one that gives you the primary exposure to do the scene. In traditional Hollywood moviemaking, the key light, whether it's from a window or a lamp, would be put on the star and be the primary source of light on the set. You can have three or four keys stretched around a big set. Even when something is not exposed or defined as a key light, there's always a key light in my mind.

Q: So the window in *Klute* was lit with little more than a key light to simulate the light coming through the window?

A: Yes, the primary light was a window, and that's what you use. There are other lamps used related to seeing in the shadows which you don't necessarily read on the screen, but they're there to do what's necessary. I'm not a great lover of back light. It's pleasing, it's very pretty to look at in conjunction with other things—a girl has pretty hair, you get a back light. It came out of the early days of black-and-white photography in order to separate actors from the background, but then it became an aesthetic tool. I never really used it in black-and-white either. When you're shooting in black-and-white you're working in values. You're working in black, white, and grays. When you separate someone from a background you're doing it in values, darker background, lighter foreground, or vice versa—I prefer that. Back light is glitzy and high-tech, people love it. They use it on television. It's pretty. Every time I set a back light I hate it. I turn it off unless it's the sole source of illumination, like when an actor moves from a front light into a back light and that's all there is—that's kind of interesting.

Q: The window scene in *Klute* is lit in natural back light.

A: Right, you just use enough fill light so you can just barely see into their faces—sometimes.

Q: Do you tend to take different lighting approaches to each actor in a film?

A: Yes, what you really want to do is to photograph the movie, but you have to be cognizant of the people that are in it or you're not doing your job properly. There are some people where you could put up a light and no matter what, they look great. On *Klute* I was always cognizant of where to put the key light with Jane Fonda and where to put it with Donald Sutherland. In some situations you have to make changes so that they look better. Jane was easy because she was beautiful. All actors worry how they look. There are times where they don't care whether they look good or not, depending on what the scene is. If you really have an outstanding looking girl in a movie, it makes life a lot easier because it doesn't matter where you put the key light. No matter what happens, they look terrific, but there are others where you are spending a lot of time. When the movie becomes subservient to the lighting of the star, you have lost the battle. Then you're going to hurt the movie because every decision you make about lighting is predicated on what she or he is going to look like.

Q: You photographed Barbra Streisand for *Up the Sandbox* after she had worked with veteran Hollywood cameraman Harry Stradling on many pictures. What was it like to work with Streisand?

A: I had a very good time with her. She's very bright. Harry Stradling put cross hairs in front of a woman's face and *bang*, that's where the light went.

Barbra would prefer the key light right between her eyes, but you can't always get it that way. Harry Stradling lit a movie in a certain way—I don't light that way. If I start lighting actors one way and the movie another it looks stupid. We worked it out very well. I thought Barbra looked great and she was helpful. She will work with you.

Q: Throughout your career you have captured the many looks of New York City. How would you describe the New York presented in *Klute*?

A: The idea was to compress this world Jane Fonda was living in so it was more claustrophobic and had an underground feeling. The villain is like the mad scientist living on the top of this glacier-like building, looking down on all the rest of Manhattan.

Q: When you are lighting a shot, how do you know how it is going to record on film?

A: The biggest danger is doing anything by habit. Decide in your mind what you want it to look like on the screen. From a technical point of view, you have to know what to do in order to make it look like that because your eye is selective—film isn't. When you look at it by eye while you're photographing, you won't see what you're going to get in the screening room because exposure of the film you are using is in direct proportion to what you want to see on the screen. You have to know how to do that predicated on how much underexposure, how much overexposure, how much normal exposure. Most art, if you want to call film an art, comes out of craft. A lot of people deny that fact in this business.

Q: Do you use filters?

A: I do, but it's like the rest of the philosophy, they're in there when I need to do something, but they're integrated with what's happening on the screen. I've used a lot of filters, you're just not aware of them when you're sitting there watching the film.

Q: Is that because you use filters to correct something that needs to be corrected?

A: That's about it. I use a lot of graduates, diffusers, and low cons when I'm shooting, but they're not as defined as the way some other people use them. Often you want to control exposures in skies, even inside rooms. Graduates are neutral-density filters which control exposure, but they're graded. The English call them graders and they're from the top to the bottom. There's more at the top and less at the bottom, so you can place them to control certain exposures, like in a sky. They are technically applicable and very fast, rather than trying to light something to reduce the amount of light. You can use them inside on a window. Occasionally, I'll put color in them, but in general terms I don't. I'm not in favor of a lot of smoke either; a lot of cameramen use smoke. Sometimes it looks like 911. You say, "There's so much smoke. I can't see anybody in the backgrounds anymore!" Atmosphere is very pretty, a limited use here and there is fine, but the actors and the crew are sucking on this smoke for four months. It also holds you up.

Q: You seem to achieve diffusion primarily through lighting and lenses.

A: Lenses, lighting—selectivity. In the movies, somebody uses one thing, it breaks out like the plague. I used a brassy yellow in the three *Godfather* films. That color broke out like the plague on all these period movies. It looked dumb because in the *Godfather* films that was only one element that was woven into the lighting, the shot structure, the wardrobe, and the sets. People called up and said, "We want this to look like *The Godfather*—now what do I do?" It's really a culmination. It's everything: art direction, lighting, acting, it's selectivity—it's a whole bouillabaisse.

Q: What is your photographic approach to a period movie?

A: Period movies are a tableau form of filmmaking. They are like paintings. If you're going to move, don't move with a zoom lens. It instantly lifts you right out of the movie because it's such a contemporary, mechanical item. It's not right for the turn of the century. Tracking can work. You lay it in at the right level and you're not really aware of it. On a period movie, you should put distance between you and the audience visually. They usually do this great wardrobe job on period movies and everybody shows up with their pretty cars or horses and all the props are great. Then, along comes some guy who's going to photograph this on the very latest Eastman stock and with the very sharpest lenses and when he's done, the visual is so defined, it's so immediate, it looks like it came out of the one-hour photo service. The visual is so contemporary it looks like a party with everybody dressed up walking around in period clothes; it does not put you back to where it belongs.

Q: *The Godfather*, directed by Francis Ford Coppola, is a period film which really captures the 1940s. What was your visual approach to the period?

A: The idea was, I made the wedding exteriors look like a 1942 Kodachrome.

Q: How did you accomplish that?

A: The film stock that was used and the choice of exposure.

Q: Did you have a tendency to overexpose the exterior shots of the wedding?

A: Right, what's going on inside being dark, while the wedding is going on outside.

Q: Was the wedding covered with multiple cameras?

A: Yes, some of it was. It went on for about a week. I felt most of it needed sun. This extraordinary Italian wedding was going on outside, then inside the house in the dark, the Don was conducting his usual business which is on the dark side of life. So it took a very simple idea, light and dark, and it made good cutting relativity-wise. It's a startling revelation in the opening when you're watching the Don. We hold back a little and then finally, *bang*, we cut around and Brando is sitting there with his cat.

Q: How did the studio react to the lighting approach on *The Godfather*?

A: Paramount was giving Francis a terrible time while he was shooting the movie. They almost fired him, and I don't think they were too happy with some of the things I was doing. I was being difficult about the way a lot of things should be. Francis wanted to go to Sicily, and we didn't get the money until way, way into the movie because the studio wasn't sure. One day they suddenly woke up and realized they didn't have some exploitation movie on their hands—that's what they wanted to make. When they suddenly realized, "Wait a minute, this is working out a little bit better than we thought," that's when they gave Francis permission to go over to Sicily.

Q: Was Rembrandt a specific influence for your work on *The Godfather*?

A: No, not at all. I like Rembrandt, but more people refer to what I do as Rembrandt than I refer to Rembrandt. It's just because Rembrandt painted in those tones. I have other painters who are more favorable in my mind. I like Sargent and Vermeer, but I don't really relate that to what I'm doing. A lot of directors like to bring pictures to show you. I can understand, it's hard for them to relate to anything because they don't shoot—they direct. The only thing I relate to in art is great light and beautiful imagery. I only specifically tried to reproduce a painting once. On *Pennies From Heaven*, I had to reproduce a couple of Edward Hopper paintings, *Nighthawks* and one other, and make them come to life, but beyond that, no.

Q: Hopper's use of light lends itself to cinematography.

A: Yes, it does. Hopper, however, and a lot of artists, paint in two or three different perspectives, so it's very difficult to totally reproduce the painting because the perspectives are different. He might paint one perspective in the foreground and an entirely different perspective in the background and something else in the middle. It all goes together nicely as a painting, but as I discovered when I was doing it, it's definitely different.

Q: The daylight in Don Corleone's office in *The Godfather* streaks through slated wooden blinds on the windows. How did you achieve this effect?

A: That was shot in the studio, and it's lit from the outside through tracing paper on the windows. That same kind of feeling happens again in the boathouse in Lake Tahoe in *The Godfather, Part II.*

Q: What role did the cinematography play in aging Marlon Brando for *The Godfather*?

A: Brando came up with his make-up. At that time, Marlon was a young man, so you have to light old-age make-up in a manner where someone looks old. It was properly applied, but overhead lighting helped make it look right and also to make the movie look right. People say, "You couldn't see his eyes." Well, you weren't supposed to see his eyes. You did finally see his eyes a lot. As I would watch Brando talk, my thought was, "I don't want people to see what he's thinking right now, they will in a minute." Brando understood all of this.

Q: What about Al Pacino's eyes in *The Godfather, Part II*?

A: The whole idea was to transpose Brando and Pacino in the boathouse scenes in *Part II*.

Q: In that scene, Pacino's eyes are in shadow.

A: Right, he becomes his dad.

Q: How many cameras were used to film Sonny's assassination scene?

A: About six. There were different cuts involved for Jimmy Caan, in the car and when he finally got out of the car. We had coverage that had to be done. You have the intro where Jimmy pulls up and then the shooting starts. The tollbooth is being shot at, there are cuts of the windows breaking, and you had long shots. You had to look at all the schematics where the effects people had laid all of their explosives to know how to lay shots down. It was a lot of shooting in a very short period of time. So you get the most cameras set in the right positions to cover Sonny being shot, and then you have to re-set everything to get closer cuts of the shooting because anything really close is in the way of the long shots.

Q: Did you use different focal length lenses on the six cameras to get different size shots?

A: We did, but within reason. You don't want to set long shots and then put on 300mm lenses because it will look that way.

Q: Did you use reflectors to control the natural light for the exteriors on *The Godfather*?

A: I almost never use reflectors; if I do anything, I'll just use a piece of bead board or a white card and bounce that, but on a long scene, usually I'll just set a light. No, there wasn't really a lot of light used anytime.

Q: In the scene when Michael talks to his bodyguard who is eating lunch in the barn, the door is open, it is very sunny outside, and the interior of the barn is illuminated by a single naked light bulb. Pacino is in shadow because the sun is behind him, but clearly we can see his face by the light falling on him from the bulb. Normally, to get a good exposure for the interior, the exterior would be burnt out. How did you capture this shot?

A: The film will perform based on what you want to see—overexposure and underexposure of what they technically call the shoulder and toe of the film. If you understand how far you can go with both ends and still get visual registration on the screen, then you can do it. So you boost or reduce light depending on how much of the spectrum you want to watch from top to bottom. You don't want to overexpose completely on the outside. Then you have to set an appropriate exposure on the inside. You may want the inside to feel like it's underexposed. As long as you understand what the film can do after you reach the point of what you want to do when you're lighting—it's math. In order to visualize what it is you have in mind, you have to have the technical capability in your head to make it work.

Q: Rather than approaching a scene with a formulaic lighting plan, as was often practiced during the Hollywood studio era, you appear to rely on your own visual perceptions.

A: The studio lighting system in the thirties and forties really was beautiful to look at. A lot of that style came from the fact that cinematographers had to deliver a certain persona of movie to audiences. Actors and actresses had to look a certain way. Warner Bros. and MGM had their own look and their own sound—that's what they delivered.

Today, people go on location and bring their staff. The staff sets about to redesign, redress, and fix the whole location. You say, "Why are we here?" There's no point being there if you go in and redo the whole place. The trick is, how do we reproduce this? You either take advantage of what's there or you shouldn't be there.

Q: You really came into the business at a time when the studio system had just been dismantled. *The Godfather* set a standard that each film had to have its own look.

A: The Godfather changed moviemaking completely. The whole approach was different. People saw visuals in *The Godfather* that made it possible to do things today they were never allowed to do. Now, I look at movies I thought were well done and I think the lighting is so bad, a very formulaic, awful lighting. I'm really glad that part's changed.

Q: What was your approach to the Sicilian sequences in *The Godfather*?

A: To photograph the scenes in this special, beautiful, strange, magical, fairy-tale gangster place everybody's heard about. Francis and I discussed the premise. I said, "This place should be sunny Sicily, it should have a dimension." So everything selected there on *The Godfather* and *The Godfather, Part II* was done with this premise. If you shoot with that in mind, you make decisions that are pertinent. I had Technicolor Rome develop this material. The look of that laboratory is different than the Technicolor laboratory here. We went to Sicily on both movies at the end of the movie, only on *Part II* we had been shooting for almost a year, so it was exhausting.

Sunny Sicily. Well, Sicily is not sunny all the time, any more than any other place. We went to Sicily and the weather was so bad. It was like boras and storms blowing in from Africa. We sat there for a whole week. Finally, Francis got fed up. We packed up and went back to the United States. That meant packing the whole company. Trucks had to be sent back to Rome. Everybody had to get on planes and fly back. So we waited for the weather to clear, then we flew back to Sicily and started shooting again. I held out for sun in a lot of places in those movies—all that beautiful period material on the steps in Sicily where Bobby De Niro stabs the old Don needed sun. The Cuba sequences were shot in the Dominican Republic, which was another place I held out for sun. The weather was terrible a lot of the time. You were trying to get the right thing—you do the right thing.

Q: Production Designer Dean Tavoularis (*Apocalypse Now*, *Tucker*) and his art department did an amazing job in transforming New York's Lower East Side into turn-of-the-century Little Italy for *The Godfather, Part II*. What was the contribution of the cinematography in achieving this period look?

A: I perceive period in a flatter light. Francis kept saying when it's in the sun it looks more period. Although there were some pieces that were in the sun, most of it was done in the shade because the values were better. There was not as much light in the period interiors. People go through books and look at photographs of Ellis Island and that's their only real reference point. If you combine your reference point with what you feel, many times you come up with something which seems real. You've embellished it to make people perceive it as real—it's not real at all.

Q: The shots on the boat carrying the young Vito Corleone as it approaches Ellis Island are beautiful and poetic. The light has a whited-out quality. The sequence appears to have been photographed in a fog.

A: They're all flat, there's no sun. There's the basic lack of contrast. It's a softer imagery and the light is flared. The imagery is softer and not as defined, but quite beautiful.

Q: How did you accomplish the shot of young Vito on the boat where we can see the reflection of the Statue of Liberty on him in the glass porthole?

A: Dean Tavoularis was kind of stumped with that. He said, "The Statue of Liberty?" I said, "Just do a big, black-and-white photo blow-up of it.

We'll put it outside the window and I'll do something with it." It was done in Rome.

Q: Where did you shoot the interior of Ellis Island?

A: That was a fish market over in Trieste. The apartment house scenes were done in Rome. Part of it was done in Los Angeles, part of it was done in New York—it was shot all over the place. The scenes with De Niro on the rooftops were stretched over a long period of time because the weather wasn't good. The sun was out and we had to match the other shots.

Q: The shots on the roof were very effective. Your compositions were straight on, framing De Niro in profile as he ran from roof to roof.

A: Right, it's a tableau form.

Q: What do you mean by a tableau form?

A: It is more of a proscenium style—theater-like.

Q: Where did you shoot the scenes in *The Godfather, Part III* which are supposed to take place in the Vatican?

A: There's another good use of people in space. That was done in a castle, north of Rome. It was a very old, big place with a moat around it. That place is high, from the windows to the moat on the ground. To put in the lighting, we had to scaffold the whole side of this castle. The lights were about three to five meters outside the window.

Q: What was the challenge filming the newsroom studio set in *All the President's Men*?

A: Reproducing the real newsroom. There were eight- or nine-foot ceilings—all fluorescents.

Q: Were they standard fluorescent tubes?

A: Yes, the tubes were Cool Whites. The green was removed in the printing. You have fluorescents now that burn at the Kelvin the film is designed for. At that point, they weren't available. If, however, you are going to shoot a scene in a huge supermarket, you are better off to just match up two or three units on the floor for fill light with the same fluorescents that are there, then print the green out in the laboratory, because that's a lot of fluorescents to change. It's labor intensive, it doesn't pay—just shoot it and correct it in the lab.

Q: In *All the President's Men* there is a great overhead back-tracking shot on Woodward and Bernstein in the library as they research the Watergate case. It is the kind of visual storytelling which makes you feel the camera is revealing something emotionally. In the sequence, it looks like the editor divided the shot into three segments linked by dissolves. Was that originally a continuous shot?

A: Yes, it was one continuous shot. The idea was, Woodward and Bernstein were looking for "a needle in a haystack." There was no way to get a crane in the Library of Congress. Also there was no way to get high enough with a crane. We put a winch and a cable in the top of the Library of Congress, and that winch actually pulled the camera up. It was done with an Arriflex and some stabilizers to keep it from shaking. That was done before we had video assist. I figured out on paper how much we'd see at a given distance. The grips had a guide line to guide it visually, because it had to go up more or less at an angle. My assistant built a radio-controlled focus system.

Q: You worked with Production Designer George Jenkins on several Alan Pakula films and on *The Paper Chase*, which was directed by James Bridges. How did you collaborate with Jenkins?

A: George comes from the old school, which is very helpful when you're shooting certain kinds of movies because he understands how things have to be done in order to shoot properly. Certain sets have to be on a platform, spaces have to be between sets and walls, certain things have to be done in glass and so on. George is a very good reproducer. He reproduced the Harvard Law School in *The Paper Chase* beautifully, and he reproduced the newsroom in *All the President's Men*—that was a huge set. It took up two stages at Warner's—they took down the walls between two stages.

Q: Was any of *The Paper Chase* actually shot at Harvard?

A: Very little, just the exterior of Harvard Yard, but not the interiors. They were done on stages up in Toronto. George did a lovely job. He used to get disturbed because if I didn't like something, I just wouldn't light it.

Q: The alteration of compositional size was very effective in *The Paper Chase*.

A: That one was very well thought out. The whole front end of that movie with John Houseman and Timothy Bottoms related to who had command of the situation. We used huge close-ups of John, and demeaning shots of Timothy. Then, as the movie goes along and Timothy begins to get on top of it, you'll notice the shot sizes begin to diminish on John and begin to get a little bit bigger on Timothy—until finally they're equal partners shooting back and forth. It works from an audience point of view—it takes over. I recommended that movie be shot in anamorphic. I felt it would play better because of the schoolroom and the graphics in the film.

Q: The visual style of Woody Allen's films changed dramatically with *Annie Hall*. How did you get the assignment to photograph this landmark film?

A: He called me up. I went and read the script in his apartment—he wouldn't let it out. I was sitting there all by myself, laughing. I got the job and shot movies for him for ten years, a very good group of movies. *Zelig* and *The Purple Rose of Cairo* were both interesting technically, it was not easy to do either one of them.

Q: Do you think you helped contribute to the visual style that Woody Allen is now known for?

A: In some ways, but it can happen related to writing and dealing with actors. You're always doing something which is predicated on what the director will finally want to execute. Sometimes you can bring more to it when you're together for a long time. Not a lot has to be said, and sometimes it's better that way. It's *their* movie, but there's an overlapping related to structure and concept.

Q: A film like *The Panic in Needle Park*, photographed by Adam Holender, takes place on the fashionable Upper West Side, as does *Manhattan*, but Holender makes it look like a war zone.

A: Right, because you bend it another way with your point of view. It's what you choose to show. We both perceived Woody's New York as this wonderful, unthreatening city. It's a comforting, wonderful place, and then you can turn around and do a claustrophobic, uncomfortable, threatening movie. It's all how you choose to do it.

Q: How would you define the photographic look you brought to *Manhattan*?

A: Manhattan is what I call romantic reality.

Q: The Purple Rose of Cairo must have been a tremendous technical challenge.

A: When you look at it on the screen, it looks very simple, but actually it was very difficult because the movie within the movie had to be shot first. We shot the interior in an old movie theater in Brooklyn. The actors up on the screen had to talk to live actors down in the audience—all the eyelines had to match. I had to plot on a piece of paper where they were in the audience. The first thing I discovered was the eyelines change, just like moving a camera around on a set with an actor. You have to think of it in terms of photographing a live actor on the stage, only we can't move the actor, we have to move the camera to make the eyeline shift. If you stood in the middle of the theater, the actor was looking where he was supposed to, but maybe if you moved to the right or the left, the eyeline from the actor up on the screen changed. So if he had to look from left to right to somebody in the audience, that had to happen, but you may be in a different place, more to the left, more to the right to make it work. It always ended up in the right position, but not by the original design. I had to keep moving the camera because the eyeline doesn't automatically fall in. You think, "It's on the screen, the eyeline is fixed now." It's not fixed! The minute you move the camera in the theater, the eyeline of the person who is talking to somebody on the screen changes. In the wide shots, we were photographing the people in the theater and the actors on the screen all live at the same time using front interlock projection of the movie on screen. No matte shots. It was time-consuming, but it finally became entertaining and effective.

Q: So the editor, Susan E. Morse, had to cut all the sequences in the black-and-white film first.

A: Yes. I photographed the black-and-white first. She had to cut everything, then it was projected on the screen with the audience in the theater and I photographed it again—this time in color.

Q: What was the concept behind the warm colors inside the movie theater?

A: If you were to take the premise of somebody going to the movies to escape the depression, what you want to do is shoot it in black-and-white and have them walk into a color world. Here we had a color movie, and she was walking into a black-and-white world. What you have to do is make this color movie work so when she finally walked into the theater it was something special to watch this black-and-white movie. It had to be a warm, comforting place.

The interior of the theater was tricky to light because I had front projection, which has to be exposed properly, and then I had little glowing lights in the theater, which has to be done properly. Even though it's a fantasy, you've got to believe it. The film on the screen had to look like 1930s' black-and-white. *Zelig* is done very well, but a lot of it is not exactly the way it was, it's what you perceived it was. It's the same in the black-and-white movie in *The Purple Rose of Cairo.* What is reality? It's what you perceive reality to be!

Q: How do you achieve that?

A: I have to go with what I think is working. As in *Zelig*—does this feel like Hitler in the 1930s? I'm using a reference all the time, but many times you have to bend the reference in order to make it work, so it's not exactly the same. If you go to the heart of the imagery used in *Zelig*, the original newsreels, you'll find they were a lot better than that.

Q: You denigrated the quality of it?

A: Right, but in many cases if I made it better than that, you would not perceive it correctly. In *The Purple Rose of Cairo*, the period photography on the screen is a little bit over the top. It's a little bit bigger-than-life, it's got more air in it than it should have in order to make it work in these particular circumstances.

Q: Because of the nature of *Zelig*, was it scheduled differently than an average movie?

A: Yes, I had to pick out footage after Woody had chosen what he wanted to use. You have to photograph shots like Woody with Hitler so it would intercut. The lighting has to be the same when you photograph it as it was with the Hitler material. To make it match, you had to know what was going to happen to it by the time you've finished duping it. That was a lot of work.

Q: In the Woody Allen movies you photographed, there are many examples of scenes where the camera is shooting in an extreme long shot. In the opening of *Annie Hall*, there's a shot of Woody Allen and Tony Roberts walking where the camera is so far away we can barely see them. We hear them in close-up perspective, but we don't see them until they walk into the camera. It this something you contributed?

A: It's something I talked Woody into. I said, "You can start talking way up there—we don't see anything. You can materialize, and then we'll start dollying with you."

Q: Another technique often utilized in the Woody Allen films you photographed is characters will walk out of a shot and continue to talk as the camera holds on the empty frame.

A: Right. Woody would say, "But they won't see me," and I said, "But they'll hear you, and then *boom*—you come back in again." It's got a certain pizazz to it, it's got a kick in the pants that's very funny.

Q: What is the role of the camera operator and the assistant cameraman?

A: Operators and the assistant cameraman work for the cameraman. The camera operator physically executes the shot at the level its been discussed. You lay it down, you rehearse, and then you shoot it. I lay the shot out with a director and the camera operator executes the shot at the level its laid out. He has to keep his eye on everything so he can properly communicate what's happening. Video assist has been helpful. Although I can really stand in back of the magazine and see whether the operator is doing the right thing, it takes the guesswork out of what's really going on from an operating point of view. It won't take the guesswork out of actors performing, and many directors still make the same mistake—they watch the monitor. You really can't see what's going on. The next day in the screening room, every performance they thought was great on the monitor won't be good, and every one they thought was bad will be good. It is entirely different performance-wise on the screen. That's why cutting on videotape is not a good idea, because you've got to constantly relate to it up on the screen. You've got to take it in and look at it on the screen—it's different!

A very good operator is helpful because they've got to see and relay information. They're the closest person to communicate with the actors. Some actors won't hit their mark properly; the camera operator has got to communicate that he or she missed it. So it's an orchestration of people, getting the right information—without stepping on toes.

Q: I would think the camera operator has to be able to anticipate the movements of an actor. There isn't a lot of camera movement in *The Parallax View*, but the camera often follows Warren Beatty, who is constantly moving.

A: Yes, you really have to anticipate to follow Warren, because most of the time he's not doing the same thing twice. It's like playing the piano—as an operator, you don't really think about whether you're going to turn the wheel to go this way or that way, you just go. You have to be good technically, but you also have to be good in explaining to some actors that this is okay, this is not okay.

I was an assistant cameraman for many years. The assistant has got one of the worst jobs on the set because he's responsible for all the camera equipment, all of the gear, all of the mechanics of keeping it running, all the mechanics of film changing, loading, and the filters. Everything happens very quickly. I may ask for a filter, or you might make changes at the last minute. The assistant has got to be ready. They've got to have all of that at their fingertips. They must have a lot of technical information when you ask him for it. The focus puller is the first assistant, and then there's a second assistant who does the slate and loads magazines. It's a chain, and a good second assistant cameraman is very important to a first because they keep all the mags and all the paperwork. They keep the running time on scenes because you want to see whether you can get another take on a magazine, you don't want to cut it too short. The better an assistant is, the better it is for actors and certain shots because they won't miss focus. There are some assistants who are remarkable the way they can pull focus, others are not so good—it's a tough job.

A good camera operator is very important. There are cameramen in this country and in Europe who like to operate at the same time as they are acting as director of photography. Operating for the director of photography is a kind of disease because you want to shoot it the way you picture it, but then you never want to give that up. When you're operating, it's very difficult to understand what's happening with lighting. If you are completely imbedded in operating, you're unable to watch what the actors are doing in the structure they are supposed to be doing it in.

Q: So you'd rather stand with the director and watch the scene. Do you look at the video assist during a take?

A: I'll watch it for the operating. I can split my vision and look over, then I can see whether the operating is correct—but I can't deal with operating and lighting a movie. Sometimes I'll say, "Do you mind if I make a shot because I want to see something?" I'm a good operator, but I couldn't possibly deal with everything I deal with and do that too—I find it too tiring.

Q: What are the different aspect ratios available to the director of photography, and what affect do their dimensions have on the viewer?

A: In their heyday, the principal form of photographing and presenting a movie was in 1.33:1, which is a square format. If you look at old movies on television, you're seeing them closer to what they were on the screen back in the thirties, forties, and fifties. Television cuts some of the sides and the tops off, but it's still square. When television started to come in, the movies began fighting for their life. A lot of other formats began to pop up: Vistavision, CinemaScope, and Panavision. Pictures like *The Robe* helped to introduce CinemaScope. Then they came out with kind of a fake wide-screen, which movies like *From Here to Eternity* were shot in. Really all it is, is 1.85:1, which is basically the standard format today. That particular system worked when it was first brought about because they would project it at superwide angles, and you got the impression you were really watching something wider than it really was. Then there was VistaVision, which was also a wide-screen format—it used more negative area. Instead of the film running vertically, it ran horizontally across the camera so the magazine was laid flat. You got a picture similar to what you get with a 35mm still camera. It was wider, with more negative area, so you got more resolution. It's used mostly for matte work today. Generally, two formats are used today: 1.85:1 and anamorphic. Of course, both of these formats end up on television. Usually, on television the anamorphic or the wide-screen version ends up with pan and scan. You don't see the whole image all at once, it's too wide to get on television. With standard 1.85:1, essentially you're seeing what you saw in the theater, but with more top and more bottom.

Q: How do cinematographers work with the sound crew?

A: I try and make it easier than I used to. In the old days, the director of photography set a key light and the sound people had a mike over the actor's head. You used cutters in front of key lights to cut the spill off the wall. Sound could then move their boom around without throwing light shadows all over the walls. It was a major pain in the ass. That has changed now, with soft light and overhead lighting. Now sound people don't have quite as difficult a time trying to hide the shadows.

Q: What kinds of scripts are you attracted to?

A: I like psychological dramas. If you want to kill somebody on the screen, I think it should be elegant on a visual level. There should be romance in it.

Q: How do directors communicate to you what they want a film to look like?

A: Directors relate in different ways, but usually how they feel about the emotional content of the movie. It was Alan Pakula's idea that everything in *Klute* should be underground, claustrophobic. Alan would relate to things emotionally. It's mostly a lot of talking—exchanging ideas. I always ask the director, "What do you want to see on the screen? With most of the directors I've worked with, I'd lay the shot down, they'd look at it and say, "Good," or "Not good, let's do this instead." That was the process. I always picked the lenses and the set-ups, but they were always predicated on what a director wanted to achieve. It wasn't me arbitrarily doing something. It would be a discussion—cause and effect. Many times, a director can't figure out how to do something and he appreciates having an idea on how to get through it. It's a terrible burden a director is carrying. If a director can feel confident he's got a good cameraman, he's relieved of worrying about certain responsibilities. Having to deal with actors and the making of the movie is so difficult. Having to deal with me is difficult. So whatever the director doesn't have to be preoccupied with is helpful.

Q: Where do you see the craft of cinematography heading in the future?

A: What's probably going to happen is technology related to movies and the visual arts will become a kind of highly polished stainless steel ball, but with very little texture. So you'll be able to do anything. It's happening now because there's a very interesting crossover with digitized imagery in film and video. It is quite wonderful because you can do a lot of great stuff.

I'm not one of those guys who likes to make film sharper and sharper technologically and make lenses sharper and sharper, because pretty soon there's no distance between you and the audience. The imagery becomes reality—which is no longer fun to watch. You don't have to see every pore, pretty soon you'll have videotape. Pretty soon you'll have an unappetizing image. It's sharp enough now! I enjoy film. I thought film had a much better quality about it fifteen years ago than it has now. The emulsions were better. They were more consistent. They had better repeatability, and the quality of the image in my mind was more interesting. You look at an image on a piece of film and you say, "What's wrong with this thing?" You can't lay your hands on it. It's not doing the right thing. You're fiddling with it. You're looking at it and you're testing it. It's been upgraded and downgraded all at the same time.

There's a kind of deadening of the senses, at least in this country, so many things have been devalued. It's very hard to deal with things properly when so many people have been so desensitized. One of the big problems with many directors now is they remove themselves from the actors. They're sitting in the back room with a television monitor, talking to actors through microphones. They're not there anymore, and film is a very organic medium—that's what makes it so magical. That's all getting swept out to sea. So I don't have too much hope for good organic chemistry, both visually and technologically. I think it's going to be slick, but I don't think it will necessarily be moving.

3

Miroslav Ondříček

Miroslav Ondříček, ASC, was born in the former Czechoslovakia, where he was a child actor in the theater and cinema. He became intently interested with what was going on behind the lens, and began to work in a camera factory and a photo lab. This led to the study of still photography in Prague, and an apprenticeship (through the camera department system) of assistant cameraman, focus puller, and camera operator. Work in a motion picture studio led to Ondříček entering FAMU, the national Czech film school where he continued to study his craft.

In the sixties, Miroslav Ondříček became part of the Czech New Wave, led by Directors Milos Forman, Ivan Passer, Jan Nemec, and Jiri Menzel. He was director of photography on Forman's *Talent Competition*, *Loves of a Blonde*, and *The Firemen's Ball*; Nemec's *Martyrs of Love*; and Passer's *Intimate Lighting*.

In August 1968, the Soviet Union invaded Czechoslovakia, and Ondříček left his homeland with Forman, traveling to the United States to photograph *Taking Off*. He also worked in England with Lindsay Anderson, and was the director of photography on *If . . .* , *The White Bus*, and *O Lucky Man!*.

In America, Ondříček continued his longtime association with Milos Forman and received Academy Award nominations for his cinematography on *Ragtime* and *Amadeus*, which won the best picture Oscar in 1984. Ondříček also has had long artistic relationships with George Roy Hill, photographing *Slaughterhouse-Five*, *The World According to Garp*, and

Funny Farm; and with Penny Marshall on *Awakenings*, *A League of Their Own*, and *The Preacher's Wife*.

   Miroslav Ondříček views his cinematic role as a filmmaker who gets involved with every aspect of a film's visual design. His poetic lighting, delicate camera movements, and rich pictorial renderings translate words into images. Ondříček observes, "You photograph a drama, you photograph a story that you are selling—this is the movie."

SELECTED FILMOGRAPHY

1963 *Audition/Talent Competition*

1965 *Loves of a Blonde*
      Intimate Lighting

1966 *Martyrs of Love*

1967 *The Firemen's Ball*
      The White Bus

1969 *If . . .*

1971 *Taking Off*
      Slaughterhouse-Five

1973 *O Lucky Man!*

1979 *Hair*

1980 *The Black Sun*
      The Divine Emma

1981 *Ragtime**

1982 *The World According to Garp*

1983 *Silkwood*

1984 *Amadeus**

1985 *Heaven Help Us*

1986 *F/X*

1987 *Big Shots*

1988 *Funny Farm*

1989 *Valmont*

1990 *Awakenings*

1992 *A League of Their Own*

1996 *The Preacher's Wife*

*Academy Award nomination for best achievement in cinematography.

Q: How did you become a director of photography?

A: I was born in Czechoslovakia, now the Czech Republic. I love movies. I was a child actor and started as an extra, acting in the theater and in a few movies. I was more interested in being behind the camera. It was very difficult to get into the Czech movie industry. I had a good social background, my mother and father had a shop. My family and the officials sent me to working-class people for one year, where I worked in a factory which had many young people. Then they sent me to another small factory, where I worked with still photography cameras. From 1950 to 1953, I worked in a film laboratory, printing, developing, and editing titles and subtitles. I got a really good technical background. Then I went to the Graphic School of Prague, where I studied still photography. I became an assistant cameraman, focus puller, and operator. The studio sent me to FAMU, the Czech film school, in 1956. The film school took four years, and you studied everything: photography, lighting, music, and acting. Milos Forman and everybody went to the film school. In the early sixties after I finished film school, I started to photograph movies. This was the coming of the generation of people who started the Czech cinema.

Q: When did you first meet Milos Forman?

A: I knew of him before I met him personally in 1960. By this time, he was a first assistant director and I had become a camera operator. Then he became a director and I became a director of photography. The first movie I made with Milos was *Audition/Talent Competition* in 1963.

Q: What were the conditions like in Czechoslovakia when you photographed films like *Loves of a Blonde* and *The Firemen's Ball* for Milos Forman, and *Intimate Lighting* for Ivan Passer?

A: You must understand that inside a Communist government some things cannot work very well. *Loves of a Blonde* and *The Firemen's Ball* were done on real locations. Milos cast real people. My wife's uncle played the father in *Loves of a Blonde*. Milos said, "He must be in my movie!" Both *Loves of a Blonde* and *The Firemen's Ball* were done in a small town of thirty-five thousand people. Everybody knew each other. We were working very free. Milos gives so much freedom to the actors. I like to bring a little life to the screen when I photograph people. I don't like the actor to stand and look. I hate to make marks. Sometimes you have to do it, especially when you have a young focus puller. The maximum is for the actors to be free—it's the only way to work.

Q: What you are describing is similar to the freedom documentary filmmakers have.

A: I started in a documentary studio. Before I went into features, I made newsreels and television news. I like documentary pictures very much. I flew to China with Pavarotti just for fun to make *Distant Harmony*. I like to do all movies.

Q: Did you operate the camera on *Loves of a Blonde* and *The Firemen's Ball*?

A: Yes, as a young guy I operated myself. I did everything myself: focus, lighting, composing. I like to know the style, the coverage for each scene. I know how it is going to go together. I know which way to go, to a master shot, to a close-up.

Q: So it's important for the director of photography to understand the editing process.

A: Yes, because I prepare everything we are filming for editing. The editor can only edit what I am filming. He can't use a master shot if he doesn't have it. He can't make a close-up if he doesn't have it. This is our job. I don't have editors coming to the set to talk about the scene. No, this is our power with the director.

Q: When did you first work with British director Lindsay Anderson and why was *If . . .* shot in black-and-white and color?

A: I first worked with Lindsay on a short film, *The White Bus*. At the end of that movie, he had scenes in black-and-white and color. After that, he talked about making a whole movie in color. I wouldn't have liked the whole film of *If . . .* to be in color. The homosexual scene when the character is looking down for the young boy, couldn't be too colorful—this is a black-and-white scene. This picture was very hard to design because Lindsay lived in a school like that. It was unusual for me because there was never a school like this in my country.

Q: You worked in England with Anderson on *If . . .* and *Oh Lucky Man!*. Is the British style of filmmaking different than the Czech or American systems?

A: Half of *Ragtime* was shot in England. Actually, the British system is very similar. Truly, there are not many differences between people. When you shoot in France, the French are not so much on coverage. The only differences are between the rich and poor.

Q: Are filmmakers pretty much the same all over the world?

A: All over the world. They are poetic and romantic. Of course, it's different if you make a movie in a studio. The studios here are different, because the technical background in computers costs so much. By now, cameras are all the same. In England and in France they use the Panavision camera. I use Panavision.

Q: Why are Panavision cameras so widely used?

A: I like this camera because it's quiet. You can hand-hold it. You have a mount front and back. After the years and years I've used it, I haven't had any problems. The color balance is very important for a color picture to give you the best skin tone. With Panavision selected lenses, you can have the lenses match 95 percent.

Q: How do you know what lenses to use on a film?

A: For me, a good lens is everything. On most of my pictures, I only use two lenses. On *Ragtime*, I used an Arriflex BL and only two lenses, the 55mm and 85mm, for the whole movie. On *The Firemen's Ball*, I only used a 75mm and 25mm lens. On *Hair*, I used a Panavision zoom because of the music and dancing.

You and I are sitting here talking. You are not walking and talking in one corner of the room. You are not going to stand up and go to the kitchen. In some movies, everybody must move all the time. "I LOVE YOU!" "I HATE YOU!" Then they stand up and walk out. This is a phoney arrangement. In classic Chinese opera, the characters are in a frame. It is mostly a black-and-white background and only two or three persons make the composition. This is a different culture. Another movie with a lot of camera movement is *O Lucky Man!*.

Q: The camera movement in *O Lucky Man!* is very effective. When the Alan Price group is playing, you are constantly dollying the camera.

A: Yes, because of the music and a lot of scenes with walking. On a movie like *The Firemen's Ball*, I wouldn't be moving the camera so much. In *Intimate Lighting*, people would be sitting at the table and eating chicken and I dollied around 360 degrees. This movement is for me, the cameraman—not for the people I'm photographing.

Q: Did you design the camera moves for *O Lucky Man!* or did you work this out with Lindsay Anderson?

A: On 90 percent of my movies, I design the photography. Some ideas come from the script.

Q: Why was the bombing of Dresden sequence in *Slaughterhouse-Five* photographed in Prague?

A: We shot it in Prague because East Germany wouldn't give us permission to film the Dresden scenes. They were shot in Prague with just me and my focus puller, no operator—nothing. The director, George Roy Hill, came to Prague and stayed there for two weeks. We went through the script page by page.

Q: The color in many of the films you have photographed is desaturated. What is the philosophy behind this?

A: This is my aesthetic—it is like traditional painting. *The Firemen's Ball* was originally planned to be shot in black-and-white, and I battled for color. I worked with a friend, Jaroslav Otčenašek, who was a very gifted painter. He came up with the idea of using brown, which is the color of the Fascist uniform. I painted the interior walls brown three times because one time there was too much brown/blue and one time there was too much brown/yellow. I worked with Jaroslav Otčenašek and selected every gold color. The original fireman's costume was dark blue, which looked awful. I went to find the fabric to make the costumes.

Q: So you get involved with the production design of a film.

A: I am filmmaker—I like to make movies. To light a scene, I must first ask, "What are you photographing?" I don't know why you would pay me just to put the camera on the set and say, "Okay, lighting—put the 5Ks, 6Ks over there." I don't know why I would be there. I don't get jobs like that. I like to be part of the filmmaking process. My son just finished film school in Prague for directing. He made a short movie and he liked to do everything: editing, camera—this is the filmmaker. I am more a filmmaker than anything else.

Q: When do you like to begin on a project?

A: I always like being on a movie many months before I start shooting. I was on *Ragtime* for four months with Milos Forman. When we were in London, Milos said, "Maybe I'm going to do *Amadeus* in December of 1980." I had three years and got 90 percent of the locations.

Q: You have photographed many period movies—*Ragtime*, *Amadeus*, *Valmont*, *A League of Their Own*, and others. What research do you do? How do you learn about the lighting in that time period? Do you look at paintings and photographs from the era?

A: Yes. For *Ragtime*, I spent a lot of time studying photography. I stole this period from photographs by the old still photographers—all the old East Side streets, the waterfall—these are all famous black-and-white pictures from the 1890s. How would you know how this period looked? It was the same on *Amadeus*. The costume designer and I went to Vienna and Salzburg. I looked at the paintings for the hats, the shoes—every idea came from the old paintings.

Q: What paintings did you look at in preparation for *Amadeus*?

A: The French painter, Fragonard, and Shikanedr, the very famous Czech nineteenth-century painter who painted Prague in this period—this is *Amadeus*. His family had a theater in Vienna which opened *The Magic Flute* for Mozart. On *The World According to Garp*, I had my best partner for designing pictures, the production designer, Henry Bumstead. We selected and looked at photographs. I won't ever forget this gentleman, "Bummy."

Q: There are many wonderful performances in *Silkwood*. What was it like to photograph Meryl Streep?

A: Meryl Streep is fantastic because she is one of those actors who is not thinking about how she looks. She's thinking about her character and the atmosphere her character would create. Many big actors are more careful about how they look—not how to play the character. I enjoy a good performance. Cher was fantastic.

Q: You often use back light to light an actor's hair and the outline of their body.

A: This is always realistic. I don't exactly like lighting the background.

Q: How did you prepare to work on *A League of Their Own*, directed by Penny Marshall? Were you familiar with the game of baseball?

A: Prague has two baseball teams. I never understood the game before, so I went to see baseball games in the Czech Republic for one month and this guy told me everything. Penny called me after *Awakenings*, and she gave me tapes. I had one and a half years to work on the project. I also looked at a lot of period pictures.

Q: Where did you get your ideas for framing and composition?

A: At first, nobody wanted to shoot the film in wide-screen. I pushed for the film to be made in wide-screen. I found many wonderful compositions for wide-screen in a very famous painting from 1925 in the Chicago Museum. I showed it to Penny and she pushed Columbia. They said, "No, no, no," and after months, they said, "Okay, let's go to wide-screen."

Q: Did you use multiple cameras to film the baseball sequences?

A: Yes, because you must understand these girls never knew how to play baseball. Also, every actress had many doubles. Geena Davis had a double for running, a double for hitting, a double to go backward, sideways— everything.

Q: How did you approach exterior light when you were shooting the baseball sequences in the stadiums?

A: I fought with Mr. Greenhut, the producer. He wanted to cover the baseball scenes from seven o'clock in the morning until 7 o'clock in the evening. I had a very big battle every day. I had a very good time preparing the film. I stayed in the stadium throughout the day and saw how far the shadows would go. I designed it so the hitter always had back light. On a sunny day, the catcher is working in back light all of the time and looks into the light. It is very difficult to catch the ball. The shade moves over the people sitting in the seats. For the whole morning, the people in the stands had sun in their faces and the shade came in the afternoon. Nobody ever started a baseball game at seven o'clock in the morning. I shot the stars in the dugout in the morning. Eddie Quinn is the best grip in the world, he made me a roof to cover the sun. Baseball is the one game in the world you cover in 360 degrees. It is played all over the grounds.

Q: Is it difficult to light for multiple cameras?

A: Of course, sometimes we can't use multiple cameras because of the shadows. How are the lighting conditions? How big a background do you want—especially for this movie because the stadium always looked full. Penny and I only had a full stadium for two or three days.

Q: You have worked in many parts of the world. Does each city have its own light?

A: Yes, exactly. I very much like working in New York. You can tell what hour in the day it is by the shadows. When you are crossing Madison Square Garden, you know by the light that it is one o'clock. On fifty-seventh Street in October, you will see a fantastic sunset. It's a simple city to recognize. The position of the light south to north and west to east is wonderful. It's gorgeous. You have wonderful back light on the East Side in the morning. This is why I like New York very much.

Q: What filmmakers have most influenced your work as a cinematographer?

A: Ermanno Olmi, Robert Bresson, Akira Kurosawa, Truffaut, Godard, Fellini, Antonioni—I grew up in this culture. This is my generation. I had the great chance to see Charlie Chaplin film *The Countess from Hong Kong*. He was filming at Pinewood Studios. Lindsay Anderson wrote him a letter. He said, "My cameraman is from Czechoslovakia and he would like to visit you in the studio." Chaplin invited me. I sat behind him for two days and watched what he was doing. This was a big benefit. Everybody was acting, but reacting. He had absolutely fantastic energy. His eyes were like two flames. I have never forgotten his wonderful energy.

Q: Where do you think filmmaking is headed in the future?

A: I am a little worried about the new generation. Nobody has the time to listen to a story. How many people sit and read Shakespeare? Look at Broadway, many plays don't have one verse, only music. Movies mostly look like a clip. They go very fast. The movies have lost the romance. Nobody has the chance to watch the camera. The director says, "Good," and you say, "Good." There are no dailies the next day. Sometimes you see the dailies after three days, sometimes one week. You look and you say, "Good." The director doesn't have the time to watch the dailies. Everything is on video. You watch dailies at home on tape. Most cameramen are like a technical factory. You say, "How is the acting? How does it look? Does it match?" You know how wonderful a movie can be when you pick the backgrounds and the people walk perfectly. Now people don't take care about the continuity. The director doesn't say, "Please, again." *You* must say it, and nobody takes care if the actor has a jacket or no jacket, or if they looked left to right or gave a good look. No, it's only time. I'm very skeptical. Everybody said radio would finish the live orchestra. Everybody says because of movies nobody goes to the theater. I hope this panic time will finish and people will say they would like to go and watch a marvelous story. I like a movie to have time, like somebody sitting and looking—you know that they are thinking, but now nobody trusts the actor's performance. If an actor has a scene where they are sitting in the distance, everybody says, "What are you shooting? It has to be close-up!" This is ridiculous. You have the position of the hand, the whole body—this is the feeling of a movie. I hate movies where everybody has big close-ups all the time. I like to focus a movie. Why do you have a cast, if no one trusts this cast? You photograph a drama, you photograph a story that you are selling—this is the movie. Why do you have big close-ups?—this is television. I have talking heads on my television set in my home all the time.

Looking! Watching! This is very important. Look at *The Best Years of Our Lives*. In the best scene in the film, when the man with no arms comes home, there are only three cuts. *Now*, there's always a cut to a big hand, and crying, and muddled eyes, and screaming, and point of view (POV)—God POV and mouse POV because nobody trusts or knows about emotion. The computer is taking power—you're watching, you're not thinking so much. There's too much importance on perfection—the computer does it. You lose the sensitivity—the humanity.

4

Adam Holender

In 1984, the late master cameraman, Nestor Almendros, was asked which contemporary cinematographers he admired. His short A-list included Adam Holender, ASC.

After attending high school in Krakow, Poland, Adam Holender went on to study architecture. A job as a draftsman for an architectural firm led to an interest in photography, and the lure of the darkroom inspired him to join a 16mm film club. Holender entered the Polish Film Academy, where directors Andrzej Wajda and Andrzej Munk were instructors. After the academy, Holender began to work as a camera operator in Poland.

In 1966, Holender emigrated to the United States, where he was embraced by the New York film community. After working on commercials and other projects, Holender got the opportunity to photograph his first feature film, *Midnight Cowboy*, directed by John Schlesinger, which won the Oscar for best picture in 1969. This seminal New York-based production continues to resonate and influence contemporary directors and cinematographers. As Joe Buck made his bus journey from Texas to New York, Holender filmed him through the wide-open eyes of an immigrant. Using long lenses and techniques he discovered shooting commercials, Holender created a photographic view of New York as a wondrous new land, but shaded with a dark side.

Adam Holender has worked with many directors, including: Jerry Schatzberg, Frank Perry, Paul Newman, Joe Brooks, Jerome Hellman, Marshall Brickman, Agnieszka Holland, Taylor Hackford, Nick Castle, Howard Zieff, Wayne Wang, Herb Gardner, and Boaz Yakim.

A cameraman's cameraman, Adam Holender continues to create images which serve the story and the vision of the film and reflect the world we live in. From Needle Park to Washington, D.C.'s corridors of power, from the stage of a rock 'n' roll show and the sanctity of a Polish church to the interior of a funky Brooklyn smoke shop, the camera of Adam Holender captures reality with the gaze of an artist.

SELECTED FILMOGRAPHY

1969   *Midnight Cowboy*

1970   *Puzzle of a Downfall Child*

1971   *Panic in Needle Park*

1973   *The Effect of Gamma Rays on Man in the Moon Marigolds*

1974   *Man on a Swing*

1978   *If I Ever See You Again*

1979   *The Seduction of Joe Tynan*
        Promises in the Dark

1980   *Simon*
        The Idolmaker
        The Shadow Box

1984   *Threesome* (TV movie)

1986   *The Boy Who Could Fly* (with Steven Poster)

1987   *Street Smart*

1988   *To Kill a Priest*

1989   *The Dream Team*

1994   *Fresh*

1995   *Smoke*
        Blue in the Face

1996   *I'm Not Rappaport*

1997   *8 Heads in a Duffel Bag*

1998   *Wide Awake*
        A Price Above Rubies

Q: How did you become a cinematographer?

A: I finished high school in Krakow, Poland. Coming from a middle-class family, there were three avenues for any kid to go: one was to study medicine, the other was to study law, and the third was to study engineering. My father was a judge, and I had no interest in law. I hated medicine, so the only thing left was engineering. I started studying architecture. These were hard times. Education was free, but we were all ambitious enough not to want to take any money from our parents. So, as a way of making pocket money, I took a job as a draftsman with an architectural firm. I was sent to photograph a building which was going to be altered. The assignment was not only to photograph it, but also to measure and pinpoint for an architect which direction it was facing and how to go about the alteration. After doing two or three of those jobs, I found myself very interested in photographing architecture. In the following two years, I became more interested in photography than architecture.

Q: You took those still photographs with no formal training?

A: No formal training. I started taking pictures on weekends. I made a contact with somebody who had a darkroom. Through photography, I started getting involved in an amateur 16mm filmmaking club. Then I applied to the Polish Film Academy. It was a very tough school to get into. I didn't mention it to my parents. I quietly prepared myself for about six months, and passed the exam. I got in, took a leave of absence from architecture, and spent the next five years in the film academy.

Q: What was the Polish Film Academy like?

A: It was a fantastic school. Having been asked to meet with students at colleges in California and New York, I still have not found a comparable institution. It was a tiny school, there were forty-seven students in two departments—directing and cinematography—in all five years. Every professor and instructor was a leading working professional, so by the time you were through you were accepted as a member of the profession. It was not a question of, Will you be able to find work? rather which group do you want to be affiliated with. The disadvantages were, sometimes the professor was involved in filming for three, four, or five months. If you wanted to have his input, you had to get on a train or in a car and drive for a few hours to the location where he was shooting. You had to wait for him to finish his day. Then he would spend an hour over dinner with you going over your problems. If you got there earlier, you managed to hang around the set, so you saw how it was done. It was a much closer affiliation between theory and practice than any other school I have seen since I left Poland.

Q: Who were some of the professors?

A: Some of them were quite well-known. Among directors, there was Andrzej Wajda, and Andrzej Munk, who was quite influential among cinematographers in my years. The dean of the cinematography department was Stanislaw Wohl, an extraordinary human being and a fantastic teacher. Without him, I don't think I would have an understanding at all of what to do. Kurt Weber, who is now teaching in Germany, was there. I became his camera operator after I finished studying. There were many others.

Q: Did you enter the academy as a cinematography major?

A: Yes, one had to make a choice between directing and cinematography from the outset. I remember having this conversation over a cup of coffee with Wohl, who was the dean of the school. I asked him what he thought—having done both cinematography and directing. He looked at me and said, "Cinematography is a profession, directing is a hobby."

Q: Did you start your professional career in Poland?

A: Yes, I finished and got my master's degree in cinematography, then I started working as a camera operator. I came to the United States in 1966, with an extremely limited ability to speak English. I didn't have many contacts, money, or relatives. It took me a few months to stand on my feet. I had two visas—for Canada and the United States. I wanted to see what it was like, and it just so happened the late sixties were terrific in New York.

Q: Did you have aspirations about working in Hollywood?

A: I knew absolutely nothing about it. I didn't know the difference between what production was like in Hollywood or New York—even that was a discovery to me. I didn't go to Los Angeles for two years, and then I discovered that whole industry.

Q: So you became part of the New York film industry first?

A: Yes, it was just a wonderful atmosphere to be accepted into, and I'll always remember it fondly. People were extremely generous and kind to me.

Q: How did you arrive in New York?

A: I came the conventional immigrant route, by boat. My boat was not allowed to pull into the United States, so it came through Montreal along the St. Lawrence River, and I took a Greyhound bus from Montreal to New York.

Q: Just like Joe Buck, the character Jon Voight plays in *Midnight Cowboy*.

A: Yes, that image of Joe Buck seeing the skyline of New York from the bus was the image that I remember. The bus came through the Lincoln Tunnel—that's how I saw New York for the first time—and we managed to do it in the film. There's something to be said for being sensitized, being fresh, and seeing a place for the first time, as opposed to growing up somewhere and being so used to elements you no longer notice them.

Q: How did you get the assignment to photograph *Midnight Cowboy*?

A: It was my first feature in the United States. I happened to be lucky enough to be at the right place at the right time. I was a twenty-eight-year-old kid from Poland who was suddenly doing a lot of commercials in New

York. John Schlesinger, who had a British Broadcasting Corporation (BBC) background, came to New York to do this picture and either heard of me or saw some of my work in Europe and started inquiring about me. They called Roman Polanski, a friend who put in a good word for me. They were trying to decide between two actors to play Joe Buck, Jon Voight being one. They built a small set on one of the stages downtown, on Fourth or Fifth Street on the Lower East Side. There was another cinematographer who was going to shoot the first day. They asked me to come in to shoot the second day on the same set with the second actor, who happened to be Jon Voight. I didn't feel all that comfortable walking in and taking over the other cinematographer's crew—by then he knew that I was a competitor. They liked what I did and offered me the job.

Q: Midnight Cowboy is a very American film, although it was made by a British director and photographed by a Polish cinematographer. It's American in theme, but you contributed a European visual sensibility. Joe Buck was from Texas; he had never been East before, and you captured the emotions of discovery. Did the director, John Schlesinger, allow you to contribute visually to the film?

A: He did, and the producer, Jerome Hellman, contributed an enormous amount to our freedom of expression. We went for a long, six-week trip to Texas and Florida to learn about America. John came from London and didn't know much about it. I came from Poland, and we didn't know where the Joe Bucks of this world came from. The screenwriter, Waldo Salt, Schlesinger, and myself went for the longest drives through Texas, you can imagine trying to see what it looked like. We'd get up in the morning, have breakfast, fill up the gas tank, start driving, and watch the speedometer going from fifty to sixty to seventy to eighty, and the gas gauge going from full to empty, over and over again. Through all of this, we got a sense of what Texas looked like. Waldo Salt was writing the script. Both Jerry Hellman and Schlesinger made Waldo an integral part of this creative process. Whatever happened on that trip, Waldo would immediately adapt it, come up with new pages, and talk about it with John. That style of work continued, not only on locations, but even in the studio in New York. Very often, Schlesinger would stage a scene and we would have a question. We would call Waldo to come in, record it on a tape recorder—then we would break for an hour. They would go upstairs and rework the scene, and inevitably it was better.

Q: Was it difficult for you to work with a seasoned crew, fixed in a lot of their old work methods?

A: Not only that, but it was pretty much unheard of for a twenty-eight-year old kid who didn't have any track record to suddenly take the key position of cinematographer. So there was a little bit of tension, but we overcame it.

Q: I understand you had some struggles in convincing the crew to use a reflex camera.

A: Right. I came from Europe, and we were used to reflex cameras. I just liked looking at the ground glass, which is an actual frame. The guys who were working in New York were used to the old Mitchell cameras with a rackover system with a finder. If you moved the finder to the left or the right, you weren't seeing the frame, but they felt uncomfortable doing the picture with a reflex camera. I tried to convince them, and they were dismissing it as an amateur way of doing a major motion picture, so we ended up having two cameras. We compromised. Wherever I felt accuracy was needed for me to look at the shot, we used a reflex camera.

Q: What was the size of the crew on *Midnight Cowboy*?

A: It was an average-sized crew—by today's standards it would be small. To put it into perspective, it cost $3.1 million in 1969. Today, on that kind of a schedule for as many days as we shot, it would probably be a $25–30 million picture.

Q: Where were the interiors shot, and how did you achieve a natural light look throughout the film?

A: We had gone to enough abandoned buildings to see what the light looked like. The interiors were, to a large extent, studio interiors. One of the trickiest things was to match the exteriors and the interiors shot on the location with interiors done on the stage. The street for the exterior of the tenement building was in downtown New York, somewhere in Soho. The staircase where Joe Buck carries the refrigerator was in an abandoned building. However, from the point when he opens the door and they walk into the apartment—it's all studio. I really spent an awful lot of sweat trying to make that part of the same look. I am most proud I succeeded in doing that. Remember, that was a day and age where all the emulsions and lenses we have today were not available. It was still 5254 negative, and it was not as easy to work with.

Q: Was rear-screen projection used for any shots inside the bus as Joe Buck travels from Texas to New York?

A: No, some shots were handheld, we also used a dolly. The flashbacks of Joe Buck's life were mostly done handheld, and I operated the camera myself.

Q: The exposures on the bus are so naturalistic. How did you light these sequences?

A: Today's lighting equipment and emulsions would make it much easier to do. I was mixing the light. I was exposing either for interior or exterior, depending on what was happening outside or inside the bus. I either gelled the window or adapted more light inside. It was very tough because the temperatures on the bus were really high, especially in Texas and Florida. It was ninety-five degrees outside; by the time you turned those lights on, it was 120 degrees and the make-up would flow down.

There was a wonderful man, Otto Paolony, in Deluxe Laboratory in New York, which is no longer in existence. Without him, I wouldn't have been able to do it. Every time I had a problem or I wanted a clear-cut assessment, even from distant locations, I talked to Otto at seven o'clock in the morning and he would say, "You got it, there's nothing to worry about." I would say to the production people, "Let's strike this set, let's move on," without seeing it—I knew.

Q: Did you overexpose the color flash-forward sequences in *Midnight Cowboy* to give them a slightly surreal quality?

A: Those flash-forwards to Florida were overexposed two and a half stops.

Q: How did you approach the flashbacks?

A: Some of them were shot in black-and-white. Some of it was not overexposed in terms of overall exposure, but it was the contrast of light—for example, the effects of policemen's flashlights. Those were extremely hot. It was meant for a shocking wake-up, jarring light, but the negative wasn't overexposed.

Q: The long-lens shots of Joe Buck which gave the impression he was surrounded by a sea of people in New York were very effective. Where did you get the idea to use that technique?

A: I must give credit for that kind of thinking to the year I spent shooting commercials in New York. When we were doing those commercials in the sixties, we were not constricted by advertising agencies and crowds of people standing behind us. We were allowed to fool around, and by doing so, I discovered a lot of wide lenses I had never used before and close-focus with wide lenses, something I had never done on films in Poland. We would remove the screws from the lens holding the focusing ring, to focus it much closer than the lens was intended, in order to do a fingernail shot. We played a lot. Once I discovered Schlesinger was open to suggestions and was looking for an unorthodox approach, we would talk about it and out of this came long lenses, wide lenses, and all those things that were not so commonly used then as they are now.

Q: Dustin Hoffman and Jon Voight have two very different kinds of faces. How did you approach photographing them?

A: Lighting was a problem because Hoffman's skin pigmentation was much darker, he had an olive tone. Jon Voight's skin was quite white, with much more pink in it. He was also very sensitive to sunlight—two hours in the sunlight during the shooting and his color would change. When you're shooting a sequence for the whole day, or two or three days, you're in the lab worrying. Suddenly, in progression he's much pinker here and there. Also, Jon would reflect light much more, so I had to watch out for that. We didn't have any special filters or lenses for either Jon or Hoffman. We did it with light. I tried to keep a little light off of Jon Voight because of his skin coloration. Hoffman could take any of it very easily.

Q: The neighborhoods in the beginning of the film are attractive and up-scale. As the characters begin to plunge into despair, New York becomes dingy, and it moves into a cold, nasty winter. Was this a deliberate and conscious concept?

A: It was dictated by the script. John Lloyd, the production designer, did a wonderful job pacing that progression. Joe Buck was a young man who was coming from Texas, expecting the riches of New York to come his way, and as the story progresses, it's sliding down and down and eventually ends up in the horror of them going on this bus trip to Florida. So the selection of locations, the color of the sets, the choice of make-up, wardrobe, Dustin Hoffman's beard, all reflected the same thing—which was dictated by the progression of the script. If it isn't structured by somebody at the very beginning, it's a miracle if it happens at all. If it is structured, and somebody takes care to follow it up and understand it, the chances are somebody will receive it. Ninety percent of success or failure does not happen on the day you shoot—that has to be planned. Even if you prepare to 100 percent of your ability, you will end up giving up 10, 15, or 20. You will realize only 80 percent of that 100. If you prepare only 50 percent, you'll end up with 15 percent.

Q: Midnight Cowboy was restored for a twenty-fifth anniversary re-release. What were the challenges in making a new release print of the film?

A: The studio which made *Midnight Cowboy* ceased to exist. The negative wasn't properly stored and the internegatives were screwed up. When we were redoing the answer print, there was only so much we could do with the picture to revive it, but we were able to take a mono soundtrack recorded twenty-six years ago and, by the use of digital technology, we were able to transcribe each one of the instruments separately and make a stereo sound-track out of it. It really is remarkable how many sound technology advances they have made and we are nowhere with the visual end of it. They were try-ing to make a new answer print of *Cool Hand Luke*. That negative was even more destroyed than ours. Every time someone buys a studio which has vaults, somebody says, "How much does it cost? Just get rid of it!" They move it to some storage facility. Depending on how films are stored on the shelves for all of those years, whether it is up or down, some reels hold up fine and some reels don't. Humidity, heat destroys it more.

Q: How did you achieve the tough and dirty look of Manhattan's Upper West Side in *Panic in Needle Park*, and how did you work with the director, Jerry Schatzberg?

A: When we read the screenplay for *Panic in Needle Park*, I remembered seeing in Poland a black-and-white film directed by Gillo Pontecorvo called *The Battle of Algiers*. I loved this film. I mentioned it to Schatzberg. We got a print, and he agreed it was something to take seriously. What was wonderful about *The Battle of Algiers* is you really believed all that hap-pened in front of the camera wasn't staged, but that the camera just hap-pened to be there and it was really life. So we ran it a couple of times. Before we started, I shot quite a few tests. Again I used long lenses. The film stocks were slow, the lenses were lousy, and a lot of the film was happening at night. To light Broadway and Seventy-second Street at night using 600mm, 800mm lenses is a nightmare, but slowly I managed to get the mechanics of it. I explained to Ray Emeritz, a technician at General Camera here in New York, what he had to build for me so the assistant would be able to follow fo-cus with those long lenses. I am still in contact with him—he's now in his eighties, still working on machines. Ray built a large panel and a gear sys-tem for us. We worked it out over weeks of shooting tests. Knowing what you want to do and finding aids from technicians is easy once you decide, "This is the way to go."

Q: Were those long takes that follow Al Pacino walking on the opposite side of the street dolly shots?

A: No, the camera was stationary. When you use long lenses to that ex-tent, they look like dolly shots because the relationship doesn't change. The problem for Schatzberg was he couldn't see performances. So after the sec-ond day, he was on the set looking at the actors through a pair of binoculars. It was so far away, but by doing it, we were able to get that look of the stack-ing up of the perspective of people. After three days, the producer, Dom-inick Dunne, got a call from Darryl Zanuck, the head of the studio in Los Angeles. He said, "What is this Holender doing? It's supposed to be a New

York picture. I don't see any New York there!" We said to Dominick, "Tell him this is the way we want to do the picture. We have an idea." So he called Zanuck and said, "That's the way we want to do it," and Zanuck apparently said, "Well, it's cheap enough, let them do it."

Q: Panic in Needle Park looks so much like a documentary. Were those studio or practical locations?

A: They were mostly locations, hotel rooms, and a variety of places, but they were all lit. We were basically doing the same kind of lighting approach as *Midnight Cowboy*. By then, I was much more comfortable. *Midnight Cowboy* was a real pain in the neck because none of the technicians on the crew were used to lighting sets the way I wanted them lit. The lighting instruments were not available. Soft light was considered only for portraits by still photographers.

Q: Were these lighting instruments available in Poland? Many Polish films have that soft-light look.

A: Right, but in Poland we built the instruments for soft light based on still photographs by American still photographers. We saw the work of Irving Penn, Art Kane, Richard Avedon, Bert Stern, and all these still photographers using soft light. We wanted to do that in film. Those instruments were not available, but they're simple to do. You ask somebody to do something out of metal. You bounce a light so somehow it works. We started doing it in Poland. Then I came to the United States thinking the lights were going to be fantastic, and I walked into the studio—nothing, just Fresnels and hard lights. I said, "What happened to the style of all those American still photographers?" "Oh, those are only for amateurs and still photography, we don't use it in film." "But this is how I want the film to look." "Oh no, we don't have anything like this." So I started taking those Fresnel lights and bouncing the light, doing things nobody felt very comfortable with.

Q: What is a Fresnel light?

A: A sharp light, a sharply defined shadow—basically a concentrated beam of studio light, not natural light as you see from this window falling on my face.

Q: Couldn't you have adapted some of the lights Richard Avedon and other still photographers were using at the time?

A: No, those were studio bank lights. Eventually, the film industry caught on and started building soft lighting instruments, but after years of resistance. They tried to keep it away; when they couldn't, then you go and get change.

Q: Street Smart has a great New York look, although it was shot in Canada.

A: Ninety-nine percent of *Street Smart* was shot in Montreal. I had a streak of those. *The Idolmaker* was a New York, East Coast picture shot in Los Angeles. *Street Smart* was a New York picture shot in Montreal. Then I did *The Dream Team*, which was a New York picture shot in Toronto, and *To Kill a Priest*, which took place in Poland and was shot in France.

Q: Was *Street Smart* as much of a challenge as *The Idolmaker* in capturing a New York look?

A: No, it wasn't as much of a problem because the look of Montreal is much closer to the look of New York than Los Angeles exterior locations are to New York. Shooting in Los Angeles for New York—you're talking about difficulty! New York has humidity in the summertime, which diffuses light. Los Angeles light is as hard as it comes, it's directly over your head—it's just very tough to match.

Q: The soul food restaurant that the Morgan Freeman character used as an office to do his business as a pimp had a very authentic New York look to it.

A: That was shot in New York, in Harlem on Lenox Avenue on 126th Street. We had five days or so in New York at the end of the schedule. That's how studios always think: let's shoot 95 percent of Toronto material and then come to New York for atmosphere. Of course, you don't want it to end up looking like a postcard, so you try to incorporate it.

Q: Did lighting the black actors in *Street Smart* demand a different approach?

A: Very much so. Actually, in *Street Smart* the problem was accentuated because among black actors, Morgan Freeman is very dark. What doubled the problem is that Christopher Reeve is pinkish white. In the scenes when they were both playing, especially in a violent scene when they are moving around in physical contact, it was an enormous task to keep the light separated from one actor to the next. I had to balance it out, it was difficult. In *Fresh*, they were all black actors, it was much easier—the tonality is the same. You learn not only how to light faces, but to use the faces as a piece of sculpture like a metallic surface that reflects light. You use the skin as a reflective matter. I would bring light out of the frame to model the face to show the angularity of somebody's facial structure by reflecting it in the skin. It works very well, and it brings the eyes out.

Q: In *Street Smart*, the characters had their own spaces which reflected their personalities. Morgan Freeman had the soul food restaurant. Christopher Reeve's loft was upscale in a manner that reflected who he was. Then there is the magazine office, and the restaurant which reflected Reeve's boss, the editor-in-chief of the magazine he worked for. Do these spaces give you the ability to comment on the characters photographically by your use of lighting and camera movement?

A: It does, and you certainly use images you remember as proper to the kind of environment you're creating. It helps you on the location scout long before we start filming. It helps you in lighting those interiors because you see these kinds of people sitting at Elaine's or in some restaurant and it feels like something you can relate to. That's why I think it's so important to get to know the fabric of life you are trying to re-create. If you don't know it, you don't know what to do. You're just making believe.

Q: Do you have a philosophy about photographing comedies like *The Dream Team*?

A: Comedy is one of the toughest things to interpret on film. Somebody has to say, "This is the kind of comedy we're doing and this is the key in which this comedy is going to work." There's a standard way of thinking that cinematography in comedy ought to be bright and flat. Nobody needs a cinematographer for that, they need a lighting technician to make it happen. If somebody told me that, I wouldn't be interested in doing it at all. Not to say that a great comedy couldn't be done by applying those parameters, but it doesn't appeal to me. Then there are great comedies. Gordon Willis, in the heyday of his relationship with Woody Allen, did some pretty damn good comedies, and they were not treated the way we just talked about.

Q: You seem to have had good relationships with production designers.

A: What gives me a good basic level of understanding with any production designer is that I studied architecture for three and a half years. Once you have that behind you, you can find a mutual language. Knowing how they think, you can also sit down with a piece of paper and lay out the film. An art director has to sit down at one point and start doing a floor plan. The cinematographer or director should be able to read it. It also helps when I talk to the grips. I know where to suspend a beam to be safe. You relate to it, not only through the experience of being on the sets, but also by knowing how construction works.

Q: Do you think that understanding architecture also helps your sense of composition?

A: Of course, but that's not the only way to get there. Somebody who paints or photographs could easily get there. A lot of people in my profession who are wrapped up in the business of doing one picture after the next do not allow themselves to recharge their batteries. They don't go to the museums often enough, they don't see those photo shows at which one can capitalize on ideas. It's nice to finish the project, get something and put it back in, read and even talk to friends, instead of just mechanically going from one project to the next.

Q: What do you look for in a relationship with a director?

A: I used to feel my way through and tried to justify this and that. As the years went by, it became clearly defined in my mind, there's no ambiguity any longer. Directors are basically broken down into two categories: directors who direct and directors who pretend to direct—nothing else matters. Those who do direct are directing in a creative fashion and in an administrative fashion. If you have never worked with the director, trying to decide, is he somebody who pretends or is he somebody who really does? That's the hard part. And if he does, what is the reason he is doing it? If the cinematographer is pursuing his own interests, not thinking what the director wants to do, he is a pompous ass. It's a conflict-ridden relationship. As soon as you answer all of those things honestly, and if you're correct in your judgements, the better off you are. I find, if the script appeals to me as a story I would want to hear over dinner conversation, that's a good sign. Now I meet with a director. If I find he indeed is someone who is interested in the process of filmmaking and if he really wants to do the film, that's another plus. So you go on. Sometimes you are fooled—you hope for the best and take it as it goes.

Q: Is it important for the director and the cinematographer to collaborate on the vision of a film?

A: Very much so. I am very much against a cinematographer who has a vision and is going to realize it no matter what. It's an ego trip. It all stems from what is written on those pages, and it is really up to the director to convey that to everybody he is working with: the production designer, the cinematographer, costume designer, composer, and so on. It is a collaborative field and somebody has to bring those elements together. If the director does everything correctly, he will bring those people together. Every time you look at a good film, it seems like everything got together. You look at films where suddenly the music is fantastic and nothing else seems to make sense. Everyone says, "Wow! Wasn't that music great?" Great for what? If you're interested in music, why don't you go to a concert, not to see a film. The same thing about the cinematography. If the film is terrible and the cinematography is good, it means that it attracted attention to itself for no particular, necessary, good reason. There are directors who chose to contact these cinematographers to do work with them. What's known as the look of that cinematographer fits the director's way of thinking about the visual end of the film. I like the work of these cinematographers, but that kind of "This-is-what-I-do" work doesn't interest me. There's a certain amount of challenge in reading every script that interests you differently and finding a visual interest different from the others you have done in the past or different from similar films done by other cinematographers. If you find an individualistic visual equivalent to express your interest in a story, it's gratifying.

Q: So, you always start from ground zero with the script. You don't start by saying, "I like back light," or "I like diffusion," or "I like long lenses."

A: Yes, depending on the reading process of the script and conversations with the director, back light, diffusion, raw stock, lenses, and filters ought to serve what you want the film to look like. Then, you apply knowledge of all of those technical elements to fit that. If you try to do that in reverse, it's idiotic. It's like a tail wagging the dog.

Q: How do you communicate with the director about the look of the film during the early stages of preproduction? Do you talk about color? Do you talk about metaphors? Do you bring in photographs? Do you screen movies?

A: All of the above. Usually in the first meeting with the director after you've read the script, either the director or I will bring in films that came to mind as a good example of treatment of this particular script; some movies done thirty, forty years ago, classics, some more recent. As the process continues, we often see those films either together or separately and we talk about it. We'll rent video cassettes and run them at night and in the morning meetings and say, "Yes, I like this, but I think we should explore it further." Still photography comes in very handily. I find myself relying on still photography more and more. Still photography is its own art form. There are books available in every book store, and exhibitions of still photographs are abundant. It's also something you can open the page to and stare at. The look of *Fresh* was based on Alex Webb's book of photographs. I was looking for something to suggest to the director and to the production designer and I found this photographer who photographed lives of Hispanics. I brought it to a meeting, and from this book came a whole slew of ideas that made their way into the film. You can now find an equivalent of this in any style that you want, it's just a question of seeking it out—it's available.

Q: Do you think paintings are effective in communicating a visual style for a film?

A: Yes, before photography became so widely acceptable, painting was it. Today, photography replaces painting because it is closer to what we do and it's usually not removed by generations. It is easily understood. You can Xerox a page or have a print of it made. You bring it to the production office, pin it to the wall. The costume designer can see it, and the set designer says, "Yes, I know what you mean." As they say, one picture is worth a thousand words. It is easily accessible. You can sense it, you can relate to it. You know that it was done through lenses on film emulsion and in a laboratory. What kind of paint did Rembrandt use, and what kind of window was he by for this one light source? It's just easier to talk about photography and it helps to demystify it. When you talk about paintings, it becomes an almost "artsy"/religious experience, which by the way, a lot of cinematographers like.

Q: What is a good way to learn about cinematography?

A: When I was studying in the Polish Film School, I remember looking at *Citizen Kane* and being totally in awe of it. So we got a reel of the warehouse scene from *Citizen Kane* and put it on a flatbed going back and forth. A couple of colleagues and I made a sketch of where the light sources were. We didn't build a set, but we arranged elements in a studio to look like what they had. Then we lit it and shot it. We sent it to the lab, got it back, put it on the editing table, looked at it, went back and said, "Okay, we screwed up because this is different." We did it four times—by the fourth time, we didn't do it as well as Gregg Toland did, but at least we got in the area of similarity. I tell students to find a still photographer they like, find a photograph—anything: exterior, interior, a portrait, a nude—I don't care what it is. You have a studio, you have lights. Light it, see if you can reproduce something you like. Use your own judgement. What is it you like? Learn the technique. Get a sense of it. If you want something changed in the photograph, change it. Expose the negative, send it to the lab. You can do it with a still camera, you'll get some sense of it. Two hours from now you have a print.

Q: Where do you see your profession of cinematography headed in the future?

A: Everybody is looking at this profession with a negative feeling that video is going to replace film, that theaters are going to close down and everybody is going to be watching films in their living room. I don't happen to agree, unless of course, extraordinary social upheavals are going to change the way we live. If people won't go out because they're afraid to go out, that's a different story, but if life continues in a fairly civilized fashion, I think possibly a new style of movie theater will be created and flourish. Those are going to be more of an event movie theater, which is going to be more reminiscent of the good days of the thirties and forties. They're going to be large, with terrific looking screens, fantastic sound systems, comfortable seats. Possibly the tickets are going to be more expensive, but people are going to look at it as an event and they are going to go to the movie theater like people go to a Broadway theater. Given a choice even today I try to avoid these little multiplex theaters. Going to The Ziegfeld here in New York is a treat. It looks so great and it sounds so good—so why wouldn't other people want it?

5

Don McAlpine

Don McAlpine, ASC, was born in Australia. His interest in still photography began when he exhibited in amateur contests. In the late 1950s, he became a teacher of physical education and science in high schools for the New South Wales State Teaching Service. He began to use a motion picture camera to analyze sports activities in his physical education course. While employed as a teacher, McAlpine started working as a freelance news cinematographer. In the early 1970s, he met Director Bruce Beresford and photographed *The Adventures of Barry McKenzie*, which was McAlpine's first feature film.

The seventies was a flourishing time for the Australian cinema and McAlpine was a central figure in that country's New Wave through his work on *The Getting of Wisdom*, *Don's Party*, *My Brilliant Career*, and *Breaker Morant*.

An early morning telephone call from Director Paul Mazursky led to McAlpine's American film debut on *Tempest*, followed by further collaborations with Mazursky on *Moscow on the Hudson*, *Down and Out in Beverly Hills*, and *Moon Over Parador*.

In addition to his longtime associations with Bruce Beresford and Paul Mazursky, McAlpine has worked with many directors, including: Richard Franklin, Tom Jefferies, Gillian Armstrong, Peter Collinson, Peter Wener, Paul Newman, Mel Gibson, Roger Simon, John McTiernan, Alan Pakula, Martin Ritt, Ron Howard, John Badham, Phillip Noyce, Chris Columbus, Baz Luhrmann, and Lee Tamahori.

A meticulous craftsman, Don McAlpine brings many gifts to the films he photographs. His lifelong love for the outdoors translates cinematically into crisp images of forests, lakes, and morning skies. His view from down under has brought Australia to the world and has captured America with an explorer's sense of discovery.

SELECTED FILMOGRAPHY

1972   *The Adventures of Barry McKenzie*

1976   *Don's Party*
          Surrender in Paradise

1977   *The Getting of Wisdom*

1978   *Money Movers*
          Patrick

1979   *The Odd Angry Shot*
          The Journalist
          My Brilliant Career

1980   *The Club*
          Breaker Morant
          The Earthling

1981   *Don't Cry, It's Only Thunder*
          Puberty Blues

1982   *Now and Forever*
          Tempest

1983   *Blue Skies Again*

1984   *Harry & Son*
          Moscow on the Hudson

1985   *King David*
          The Fringe Dwellers

1986   *Down and Out in Beverly Hills*

1987   *Predator*
          Orphans

1988   *Moving*
          Moon Over Parador

1989   *See You in the Morning*
          Parenthood
          Stanley & Iris

1991   *Career Opportunities*
          The Hard Way

1992   *Patriot Games*
       Medicine Man
1993   *Mrs. Doubtfire*
       The Man Without a Face
1994   *Clear and Present Danger*
1995   *Nine Months*
1996   *William Shakespeare's Romeo & Juliet*
1997   *Bookworm*
       The Edge
1998   *Stepmom*

Q: How did you become a cinematographer in Australia?

A: I had a background exhibiting still photography in amateur photographic contests. In the late fifties, I was in the New South Wales State Teaching Service as a teacher of physical education and science in high schools. In my physical education course, I started to use a motion picture camera for analysis of various sporting activities. I worked in conjunction with a lot of the coaches preparing teams for the 1956 Olympics in Melbourne, so I became moderately proficient with recording motion on film. When I was schoolteaching, the television news department where I was doing freelance work gave me the nod and suggested I apply for a job at the television station. I went to see the guys in the camera department, who said, "Your work in news is pretty good, but you don't have any technical background." So I raced home and bought two great books: *The Principles of Cinematography* by Wheeler, a very technical book, which explains the mechanics related to motion picture cameras up to that point in the fifties; and Cox's *On Optics* which is a Focal Press book. I studied them like a university subject. I went to the interview, and there were five gentlemen, obviously old cameramen—they all looked a bit disheveled. The chairman said, "We know about your work, but there's a note here you're probably a bit deficient on the technical side." I said, "I was told that, and I've done a bit of work trying to help educate myself." They said, "Oh, that's good—why did they change from sixteen or eighteen frames to twenty-four frames when sound came in?" So I started on a long dissertation about the response of galvanometers and the frequency you get as the film goes past the surface. Eventually, I started to look at these guys and they showed either dismay or incredible interest because they had never heard of it, and I realized very quickly I was about to make a complete ass of myself. I wound it up as quickly as I could, and they said, "That's very impressive." They asked me a couple of other questions, I managed to modify the answers down, and got

Principal Photography

the job. That's the way I got into the business. I was a technical person who got very much involved. I've been involved in theater all my life as an amateur. I didn't get inspired by any great guys. I never went to film school. I went to the film pictures to enjoy them. I never went to study them.

I was a stringer cameraman for television. As the teaching service started to get concerned about my extracurricular activities, I was offered a job as an assistant cameraman in television. So I left teaching. While all this was going on, a ground swell of people involved in film as an expressive form were all over the place, and were very well supported by an experimental film fund run by the government. This all just kept going ahead to the point where one prime minister of the country was so visionary and so well advised that he then decided to start a film bank. One of the people they got back from England to run it was the director, Bruce Beresford, an Australian. The first film financed by this government bank was *The Adventures of Barry McKenzie*. I'd done some work on award-winning, dramatized documentaries. By then, I had worked my way through television and had become a cinematographer working in current affairs, dramatized documentaries, and small dramas. I then transferred to the Australian Film Unit, now called Film Australia. It is a similar organization to the world-renowned Canadian Film Board. In a few years there, I became chief cameraman. I was granted leave, and did *The Adventures of Barry McKenzie*, the first of the films of the Australian New Wave, with Bruce Beresford.

Q: As director of photography on Bruce Beresford's *Breaker Morant*, *Don's Party*, *The Getting of Wisdom*, Gillian Armstrong's *My Brilliant Career*, and many other films, you were an integral part of the Australian New Wave in the 1970s. What was the film industry in Australia like prior to this period?

A: Before the seventies, there was no indigenous film industry in Australia in my lifetime. There had been quite a strong film industry in the twenties and early thirties. Then the Americans came in, bought it all up, and closed it down to avoid any competition for their product in Australia. From the early thirties, Australia was used as a location for many films from England. There were sporadic attempts by individuals. Charles Chauvel did a film called *Jedda*, and there were a couple of other films in the forties and fifties. It all died, it couldn't be sustained as an industry. In the early days, there was always a core of craftspeople, technicians involved in newsreels, in documentaries, which was a pretty lively form in Australia, and in cinema shorts and cinema commercials. When television came in, there were television commercials, but there was really no sustainable motion picture industry. In the late fifties and early sixties, there was strong support for the arts in all forms and in filmmaking in particular. It was an experiment to see if anyone could make a film. I was involved in a lot of these.

Q: What are the principal similarities and differences between working as a director of photography in Australia and America?

A: The biggest mistake I made when I first started working in America was assuming because of our parallel histories as pioneering countries we were of similar background—entirely wrong. The individual in America is supreme, there is far more concern in Australia for the group, the society. In America, much time is spent in excessive organization, which generally becomes a negative force in any creative effort. You're just organized to a point where you cannot show any degree of flexibility. In Australia, we'll organize it pretty well. The classic situation in a moderately budgeted Australian film is that the production office is generally manned by a line producer, one assistant, one accountant, and a runner. That's all that would be set up to organize a film. Here, on quite a modest film, there could be three times as many people as that.

Q: What is the make-up of the camera crew in Australia?

A: Identical. There's the director of photography, an operator, then you must have a first assistant or focus puller and a second assistant or clapper/loader. If it's a project that's using a lot of film, then you need a loader to keep the film coming. That is one department that does work almost identically in any country I've worked in. I've had the fortune to work in Australia, England, Germany, France, Italy, and in Asia. Basically, the camera crew is a constant because you need those people. They're the only people who work all day on a movie crew. That's anywhere in the world. The relationship between myself and the operator is personal and varied, but everyone else is performing identical functions, no matter where you are or what language is being spoken. I feel comfortable in the camera department with good people, no matter where I am.

Q: Breaker Morant takes place principally in one room. What were the challenges in filming the courtroom sequences?

A: We turned an old cinema into a stage. That courtroom was made out of plywood and corrugated cardboard. It was a well-designed, but cheap set. Bruce Beresford and I shot most of the graphic, isolated exteriors on a Sunday with nobody. The crew was working incredibly hard. We didn't want to ask them to work on the Sunday. So Bruce and I would just go out with a couple of horse wranglers and shoot the carts going across. A lot of the big, wide shots that gave the film space were shot in a very short time. Basically, it is a courtroom drama. We managed to deceive the audience into thinking it was something much grander. You'll find a lot of energy in the courtroom is borrowed from the scenes we shot outside. We used split diopters and all sorts of little tricks to enliven the courtroom scene. Wherever we could find an excuse to move the camera, we moved it.

Q: What is a split diopter?

A: A diopter is a bifocal lens. It's just cut in half. The screen is split, so you can have half of the shot focusing at ten feet and the other half focusing at four feet. So you can have a man sitting close to you and the person he's talking to, who is much farther away, are both in quite sharp focus—which we did on *Breaker Morant*. There's a dividing line, but in that film we used the cords that operated the windows as the line. If anyone looks at it closely, you'll see a slightly different focus in the texture of the wall, but nobody does. As long as you don't sustain the shot or push it to a ridiculous point, the audience will buy it. Split diopter lenses are ideal for courtroom scenes because people stay still. You could use them a lot more when you're with a director who will understand they are great to use for that small cut. Most younger directors want the whole scene to go right through, from beginning to end. The actor is going to move across this focus line and you can't use it.

Q: Were the courtroom scenes in *Breaker Morant* shot with a single camera?

A: All single camera. All of the Australian films were shot with a single camera. Chris Columbus, the director of *Nine Months*, is basically from comedy, and always has a second camera available. It's often a big compromise for lighting and in detailing both cameras. If you shoot an actor in a place for one camera, then it doesn't work on the other camera. From the actor's point of view in a two character scene, one actor is being presented on one camera and two actors are being presented on the other. I would much prefer to work very, very fast. You can almost work as fast with one camera as you can with two. A second camera certainly has its place for stunts, special effects, high camp, outrageous comedy. We shot stunts on *Nine Months* with four cameras, but for the bread and butter work, one camera is the way to go. I'm not a strong advocate of two cameras as a day-to-day thing, but if the director insists on it, I've got to do it where I can.

Q: What was the shooting ratio on *Breaker Morant*?

A: Breaker Morant was about ten to one. Because of economy, we shot eighty-five thousand feet. Since then, in America I've done several films that went over a million feet. We shot movies at eight to one in Australia. When you consider the run up and all the rest, it isn't eight to one of useable film because there's a lot of film consumed in clappers and running down after the scene. Also, you get all those unpregnant pauses.

Q: Breaker Morant concludes with a military execution scene which takes place at dawn. Was any additional light utilized to photograph that sequence?

A: The firing squad scene was shot over two mornings at dawn. There was no lighting involved at all, it was all sunlight. I insisted everyone be there an hour before sunrise. The hour was in case one of the trucks broke down. Everyone was there precisely one hour before and they were standing around waiting. It was cold. Of course everything worked perfectly, so they got a bit angry, but it was a fine scene. It was shot with military precision. I had two cameras. The whole scene was rehearsed in my mind, with the crew and the director. It was all virtually single shots, and we just moved to another situation. Within those half-hour breaks, we achieved up to twelve different camera angles. It was very, very fast. I must admit, I was a bit tense because that film was on a very limited budget and we only had those two mornings. We didn't quite have the star system you've got here, but Bryan Brown was sitting on the chair discussing his motivation with Bruce as the sun was coming up. I yelled at him that his motivation was I'd smack him in the mouth if he didn't shut up and get on with it. That's something you certainly couldn't do in Hollywood. Then the scene putting the bodies into the wagon was shot about an hour after. We were trying to keep that same morning light.

Q: Don's Party had many characters and complex blocking. How did you and Director Bruce Beresford work out the camera positions?

A: Don's Party was shot at night in a real house. Alongside every scene in the script we had a floor plan of that house. Each actor was given a color so we knew exactly where each and every actor was at any given time in the film. A character would be drinking at the bar for a half an hour of the film—then he walked over and stayed talking to this girl for forty-five minutes. Every time that corner of the room was seen, he would have to be talking to that girl. Everyone was in place for every angle.

Q: It sounds like the actors had to be very precise in their blocking.

A: It was pretty rigorous. Improvisation is a luxury I became involved in when I got to America. Most Australian films haven't the budget. *Mrs. Doubtfire* was miles and miles of improvisation, but you'd find probably 80 percent of the film was still the original script. There are improvisations within the original script and working with a talent like Robin Williams, but it's amazing, often even with all that work it still gets back to the script. That's the only way a movie hangs together.

Q: You've worked with two wonderful improvisational actors, John Cassavetes in *Tempest* and Robin Williams in *Mrs. Doubtfire*. Is there a differ-

ent approach in filming the work of an actor when you don't precisely know
where they are going to be at any one point?

A: Yes, that situation is an occasion where two cameras are justified because you may be on a close-up, then right alongside of it you sneak in a
camera shooting wide. Then, if the actor goes bananas you've got a chance
of keeping up with him. If you're too tight, it just gets very distracting. If the
actor is moving fast, that's the classic place where two cameras locked side
by side works quite well. If you can't really anticipate what's going to happen, then two cameras are great.

Q: How did you get the assignment to photograph *Tempest*, directed by
Paul Mazursky?

A: Tempest was my first big American film. I'd shot a couple of films in
the Philippines and an American movie in Australia. I got a call in the middle of the night from this guy, Mazursky. He rang me at three o'clock in the
morning because he got the time wrong. I said, "It's three o'clock in the
morning, I'm thrilled you rang. Ring me back in fifteen minutes, I'll get up
and have a cup of coffee and I'll be able to talk to you." In the interim, I managed to get a book out and found out who Paul Mazursky really was. He rang
me back, and we struck a deal there on the phone. He said he would pay me
to meet him in Athens, Greece for two weeks and if we got along together,
he'd keep me on the movie. The script was a little strange to me. I didn't
fully get some of the American cultural background to the characters. We
met formally and had a lot of discussions. From that point on, I started to understand what the movie was about. I needed Paul to interpret some of it.
The topography of the places we were shooting was something I'd never
seen before. So because of my lack of knowledge and experience, I did have
to develop a vision. Of course, by the end of the two weeks I could see the
movie and we shot it.

Q: What was the visual concept of *Tempest?*

A: It had to fulfill the John Cassavetes character's requirement of a magical place. The whole place had to have an illusion of reality to take him away
from the life we'd seen him live in New York. It had to be that mystical place
a lot of people were trying to escape to. It was a fulfillment of the midlife cri-
sis of the character. The audience had to feel the infection of that place in
Greece as Cassavetes might feel it. There had to be a slight feeling of opulent excess in New York. The balance between those two places were the
two sides of the scale of the film.

Q: What photographic elements helped to create the magical world in
Greece?

A: The light—it's cloudless. We had a lot of trouble getting cloudless skies. We'd shoot scenes, and in the afternoon the clouds came. It was supposed to be an idyllic world for this man who had lived in a terribly delineated square, boxed world of New York. There were quite brilliant, massive slabs of color and totally irregular shapes. The production designer, Pato Guzman, and Paul flew along half the coast of the world searching for that little magic bay that created the illusion. That bay was a beautiful spot. They didn't arrive at a bay and say, "We'll turn this into it"—that was that place.

Q: The scene where Susan Sarandon, who plays mistress to the Cassavetes character, and Molly Ringwald, who plays his daughter, sing "Why Do Fools Fall in Love" in the water is a gorgeous moment. The two women have a special enchanting beauty about them. How did you capture this on film?

A: It's never the immediate detail. I mean, I had Susan beautifully back-lit with the water splashing around her. You can talk about the quality of the light, which was correct for the scene, but I think we had gotten the audience into wanting to perceive her in that way. That's what you're doing all the time. You're creating a situation. If it works, they're seeing more than they're actually seeing. They're seeing more beauty because they feel the beauty that you did at the time. You felt the wonder that emanated from the Cassavetes character. The performances are great, but it's that cumulation which takes it one step into wonderment. So when the audience sees it, they have an entirely different reaction than if the same scene was used to sell Coca Cola. I could shoot that same scene in a way you'd be intrigued and amused, but you wouldn't look at it for that wonderment the situation creates. That's theater. That's what it's all about and we're part of theater.

Q: How did you work with Director Alan Pakula on the film adaptation of the play *Orphans*?

A: To me, it's in many ways the best work I've done in America. Alan Pakula is wonderful to work with, probably of all the directors I've worked with, the one who analyzes each and every part of the film to the near absolute degree. We lived close together in New York. In the morning, we'd pick him up in the car and talk about the scene going to work. We'd arrive, go into an office, and talk about the scene for another hour. Then he'd go and talk with the actors for an hour and a half. I'd go talk with them for a half an hour about how they were going to do it. Then we'd get the principal crew people in and talk for another half hour. After lunch, we'd come back and rehearse the scene in detail. We had a second team of three wonderful actors who mimicked both the dialogue and performances. We set up quite an interesting system of working within that house on *Orphans*. It was a very complex design. We were endlessly moving through all those rooms. The interior of that house was all a set. You saw an exterior house, which was left as a construction office for a development. They just demolished the whole thing and left this one house. You walk around inside that house, and inside other houses, and then you adapt. You say, "Where would the light come from if I was sitting in this room?" It's pretty obvious here that the light is falling on your face and there's only subdued ambience on this side of my face from a little bit of the practicals up on the ceiling. If I was shooting a close-up of me on a stage and I wanted the audience to believe they were really in this room, it's the way I'd do it. Most times, it really is just reproducing and enhancing reality. You just take reality so many steps beyond the reality the language of the film demands.

So then we'd start rehearsing the crew about which lights would change as the characters would go through rooms. About four or five o'clock we'd start to shoot a five-minute sequence. We might shoot it once or twice—it could take three-quarters of an hour—and then we'd very quickly do three, four, six, or how many close-ups there were to match that sequence, and we'd finish the day by seven. The efficiency of the work was amazing, even though sometimes the crew would be sitting around for six hours playing cards while we were doing all of this preparation, but it all worked for that particular, enclosed part of the film. We kept on-schedule and made an interesting film.

Q: What tools are available to you as a cinematographer to enhance the look of the production design and to create a visual style?

A: The first tool I've got is camera placement, where I place the camera, the height you shoot from. Many times, shooting low-angle can give a character power. A high angle often makes a person feel vulnerable and lost.

I have the lens. I can have a full-length shot of an actor on an extreme wide-angle lens and it will say something in that situation. It will say something extremely different than a full-length shot of the same actor with a long lens, fifty yards back. You can't lay rules about what these effects will say—it's a feeling, but that angle of view which is created by the focal length of the lens you were using—from taking a real wide view of the situation to a narrow view—is a wonderful tool. You can isolate people from the environment. You can lose people in the environment. If you work by rules, you've lost, but once you raise or lower the camera, you're taking away a normal view. It's a view the audience wouldn't have of that situation if they were there, and you're asking and telling them something differently.

The camera can move laterally, sideways, or it can stay still. Movement has to be for a reason. It can be a very simple reason—you want to keep up with the movement of the actor. It can be movement to transfer the interest from one area of the scene to another. It's all complex and all related to a particular situation, but it will say something differently than just leaving a camera steady. If you move the camera, you're going to disturb the audience in some way, and the degree you disturb them is something you've got to be very aware of.

I've got the lighting, which can be a very powerful tool, a very powerful statement. Knowing how to light is an accumulation of a lot of experience. Lighting can reveal a face, hide a face, create any mood.

The film stock itself is chosen to adapt to the situation. If you're working where there isn't a lot of light and you want to use available light, you have to use a fast stock. For exteriors, you use a much slower stock.

The degree you expose this stock is another tool. If you overexpose and it's bright, you're making quite a clear statement; underexpose it, you're making another statement. Nowadays, the skill of using film stocks isn't quite as fine as it used to be because the stock was far less sensitive to a wide range of colors and lights than it is now. As long as you basically expose film so that there's a strong image on the negative, then in postproduction you can turn a sunny, day-lit scene into a dark, moonlit night scene. You don't want to have to do that very often, but that's the range you have back in the laboratory.

Understanding what these movements, what this height, what this lens will do, is the craft. It's like words are to a piece of literature. These are the words I've got and there are a lot of them. They get very complex.

Q: What are the general principles of working with light?

A: We work with two sources of light. There's daylight and manufactured light. Sometimes it's a combination of both, but normally in commercial cinema you can't sustain a combination of both because the sun goes behind a cloud and the sun moves. If the sun is shining through a window at forty-five degrees at ten o'clock, it's not going to do that again until ten o'clock the next day. So you just can't rely on that. The source of light all over the world is the sun. There are only two things that can vary it: the topography and surface that reflects the sun, like a green field, a sandy beach, black rocks, the water; and diffusion, mostly being created through a cloud. The sun is quite different in cities. In London, the fog makes the sunlight beautiful, it's like having a big silk, a big diffusion right on the sun. You still get your direct sun, but the shadow areas are just automatically filled. With the dark red earth of the center of Australia, it's the total reverse. There's zero pollution, the sun just beats through like a knife and very little is reflected back. You've got extreme contrasts. Those are the only differences you're working with all the time. I was working here in San Francisco down on a beach by the water with the sun, and a little bit of pollution here did help, but it still is a beast to work with in the sense of being a harsh light. For most film scenes you don't want that harsh light and you're fighting against it. So it really is not quite such a big deal as some cinematographers pretend it is. It's one source in the sky—it does change angle as you proceed to get away from the equator area north and south and with the season, but it's still just the sun and the earth.

If you're doing an outrageous comedy in full sunlight, like a lot of the scenes in *Nine Months*, you must get enough fill light in on the actors' faces so you could pretty clearly read what's going on. Of course, if the audience ever gets the feeling there's a light involved, then I feel like I've failed.

Q: So the art is in making the lighting look as if it's part of the available light source in the scene.

A: Yes, the mind, in conjunction with the eye, is wonderful at being able to go into shadows. The film hasn't got the physical or mental capacity to do that. So you just try to go up to or somewhere below, but never past that line where it looks like you've lit. This, in actual fact, involves massive amounts of light to make sure it looks like there's no light there. To get the feel of a person walking towards the light if they move forward or back three, four, or ten feet, you've got to have a lot of light a long way away. It's a very expensive and time-consuming process to get that effect.

Q: What are the qualities of the magic hour, the time of day when the sun is beginning to set?

A: The light is virtually nondirectional, as it is on a heavy, cloudy day. The light level is very low and the sky brightness relative to the ground brightness gets much closer. So you could shoot the sky and it looks dark. You can introduce illumination, like simply carrying a candle, and it will work if you're game to wait long enough. Magic hour often is an opportunity to shoot a scene over a very wide area that you couldn't afford to light and to convince the audience it's night, moonlight, or a diffused night, because any lights you have on in houses or you prelight will look like lights on at night. One real set-up with multiple cameras is all you ever are going to get with magic hour at the precise moment. It's fun sitting around trying to get the precise moment. It's a real gamble. Your meters can do it, but it gets back to your intuition about what will work. In summer, the sun rises vertically and sets vertically, thereupon, magic hour's shorter. In winter, depending on the latitude you're at, the sun comes at a much more acute angle and apparently rises much more slowly. I don't think there is any more light at either end of the day, except maybe in industrial areas where the pollution level may be higher and diffuse it a little earlier. Most people get worried about shooting magic hour in the morning because they're working away from a window of opportunity. At nighttime, you're working into a window of opportunity. It's psychologically better to start when it is too bright and then build down until the point where it's too dark, and then build up. It doesn't phase me particularly either way. Logistically, you find it's much easier to get a hundred people together at dusk than it is at dawn.

Q: The sequences which take place in Moscow in *Moscow on the Hudson* were shot in Germany. How were you able to capture the look of Russia there?

A: The drama is more important than the truth of the way you work. The story required reasons for the character wanting to leave Russia, and so it was always cold and drafty. It was shot in Munich in the middle of summer. We had five hundred extras, all done in very heavy, cold gear standing in line on a street. We always had the streets shaded, even if the sun was shining, and always underexposed a bit to try and keep that feeling of a solemn, ugly Moscow. Now, I know the sun must shine as brilliantly in Moscow in the winter as it shines in New York, but we're adapting the light all the time to tell a story.

Q: The scene in which the Robin Williams character defects to the United States was shot on the cosmetics floor in Bloomingdale's. You were able to capture the high-key, glamorous lighting designed by the industrial lighting designer for Bloomingdale's. How did you light this scene?

A: I only enhanced it a little. Basically, I used the lighting that was there. We had to add a little bit of the overall fill light because there were too many areas of darkness for the film stock to handle. So many of the fixtures there were green fluorescent. We had to either replace or color them with gelatin filters so they didn't look like ugly patches of green through the store. That's all we did. We had to get in at night after the store was closed, so it was fast and furious work, and I mostly used available light.

Q: The shot of Robin Williams and Maria Conchita Alonso in the bathtub had a lovely romantic quality to it. How did you capture that on film?

A: We had to create a romantic feel in what was a very down-market little apartment. You can't turn it into an Arabian boudoir all of a sudden. So the illusion I had to create was a scene lit from one practical lamp. I enhanced that with a soft light support, but never got away from the fact that it was that one light. The accumulation of all the efforts that went on before and at that point enhance the scene. So often, high moments in mine and most other people's films never quite have the impact in dailies because there it's just a shot, but in a progression, you've managed to create some magic and that's the wonder of what we do to write it.

Q: What was it like to shoot in a jungle for *Predator*?

A: The real problem in a jungle is the old cliche, "You can't see the forest through the trees." If you are in a real jungle, then the back wall of where you're working is about ten feet away from you. That's all you see. As it thins out, you might get to twenty feet. So you can't work in an absolute real jungle. You've got to work in modified jungle, in which you have a lot of people cutting out a lot of the undergrowth. We shot *Predator* in Mexico. Most of the jungle in the film was replanted. You have to select the areas you want. You've got to put the light twenty feet away and it's obliterated by trees before it reaches the subject. If you put the light near the camera, it would look like you were shooting a home movie because the foreground trees are always going to be stronger lit than the background trees. So I just didn't bother lighting. I went in with a fast stock and 99 percent of the time we used no lighting at all for the daytime sequences. That requires a certain amount of skill in exposing and adapting as the day goes by—it's real tricky.

Q: What is involved in shooting a night exterior?

A: It's not much of a problem in an urban situation because there are always streetlights, shop lights, and you enhance and support these lights. As soon as you get outside an urban situation, you really are in a problem. When somebody walks through a forest at night, you can pass them two feet away and you'd never see them. So you really are extremely limited, moonlight is the only excuse you've got. You can see a beautiful moonlit night out on the desert or in the mountains for miles. It's obviously a reflected sunlight, but it's impossible to reproduce that. So at night you have to limit your depth. The only way of getting any real depth in these situations is magic hour. *Thelma and Louise* is an example where they tried to start this language of there being streaks of light going out into the desert and accepting it as night because there was nothing else they could do. It was an element that was logically ridiculous, and whether it worked aesthetically or not depends on the viewer. You've got to have something you can light. There has to be some sort of a background, or you are just lighting air.

Q: The finale of *Patriot Games* is a long, involved scene when the terrorists attack Jack Ryan's house. It culminates in a boat chase on the ocean. The entire scene takes place at night. This must have been a real challenge.

A: It's a rainy night, so moonlight is eliminated. We're at a house where there's a party going on and there are some outside lights, but then the plot says the terrorists pull the power. So you now have a situation in which it's totally black. All you can do is deceptively bring in soft ambience which would never be there in a million years. I mean, you could actually go out in that yard at night and take the lid off the magazine of the camera, handle the film, put it all back, and nothing would be exposed on the film. So you do have to go back to just absolute blind tricks. What you do is say there's some moonlight around and an ambient glow that sometimes exists at night, and you enhance it to the point where you can actually see what's going on. In that situation, I have to use an awful lot of soft light. A lot of shots were done at magic hour so there was still some level. Then they run out along a cliff at night—once again, you couldn't see a foot in front of your face, yet you've got to show the audience where they are. So you just sneak in an ambient level of light. Then they get on a boat and head out to sea. There's lights on the boat, but they wouldn't light up that much either. So you create a whole ambience at sea in the night. We shot it in the parking lot at Paramount Studios.

Exterior night in which there are no ambient lights used at all is an area that nobody has actually resolved satisfactorily. It's one of the few conventions we're still working with. The audience still accepts it, even though it should be black—you can't see an inch in front of your face. You still have to see what's going on—otherwise you could just put black film in the projector and put voices over it. I've given you the worst-case scenario, but they're the basic problems you have as a director of photography at night. It's the most unsatisfactory area I've come into, because I'm a guy who really tries to enhance reality—but reality flies out the window in those night situations.

Q: How do you work with directors?

A: I'm very much a supporter of the director, and I expect the director to support me. I very much feel it's his vision I have to interpret—if he has a vision. Some of them don't have a vision, so I have to put one in. A lot of the earlier cameramen had their vision and just did it. It was a way of doing things in those days because there was so much more mystique about their craft than there is now. Now, anyone can get a Hi8 camera and get a pretty interesting image. More and more of the directors have had some training in the field, so they're aware of what you're doing very clearly. Some of the directors in the fifties and sixties weren't that aware, and guys like James Wong Howe could do what they did. You couldn't get away with it today. The collaborations are intense. We sit side by side all day now watching video, endlessly discussing where we are, where we've been, and where we're going. So communication is endless sometimes, but good. I'm commenting as much on the performance as the director is commenting on the lighting and camera placement. We collaborate. There's an awful lot of crossover.

Q: Should a cinematographer have a visual style of their own?

A: I find "style" carried to a point can become totally boring visually. If somebody says, "What style are you going to shoot this movie in?" my answer is, "The only style I have is the style that suits the script." You do keep a concept of what the basic script is all about. Comedy might be a bit brighter than a heavy drama, but I see many scenes in heavy drama where you want a visual relief. You should get away from what you've been doing to make some real statement about what you're going to do, otherwise if you just keep it down in the same "Johnny-one-note" all the way through, it's boring.

Q: Should a film have an overall visual style?

A: There's a visual theme that goes through. It develops from the point I first start reading a script. I immediately see that film quite clearly. There will be changes, but that basic vision will stick with me until the final day I'm at the lab fine-tuning the release print. That's my craft in a nutshell. If I don't see a film when I read a script, then I'm not very interested. If the inherent drama isn't working, then I can't see the film. A script has to be a logical, entertaining piece of drama and then I can visualize it.

Whether you realize it or not, as a filmmaker you create your own language in every situation in the way you're going to communicate to an audience—a visual language. You can set certain rules very quickly and you don't usually do it consciously, you do it subconsciously. You start this style of telling a story and generally, if it's not too obvious, the audience goes along with it. *Pulp Fiction* was an extreme example of saying, "The story is going to be told this way and if you're going to enjoy it, come on board." In Baz Luhrmann's *Romeo & Juliet*, we opened with an outrageously stylized sequence that leads the audience into the character of the movie. This sequence served many functions. The most interesting to me was the way it transported the "masses" to a place where the Elizabethan English is acceptable. Lots of the more interesting filmmakers go for a more radical basic language of communicating and structuring their film. That has its own strengths and weaknesses, it depends whatever ways you support it.

Q: Can you give an example of how you translated a script into a visual conception?

A: Man Without a Face was a well-written script. When I read it, I could immediately see the character Mel Gibson had to become. I visualized a boy not unlike Nick Stahl, who played the boy very well. I'd seen enough and heard enough about Maine to know what the situation was to be like. There was some vision in my mind about the rooms. If somebody said, "Draw me that room," it would be different than the room that was finally in the film, but it would have a lot of the same elements. So, I do just pick it up and I see a movie. Some directors are actually visually illiterate because I know they can't do that. I've worked with director/writers who see the wonders of the relationships, they see the wonders of the words that they're saying to each other, but they really don't see the film that clearly. John McTiernan, who directed *Predator* and *Medicine Man*, is a wonderfully visual director to work with. Of course, it's wonderful to work with a visual director because then you're polishing the diamond, with other directors you're sometimes just out there mining the diamond. I've worked with many first-time directors; some of them are intuitively visual, some of them aren't, and some of them become visual. I worked with Paul Mazursky on four films, and it was amazing to see by the fourth film he was starting to tell me things that I told him on the first film, which we both found amusing when I pointed it out to him. I've learned endless amounts from all those people I've worked with about other aspects of this business. It's always a two-way game.

Q: Your work demonstrates a real affinity for vistas and landscapes. Why do you think you have this ability to capture the outdoors?

A: I love the outdoors. I live in a forest in Australia. I spent my most interesting vacations in the wilderness of the desert, which I love. So I do have a great passion for space and the tranquility it offers. I feel very comfortable in the remoteness in my forest. You just relate what you see to what you feel is in the script, and you find a place to put the camera which expresses that relationship with the place, the script, the drama, and you say, "Here it is." Generally, I can convince or explain to the director why the particular spot suits.

Q: How much does the director of photography need to understand about editing?

A: Because of my news background and working in a documentary organization like Film Australia, I never shoot a scene that can't be edited. Once or twice I've been challenged, somebody's editor came in and said, "I can't cut this." They just couldn't see the way I'd structured it. After work, I ducked into the editing room and said, "This is the way I shot it, put that to that, that to that," and everyone's been content. So I don't shoot anything that won't make a sequence, and usually a reasonably eloquent sequence. It's part of the gifts I think I have. Then the great editors come back and produce a scene that has enhanced what you've done and looks nothing like what you envisioned. There may be no cut that matched what you had in mind and that's the wonder of the business, but at least it will always cut the way I had it in mind. It may not be exciting, but it will always work.

This business of visualization is not really the visualization of a static shot, it's the visualization of a sequence on a screen. It is cuts, it's close-ups, it's medium shots, it's wide shots, it's tracking shots. I can see five actors play a scene and immediately I have a pattern of the way to shoot it. That's just intuitive. One of the things I do as a director of photography is make suggestions. It's just a matter of saying, "Don't you walk across here or there. You stay in this group, then go over here." It's mechanical, but it can get you into and out of a lot of trouble very quickly. In terms of production, the skills I have save thousands and thousands of dollars in the speed in which things can happen. You're planning ahead.

Q: Where do you see the future of the craft of cinematography? Will film survive the next century?

A: That Panavision camera is a means of recording a performance. There's no way I can see any threat to what's basically very cheap within the concepts of a film camera. I'm sixty now. I'll just keep working until I don't get offered work of an interesting nature. It wouldn't make much difference to me whether it was recorded on laser disc, or tape, or anything else, somebody is going to have to be out there to call the shots, to call the lighting, to do all of the things I do. The whole separate little group of people who operate and maintain the camera could be retrained or replaced by anyone operating another system, but it's still going to be a system that views the scene. What we're doing is just the next step from theater. Cinema is this very flexible, portable theater we take with us, and I can't see that form of entertainment changing. The way that people view it may be different, but I think they're still going to want to see dramatic performances and dramatic plays recorded. They're still going to have to be lit, there are still going to have to be decisions made on lenses, movement, and all the other things I spoke about. Somebody—either me or somebody like me—will be around to make those decisions and be sought after as much as people in my craft are today.

6

John Bailey

While Francis Ford Coppola, Brian De Palma, Steven Spielberg, George Lucas, and Martin Scorsese were becoming movie brat generation film directors during the sixties, a new breed of cinematographer was emerging. The seventies heralded a New American Cinema, which demanded an innovative approach to the art of cinematography. Inspired by classical Hollywood masters and the international cinema of Yasujiro Ozu, Carl Dreyer, Robert Bresson, Michelangelo Antonioni, and Bernardo Bertolucci, John Bailey, ASC, was one of this new breed.

John Bailey comes from a blue-collar family in Moberly, Missouri. He was educated at the University of Santa Clara in California, Loyola University in Los Angeles, the University of Southern California Film School in Los Angeles, and at the University of Vienna in Austria.

During the sixties, the USC Film School was fertile ground for filmmakers. Bailey attended the graduate program during the era when George Lucas, John Milius, Hal Barwood, Matthew Robbins, Randall Kleiser, Willard Huyck, and Walter Murch were on campus. Bailey shot as many student films as he could to learn the art and craft of cinematography.

After school, Bailey began to work with many fine cinematographers. He was assistant cameraman to his mentor, Director of Photography Gregory Sandor, on Director Monte Hellman's *Two Lane Blacktop*. In commercials, he assisted Laszlo Kovacs and Philip Lathrop. As a camera operator, Bailey worked with Charles Rosher Jr. on *The Late Show*, directed by Robert Benton, and Robert Altman's *Three Women*; with Vilmos Zsigmond on *Winter*

Kills, directed by William Richert; and most notably with Nestor Almendros on *Days of Heaven*, directed by Terence Malick.

After becoming a director of photography in the late seventies, Bailey spent the next decade developing an impressive body of work, including *American Gigolo*, *Ordinary People*, and the visually dazzling Paul Schrader production of *Mishima*.

John Bailey has worked with a diverse group of directors, including long associations with Lawrence Kasdan and Paul Schrader, and collaborations with Robert Redford, John Schlesinger, Walter Hill, Richard Benjamin, Gene Saks, Karen Arthur, Stuart Rosenberg, Michael Apted, Wolfgang Petersen, Robert Benton, Errol Morris, Jonathan Demme, Herbert Ross, Harold Ramis, James L. Brooks, and Richard La-Gravenese.

John Bailey has directed *The Search for Signs of Intelligent Life in the Universe*, *China Moon*, and *Mariette in Ecstasy*, while continuing to be a working cinematographer. A devoted cineaste, and an articulate spokesman for the art of cinematography, John Bailey is a homegrown cameraman who brings global artistic influences to American film.

SELECTED FILMOGRAPHY

1972   *Premonition*
1974   *End of August*
1975   *Legacy*
1978   *Mafu Cage*
1979   *Boulevard Nights*
1980   *American Gigolo*
       Ordinary People
1981   *Honky Tonk Freeway*
       Continental Divide
1982   *Cat People*
       That Championship Season
1983   *Without a Trace*
       The Big Chill
1984   *Racing with the Moon*
       The Pope of Greenwich Village
1985   *Mishima: A Life in Four Chapters*
       Silverado

Q: Which directors of photography did you work with when you started out in Hollywood as an assistant cameraman and camera operator?

A: My mentor was Gregory Sandor, a wonderful cinematographer who never really was in the Hollywood mainstream. He had worked in Cuba. He was Hungarian, but in style very American. He photographed two of Monte Hellman's early Westerns, *Ride in the Whirlwind* and *The Shooting*. I was his assistant on Monte's *Two Lane Blacktop*. It was my first studio picture. Gregory was a very classical cinematographer. He was a proponent of a codified system of lighting by virtue of his Hungarian training. He believed the key light should be in the direction of the actor's look and that there should be a proportionate counter-key light or a rim or hair light. The fill light was always set to a precise ratio. Greg's one-light dailies looked like answer prints, everything was set perfectly with every composition composed in balance. There was nothing ragged or erratic and, by the same token, there was nothing dangerous or unpredictable. It was absolutely classical. He was a great hard light man and he used soft light mainly for fill. I watched him work—always quietly, very simply, and always with consistency and a methodology to the work.

I didn't assist a lot of the Hollywood "big guns" like Harry Stradling, Phil Lathrop, or Fred Koenekamp because I got in the union through the back door. I was never really integrated until I became a camera operator. I did two pictures with Chuck Rosher Jr., *The Late Show* and *Three Women*. I worked with Vilmos Zsigmond on *Winter Kills*, a very bizarre, offbeat picture from a Richard Condon novel. I did commercials with Laszlo Kovacs, Ric Waite, and Don Peterman.

I was also camera operator for Nestor Almendros on *Days of Heaven*. As we were doing certain shots, I just said, "My God, this shot is an archetype!" Sometimes I would look through the finder and it took my breath away because it was so perfect.

Q: What did you learn from working with Nestor Almendros?

A: Simplicity. Nestor very much believed in a single source, either simulating or using existing light as much as possible. There was a purity and an honesty to what he did. He was not big on camera moves or fancy compositions. On one hand, you could say his work was rudimentary and on the other hand, you could say his work was just distilled to the essence. Depending on the individual film, the work looked either luminous or naturalistic because he surrendered himself completely to the material. I don't think he ever tried to transform it. What I learned from him was always to find a simple truth. Even if I found myself working in a complex way, I tried to keep centered on a single, clear objective because that's what he did very well. But more than anything else, what I learned from Nestor was a sense of heart and humanity. He had a very large soul and was very beloved. During the course of a production, he would sit down at lunch with different people every day to make sure that he dined with everybody on the crew. For the most part, he worked in New York and he maintained his European sensibilities. He did not penetrate or have much of an influence on the Hollywood mainstream of cinematographers of his own age-group, but he had a tremendous influence on my generation. He eventually got into the ASC, but I don't ever remember seeing him at one of the meetings or functions because he was hardly ever in Los Angeles. He hated to come here with a passion, as only a sophisticated Spaniard could.

Q: How would you classify your visual style as a cinematographer?

A: I consider myself a classicist, even though early on I did a couple of films like *American Gigolo*, which were considered innovative. I've always really loved classical cinematography and the classical filmmakers. The filmmakers I love are some of the same ones Paul Schrader loves, and Schrader was a big influence on me. I love Ozu, Dreyer, and Bresson. Antonioni is an incredible classicist, just the purity of the image. He doesn't do things strictly for the dazzle. We see more and more of that in films—the "Hey, look at me," kind of lighting and camera moves. I find the fatigue factor is so quick. There really isn't anything as ultimately stimulating, rewarding, and that has a longer hang time in your consciousness than the classical, well-composed, well-lit shot, and that's what I aspire to. There are many different ways to light classically. There's the classic Hollywood portrait lighting, there's the classic French or northern European Vermeer, soft, single-source style. The classical style really appeals to me because it is not only beautiful in its own right—it makes the viewer feel centered and really comfortable in the image—but it's also totally supportive of the drama or the comedy. The cinematography ultimately has to serve the narrative line, and classical cinematography does that best.

Q: There are so many European cinematic and literary inputs into your work, but many of the films you have photographed are very American. That combination makes for a unique visual style.

A: The mixture of the two has really intrigued me for a long time because I went to film school in the sixties when the French New Wave, films by Godard, Truffaut, Malle, Chabrol, and Rivette were really at the forefront.

Q: Were you influenced by French New Wave cinematographers like Raoul Coutard?

A: Yes, and even older cinematographers like Henri Decae, Sacha Vierny, and Henri Alekan—but also the younger ones: Willy Kurant, Jean Boffety, Pierre Lhomme—there were a lot of wonderful French cinematographers at that time. Everything about the films we were looking at was completely different from Hollywood. I was intrigued with the way they portrayed life because they weren't larger than life, they were very much of life. The films were very tactile and I loved that technique. My influences have all been European—partly because of my film school experience, partly because even though I grew up in Los Angeles, I didn't have any relatives in the business. I wasn't so interested in the studio vehicles. My love of Hollywood cinematography came much later, in the seventies, after I started working in the industry myself. Then I started to go back and really see the work of great black-and-white cinematographers like George Folsey, Arthur Miller, Leon Shamroy, William Daniels—there are so many of them. From the time I was a student, I loved Gregg Toland. As I started working in the industry, I understood there was something about American filmmaking that appealed to the whole world—the tightness, the discipline, the pacing, the moral imperative. The characters don't have too many colors of dramatic gray; they know what is right or wrong. These are some of the many elements that reside deep in our own character and psyche—those things we think of as being American. I finally had to admit to myself, "I am an American filmmaker, even though the films I really love are European films." I love Truffaut, Bergman, and Antonioni, those are my gods, but I can never make films like that. For me, the last fifteen years or so has been trying to come to terms with that. The fact that I have worked in the Hollywood mainstream as a cinematographer for so long finally washed over me. I made peace with it.

Q: How did you first come to work with Paul Schrader on *American Gigolo*?

A: I knew his reputation as a collaborator with Martin Scorsese on *Taxi Driver* and had seen his first film, *Blue Collar*. He was very hot and very hip. I was in awe of him. I also knew of his work as a critic. Paul really wanted a European cameraman, such as Sven Nykvist or Nestor Almendros, but they weren't available. Getting *American Gigolo* was a baptism of fire for me. I met with Paul several times. The first time, we talked a lot about Bertolucci and Antonioni in terms of staging, because they're both brilliant in the way they block scenes. Paul was intrigued with the formal aspects of their filmmaking. I made an impression on him, but he told my agent at the time, Jo An Kincaid, that I wasn't experienced enough, so he wasn't going to hire me. Jo An wasn't going to give up. She found out he was going to be at a party that coming Saturday night. She crashed the party, found him, got him into a room, closed the door, and said, "I'm not letting you out of here until you have another meeting with John Bailey." Paul was charmed by her, so he invited me to his house and we talked for six hours. He put up a lot of videotapes: Bresson's *Pickpocket*; Antonioni's *La Notte*, *Eclipse*, *L'avventura*; Bertolucci's *The Conformist*, which was a key film for both of us. Ferdinando Scarfiotti was going to be production designer for *American Gigolo*.

Q: Scarfiotti told me that you and Paul Schrader were fascinated with *The Conformist*. Why did this film so capture your cinematic imagination?

A: Like all the films I've really been moved by, it's not just the stylistic formalist approach, but the conflict, torment, and the betrayal of the story. *The Conformist* was thematically so powerful. To find such a personal story told against the backdrop of the great human and social upheaval of Italy in the thirties, but also to keep very close to the perspective of one man's story of loss of his soul was very compelling to me. It was illustrated in a very cool, controlled way, like moving pieces around a chessboard. The way the story was revealed in flashback, with time moving back and forth, was just the most intricately appealing maze. A lot of elements came together in that film: the design aesthetic, Scarfiotti's sense of the beautiful locations and the set dressing, the camera movement, compositions and lighting of Vittorio Storaro. It was a perfect blending of three collaborators working together—just perfect unity.

I decided to become a cinematographer the night I saw *The Conformist* at the Regent Theater in Westwood. I was an assistant on commercials at the time. We had wrapped early one afternoon, so I went to a five-o'clock screening by myself. I saw the film and was knocked out. I phoned Jim Dickson, the cinematographer I'd been doing all of these commercials with, and said, "Come on down here and see this movie tonight." He said, "I'm getting ready to have dinner." While I was waiting for him, I went in and sat through the movie for a second time. He arrived for the nine-o'clock show and I watched it a third time. I walked out of the theater about midnight. After seeing that movie, I was absolutely convinced I wanted to be a cinematographer. I told Vittorio Storaro that story much later when I finally met him. Vittorio and I have become really good friends since then.

Q: What was it like to work with Ferdinando Scarfiotti?

A: At first, I was very intimidated. Nando was like a god to me, even on the basis of the few films he had done. They were in that Italian style of quiet sophistication. He was very gracious and warm. He had that sense of being able to look at something and totally place it in a critical or aesthetic perspective almost just by virtue of his breeding, but there was nothing pretentious about it—that's what was so amazing. I had studied for a year in Europe. I had been an undergraduate in Austria. So I had started to develop some sense of aesthetics, but I came from a real blue-collar family. We had American pseudo-Colonial maple furniture and knotty pine paneling in our den and thought very highly of it because that was about as far up the ladder as my parents and our friends got. It was only when I went to Europe that I started to see the way the highly refined modernist Bauhaus aesthetic could, in the right context, go side by side with a piece of Baroque sculpture. Nando had absolute confidence in mixing materials and colors. Nando really had a vision of *American Gigolo*. It was a question of my trying to play catch-up and to photographically do the most appropriate and collaborative work possible. I started to develop more and more confidence. When you're really working "in the flow" of something, you do start to work beyond what you think your own limits are. That was the first time that had ever happened to me. It was only my second picture as a cinematographer and during the course of it, I found tremendous confidence. I suddenly found I was working on a level parallel to Paul and Nando, but able to make my own contributions.

Q: In *American Gigolo*, there are shots of light streaming through the blinds. Was this a reference to *The Conformist*?

A: It was a total homage to Storaro, to the scene when Trintignant comes to visit his fiancee. They go into the little sitting room and start to dance, and the light from the Venetian blind starts to move up and down the wall. This also echoes the black and white stripes of her dress. Of course, I had seen the Venetian blind effect in the noir films of the forties, but it had never impressed me as a dramatic or character element. In *The Conformist*, it was used very expressively. I was intrigued. Nando wanted to use these thin Levelor blinds, which were quite new at the time. Julian Kay, Richard Gere's character, was a man in transition—he never quite moved into his apartment. There were crates on the floor. Things stacked up against the walls which were bare. When I saw that set, with those gray walls with nothing on them, I started to think of how light and shadow and different colored lights would essentially define the apartment each time we were there. In a sense, the light and patterns could become a mirror to what was happening to the Richard Gere psyche—the escalating sense of isolation, paranoia, and entrapment. So I tried to find a way to plot that by using the light on the walls. It was not necessarily always as dramatic as the Venetian blind effect, sometimes it was just flashes or cuts of light. Sometimes it was just the way a light or a color spilled on the wall or a single color used to enhance that feeling.

Q: The opening of *American Gigolo* features a montage of Julian Kay driving to the music of Blondie. How did you accomplish the sweeping movements of the camera?

A: That was before you could do sweep-arounds with a camera remote or a Louma crane. The Mercedes was being towed in the center of a U-shaped plywood platform that we laid dolly track on, and it was pulled by a forty-foot-long flatbed truck which circled three sides of the car. The studio was very upset because it was an incredibly expensive shot to do and did not represent much of a page count. We did a few shots like that. It was a fairly low-budget film, it was not a film that the studio had any great expectations for. Richard Gere wasn't a star then. Originally, John Travolta was going to play the role. It was after *Saturday Night Fever*. I believe that John's mother had died and he had to drop out in preproduction.

Q: The pan of Julian matching the shirts and ties on the bed was a very effective shot. How did that come about?

A: That was a very worked-on sequence. Paul used a Pointer Sisters song, and we did shots for that sequence four or five times during the course of the film. Paul kept going back to the sequence. We shot a number of set-ups and they were cut to the song. If Paul felt the rhythms weren't quite right, he would design a couple of more shots. We'd talk about it, look at the cut sequence, and if we had an hour or so while we were waiting for something or we could sneak an hour in at the end of the day, we'd go back and do a few more shots. This sequence became the proverbial telephone booth you carry from location to location. There are some very bad lighting mismatches on Richard Gere. There are two I can think of and I still cringe at. I did close-ups of him three or four weeks apart and didn't have a match frame clip. I was pretty inexperienced at the time, I couldn't quite replicate what I had done. So I mismatched the light. This sequence was not storyboarded, it just evolved.

Q: Ferdinando Scarfiotti reconceived the Polo Lounge. In reality, the set bears no resemblance to the actual restaurant. What was the concept behind the photographic look of the Polo Lounge scenes?

A: I've collected photography for the last twenty-five years, and at that particular time in the late seventies I was collecting contemporary Los Angeles photographs by people like Jane O'Neil and Joanne Callis. Jane O'Neil had done a photograph of a closed-down restaurant in Union Station. It had hidden neon lighting on the perimeter, right around the ceiling. It had booths with an art deco feel. The restaurant Nando designed came from that photo. We didn't use neon because it would have been too noisy and wouldn't have been bright enough. So Nando designed the set with a trough all the way around the wall so we were able to put tracing paper up and light from above. The walls were all washed with pink light—that became the dominant light in the restaurant. I filled in a little bit from there. It is supposed to be the Polo Lounge, but, of course, it wasn't anything like it. They wouldn't let us shoot there anyway. They did let us shoot the scenes of Richard walking down the hallway and toward the Polo Lounge—between 2 A.M. and 5 A.M. We were in there with a skeleton crew doing two or three tie-in shots.

Q: Mishima is an intricate film with many stylistic aspects. Did you have an overall concept which helped you to capture the look of the film or did you approach it a section at a time?

A: Paul Schrader had been thinking about it for a long time. When he got me involved, he had already decided he wanted the three sections to look different. At one point, we had thought about doing the fiction (novels) section of the film in Sony's then-new, high-definition video. We went to the Sony factory outside of Tokyo, but were not very impressed. We thought it wouldn't begin to capture what Eiko Ishioka's designs promised in terms of the color, texture, and detail. We worked backwards, and said, "The most lush and opulent part of the film is going to be the designed Eiko Ishioka sections which are from the novels. So that should be a lush, brilliant, art-directed section." Working backwards, we decided the historical material would be in black-and-white. We then thought about shooting the events of Mishima's last day in video to transfer to film, but that seemed too gimmicky. So I proposed we shoot the last day, from the time that he leaves his house, goes outside the gate and gets into the car, until he's finished his speech on the balcony at Ichigaya, all handheld. Everything in his house on the last day when he wakes up and has breakfast, was done traditionally on a dolly, but as soon as he gets outside the front gate and goes out into the world, it becomes handheld. Conversely, at the end of the film, when he comes back in from the balcony to commit seppuku, from there to the end, all of the shots are totally tableau, frozen, very Ozu. The last shot was a dolly/zoom combination, but all the rest were locked-off tableaus.

There was an intention for *Mishima* to have different styles very much from the beginning. The story starts in 1930, when Mishima is five years old, and goes until the last day of his life in November 1970. In terms of the lighting and camera style, I wanted the black-and-white sections to reflect what would have been the evolving contemporary look of Japanese films. So I shot the early material with Plus X with hard lighting in very high contrast and very static compositions. As Mishima got older and we followed him through the forties, fifties, and the sixties, I went to higher speed film stocks with softer light and more camera movement. I used Double X for the last few years. This tonal subtlety doesn't read very well on video cassette, which is about the only way to see the film. It even got lost in the release prints when the picture went into general release—the black-and-white scenes all had to be printed on color stock because it had to be single-strand. The color stock did not capture the subtlety of the black-and-white. But we did have two prints made for festivals. The print shown at Cannes was black-and-white and color, spliced together. So all of the black-and-white material was actually on black-and-white stock and it was glorious to see.

Q: Has black-and-white stock changed since the studio era?

A: Yes, black-and-white doesn't look the way classic black-and-white looked because they've diminished the amount of silver in black-and-white stock so much. The silver is the key to luminous whites and absolutely black blacks.

Q: The sequences in *Crossroads* which take place at the crossroads where the devil tempted Robert Johnson have a mythic quality to them. How did that location come about and what was your visual approach to it?

A: The director, Walter Hill, is incredibly well-read. I was very interested in his knowledge of classical storytelling and Greek mythology. He sees so much in archetypes and applied it to *Crossroads*. I've loved blues music for years. Walter's an incredible blues fanatic, so we bonded right away. We looked at a lot of crossroads, lucked out and found the one in the film. It was in the middle of farmland outside of Greenville in the Delta. We were on a crane or a scaffolding to get the right angle. There was one solitary tree which was actually there. It almost looked like it was art-directed into position, but it was actually there.

Q: In the Line of Fire was a big production. What was it like to work on it?

A: By choice, I've not done very many big effects productions, so for me it was a real departure. The only other big film I'd done was *Silverado*. I had never really been interested in big genre films, but when Wolfgang Petersen sent me the script, I was fascinated with the moral dilemma, the battle of good and evil. I told Wolfgang, "What really interests me about this film is not all the chase scenes with helicopters, motorcades, and the air force. I've never done anything on that scale before. I know I'll enjoy it, but the heart of this film is the series of phone calls between Clint Eastwood and John Malkovich. If we can do a movie within a movie where those phone calls essentially lay out the film and tell the story, *that* is the challenge. They have to be visually compelling and all different. If those aren't done well, they will be so isolated and surrounded by this huge flow of space and material." So that's what I was most challenged by.

Q: The sequences in *Ordinary People* where the Judd Hirsch and Timothy Hutton characters meet for therapy sessions are also like a movie within a movie. How do you visually approach these kinds of situations within a film?

A: In *Ordinary People*, they had to meet after his swim class somewhere between four and five o'clock. It takes place from the beginning of the fall semester, past Christmas into the winter, when it verges from twilight into night. I proposed to Robert Redford to use the logic of the way light would change over these four months, starting with full daylight, going into sunset, then a late twilight, and into a full night at the end. I plotted the lighting to represent the changing season.

Q: How did you light the climactic scene when the boy goes to see the doctor late at night after his friend has committed suicide?

A: I used a very hot central light above the table where they sit and almost no fill. The only fill I used was what bounced off the floor by reflective cards. When Tim Hutton got up and walked into a corner away from that light, instead of having supplemental light I had a small light for a rim so it wouldn't go completely muddy. The logic was: if they were right in the center, they were very bright; outside of that, they were normal; and if they were in the corner, they were dark. It was as though there were a single-source light. There wasn't anything fancy or artistic about it. The feeling you got out of the scene is that he walked in, turned on the light switch that lit the light in the center of the room, and that's it. It's very severe looking, but I felt it was right. The emotion and the drama in that scene is edgy. It's such a fever pitch, it's so highly charged, you wanted something very elemental. Even though it's not elaborate or glamorous lighting, the absolute bare bones quality really served the high emotional pitch very well.

In the same way that *In the Line of Fire* had the phone calls and *Ordinary People* had the meetings with Judd Hirsch, *Groundhog Day* had the light motif of coming back to that knoll where they had the ceremony every day, over, and over, and over again. Trying to make that scene the same and yet different was very intriguing.

Those are the kinds of things that interest me as a cinematographer. People want to talk about "What color gels did you use?" and "Do you like Primo lenses?" and "Why did you shoot this film in anamorphic?" To me, this is not the essence of cinematography. When you're talking about important films seen by a large number of people and you want them to have some emotional reaction, they really don't care whether you use Primo lenses or what color gel you use, but insofar as you use those things to bring forward and illuminate an emotional, moral, or a dramatic state—that's important to talk about.

Q: There are many large-scale scenes in *In the Line of Fire*. Was it necessary to employ multiple cameras?

A: Not as much as you would think. There were some, but most of it was one camera. I've never been excited by the use of multiple cameras. The arrival of the president at the Bonaventure Hotel was shot at magic hour, so we had a very short window of light. I wanted the canopied lights to be bright and for it to be bluer outside. We only had about twenty-five minutes to shoot, and there were seven or eight shots to do. We had five cameras set up strategically so I was able to get two set-ups for each camera. That's the only scene which had extensive multiple cameras. When you're shooting in different directions, it's always a problem trying to hide the cameras. A lot of people line them up like ducks when they shoot three or four cameras and just change the focal length of the lens.

Wolfgang Petersen is a very technically dexterous director. He's got a tremendous sense of cinematic flow and movement, every shot contributes something to the sequence. He knew what he wanted. I didn't have to do as much thinking as I normally have to do, because he had things so well planned. We had a lot of time, we had a good schedule. He would prefer to have one camera get the right angle than to have three cameras get compromised angles, so our mode of working was very compatible.

Q: Clint Eastwood is a movie icon. *In the Line of Fire* was a departure for him. He plays a heroic character who has a strong romantic link to the Rene Russo character. How did you approach photographing him in this role?

A: I photographed and lit Clint in a style he doesn't ordinarily have, because he wasn't directing the movie. He's legendary for being very efficient and quick in the number of takes he does and the simplicity of the set-ups. Clint said a few things to me on *In the Line of Fire* when he thought I was taking too much time. During the rooftop chase, when Clint is running up to the edge of the precipice that Malkovich has already leapt across, Clint runs up, looks down, and decides he's not going to make that jump without backing up. There's a point-of-view shot where the camera moves up and looks over the ledge. It was a dolly shot and I wanted the camera hung out over the front of the dolly shooting straight down, even back a little bit to make it seem vertiginous. I said to Wolfgang, "This should be a disorienting shot. This is going to take a little bit of time to do," and he said, "Do it." Clint came up and saw the dolly track set-up with the camera pointing straight down and he said, "What are you doing?" I said, "It's a point-of-view," and he said, "Jeez, grab an Arriflex and just lean over and shoot it." I'm sure it would have been fine for him, but the fact of the matter is that I couldn't have shot straight down and I couldn't have done it smoothly. Also, we were shooting anamorphic. The shot lasts three seconds, but I think it's a very disorienting and disturbing shot when you see it on-screen. If I had been shooting for Clint Eastwood, he may not have wanted it done that way. But that's a director's choice. He has a different aesthetic from mine and it's an incredible one. Look at a film like *Bird*, it's masterfully made the way the story is told.

A common visual thread in all of Clint Eastwood's films is very strong, single-source lighting with almost no fill, very severe. When Bruce Surtees was working with him, you could hardly see what was going on in the frame. Jack Green now has modified that style, but has continued it to a certain extent. It's what Clint really likes. It's not the most flattering light for him, and I didn't feel at all compelled to light *In the Line of Fire* the way a Clint Eastwood film would have been lit. Wolfgang and I talked about it, and we both agreed we should make him look like a leading man—sexy and attractive. Clint is a very no-nonsense guy, and very unassuming. He sometimes felt I was putzing around a little too much. He was very sweet about it, he put up with it, and it paid off. He does look good in the picture.

Q: In the scene between Eastwood and Rene Russo which takes place in front of the Lincoln Memorial, as she walks down the steps, he talks to himself about whether she will turn around to look back at him. When she does, it is shown from Eastwood's point of view. How was that shot executed?

A: It was an enormous cheat. I wanted to shoot it on a long lens from his perspective. However, shooting from his perspective, all you would see was the cement sidewalk down below. I looked at it, we tried to set something up, and it really looked ugly. It was not at all interesting on her. So we did one shot of her walking away, which had to be done in late afternoon light. I cheated the light when they're on the steps, the sunset effect was done with lights we took up there. Several days after we saw dailies, we wanted a cutback, so we sent a Steadicam operator back with a small unit. I didn't go there because we were doing the rooftop chase. We essentially had Rene do the same action we had done before, but it was her walking, with the Steadicam just following her a little bit for the second cut on the turn and the look. It's an absolutely marvelous shot. In over twenty years as a cinematographer, there's hardly ever been a close-up of an actor that I didn't actually do, but this close-up of Rene was done second unit.

Q: Was *In the Line of Fire* storyboarded?

A: Only the material which involved motion control and matte work involving Air Force One was really storyboarded. The rooftop chase and one or two other intricate sequences were storyboarded, but most of the film was not.

Q: The rooftop chase was a wonderful action sequence. I understand it was John Malkovich's idea for his character to put the barrel of the gun in his mouth.

A: It totally shocked us when he did it. It's wonderful when an actor surprises you, surprises himself. He probably didn't know he was going to do it. The angle shooting down on Clint was all rigged and shot on a rooftop in Washington, D.C. We ran out of time for the up angle of Malkovich. The shot of him leaning over holding onto Clint, the sunglasses falling off of his face, and putting his mouth on the gun, was all done in Los Angeles at the end of the schedule. It was two and a half, three months later. At that point, we were not in the studio, we were traveling around. They set up a brownstone wall in the oil fields out near the airport off of La Cienega and Stocker. It was between two locations we were doing. There were two shots on Malkovich, one over Clint and the other a clean single. If you look carefully, the lighting is mismatched because it was a more overcast day when we shot in Los Angeles. In D.C., it was stark sun. I did everything I could with an 18K HMI key light to create a sunlight effect, but it was a miserable smoggy and foggy day in February near the end of the shoot. I could never get the sky to match in terms of color.

Q: You have directed *The Search for Signs of Intelligent Life in the Universe*, *China Moon*, and *Mariette In Ecstasy*. As a cinematographer, what have you learned about directing and as director, what have you learned about cinematography?

A: As a director, one of the things I really learned about cinematography is a validation of certain things I knew ahead of time. There isn't a single shot I would do as a cinematographer I wouldn't compromise or basically undermine, if necessary, for the sake of the dramatic moment, because that's all that really counts, and I took that with me into directing. While I had great sympathy for my cinematographers, Willy Kurant (*Masculine Feminine*, *The Immortal Story*) on *China Moon*, and Paul Sarossy (*Exotica*, *The Sweet Hereafter*) on *Mariette In Ecstasy*, in terms of anything photographic, I would be equally ruthless about saying, "No, the light can't be here because of the actor's need here," or "We've got to find another way to do the shot," or "Yes, I know you didn't like that camera move as much on this last take, but the actor was so much better and I have to move on because I've got to get three more shots in the sequence." So as a director, I'd make those decisions and compromises, but I always did them with the full knowledge that I would have done the same thing as a cinematographer. The other thing I learned was a realization of how well prepared I've been as a cinematographer. When I go in, what I bring a director in terms of thinking about the story, character development, the mechanics of the plot, the emotional line, goes beyond the literal level of what a cinematographer should do. All of the really great cinematographers are concerned with the same things. So it's been very interesting for me to work with cinematographers and see the degree to which they do or don't have those same concerns. Paul Sarossy is still young and he's very much into pure cinematography. He was very filmically literate while he was shooting the movie, but he was not concerned about a lot of the other things. Maybe that was because he felt I was sufficiently grounded in the material. It's interesting for me not to have a cinematographer propose or be involved about nonphotographic things, because I expected it. As a director, I would never feel invaded by a cinematographer who would come up and say anything about a line reading or a performance. As a cinematographer, I always try to be discreet in doing that. I wouldn't say, "Hey, that was a really crappy line reading," but there are times when you feel something has slipped by the director because there are so many things to watch. Sometimes you can see something has happened you think the director needs to know. It's not purely a photographic moment. Very few script supervisors and most people on a set wouldn't presume to deal with anything beyond the mechanics of matching and so forth.

So, when necessary, I've always felt comfortable with being a second set of eyes for a beleaguered director. I know as a director, I'm open to that. Having directed, I understand firsthand just how much there is to deal with, not just in terms of what's happening for the shot, the scene, and getting the day's work done, but all the politics, all the administrative things, all the money worries, all the scheduling, all the crap that a director has to deal with that the producers say they want to protect him from—all the temperaments and egos that go swimming around every day at any given time that the cinematographer isn't necessarily aware of, all of which the director has to deal with. Even when I was photographing *Nobody's Fool* for Robert Benton, my own limited directing experience has made me much more tolerant, sympathetic, understanding, and supportive of whatever chaos or disorientation a director may be in. Cinematographers have to be so decisive. We can't light a set four different ways and then decide which way to light it. We light it once. As a director, you can have an actor do ten takes with different line readings each time. I can't relight the scene every take, so as cinematographers, we have to learn to live with our decisions. There's an innate prejudice or predilection on the part of a lot of cinematographers to look at directors who are floundering and say, "What's wrong with him? Why can't he make up his mind? It's so easy—just do it." It's *not* that easy because there's so much going on. Unless you have actually directed yourself, sometimes it's hard to understand all that can make it difficult for a director to get through a scene. I understand that better now, having been there myself.

Q: Throughout film history cinematographers have made the transition to directing, but this seems to be happening with greater frequency now.

A: Yes, more and more. Caleb Deschanel (*Being There*, *The Black Stallion*), Jan DeBont (*The Fourth Man*, *Basic Instinct*), Mikael Salomon (*The Abyss*, *Far and Away*), Chris Menges (*The Killing Fields*, *The Mission*) John Seale (*Witness*, *The English Patient*), and Michael Seresin (*Fame*, *Birdy*) have directed. More and more cinematographers who have been working for fifteen or twenty years, who came out of film schools or art schools, out of an informed technique and a sense of film history and tradition are not narrowly working only as cinematographers, but are truly filmmakers. They're filmmakers with a full-blown filmmaking aesthetic. They happen to be working as cinematographers, and it's natural because they bring a sense of informed drama and involvement with a script and the acting to their work because they feed off of it. Their work refracts back onto it. So coming from that background, it's natural to make a transition. Even though the industry has been slow to take to it, it's a very natural stage of development for the more informed cinematographers in the same way that editing is. Everybody thinks the only way to do it is to come out of writing, but writing is not necessarily the most relevant. That may seem heretical for me to say because a lot of the directors I've worked with and love—Robert Benton, Paul Schrader, Lawrence Kasdan, and Jim Brooks—are writer/directors. I've just finished a film with Richard LaGravenese and Stacey Sher. It is Richard's debut from an original screenplay. It was thrilling to watch him becoming a director as he discovered the transition from written word to the visual shot. He is going to make important films in the future. My best relationships have really been with writer/directors because there is a sense of authorship in the material. They became directors because they wanted to protect and interpret their own material, not because they necessarily initially came from a visual or editorial aesthetic, but because as writers they felt that their material was not being served in the way they wanted to. It's kind of a back door approach, yet that's the approach the industry has looked upon as the front door. That is changing now. Recently, it seems like every other film is being directed by an actor. It makes a lot of sense on the level of acting, but not necessarily on the level of anything else. The fact so many of them have been so successful is also really a testament to the incredible skills and artistry of the people they surround themselves with—the production designers, the editors, the cinematographers. I don't mean to malign any particular actor, but many actors have basically lived between the set and their motor home and really don't know the nuts and bolts of what happens on a set because they walk onto a set when they're ready to shoot.

Q: Where do you see your future headed? Will you continue to direct and photograph projects that interest you?

A: Yes, I'm going to do both. It took three years before we got *Mariette In Ecstasy* put together. I couldn't shoot two or three movies a year anymore. So I became even more selective about the films I did. I shot one film each of those three years, and all three are films I'm very proud of. So what it's done is made me use a purifying fire to get rid of the dross and just really look for the gold of what it is I want to do as a cinematographer. I want to continue shooting. There's something so gratifying about just making a movie. A cinematographer gets to come on when it's been cast, when the money's there, when all the bullshit with the studio is either peaked or has slightly past, and you get to go out and *make the movie*—it's the best part. So I don't want to give up shooting. Robert Benton told me I'll have to give up shooting. I said, "Does that mean for you, too?" and he said, "No, no, no, you give up shooting for everybody except for me." But I won't. It is important to keep working as a cinematographer. The very cinematographers attracted to directing are the ones attracted away from it because when you direct you get to work with actors, story, and narrative. They're the very ones that should continue to be shooting movies and not guys who are just shooters. So yes, there is a dilemma there. But I fancy I can do both. If it's going to take me two or three years to do a movie as a director, it's got to be something I really want to do and believe in.

Directing *Mariette In Ecstasy* was a magical experience, the postproduction was a nightmare. Though I was also one of the two producers, I didn't have control of the film. Against my and Ron Hansen's desires, the film was recut and a plodding and lead-footed narration voice-over was added. The intention of the film, a faithful adaptation of Ron's novel, was thwarted, and the spiritual journey of a tormented young girl was glossed over with an air of sanctimonious piety. Ron and I are chagrined with the final film. It has not been released.

Cinematography is still a pretty protected domain. Even allowing for digital technology, the parameters to change a cinematographer's work are very small. Directors have always been vulnerable to producers and studios, maybe more so today. Cinematographers can still be a maverick breed.

7

Dean Cundey

Dean Cundey, ASC, is widely known as a director of photography on large-scale, complex special effects driven films. This career path began with low-budget genre films on which he learned his craft.

As a child, Cundey was interested in school theater and magic shows. For an eighth grade term paper, he had the ambition to interview television directors about their vocation. By high school, Cundey decided he wanted to become a production designer. He was on a design track at California State before transferring to the UCLA Film School after he attended a cinematography class with the legendary black-and-white master cinematographer, James Wong Howe. Howe's professionalism and artistry inspired the young Cundey to become a director of photography.

In 1978, Cundey met director John Carpenter and photographed *Halloween*, a film which helped forge a renaissance in horror films. Cundey had a long association with Carpenter on *The Fog*, *Escape to New York*, *The Thing*, and *Big Trouble in Little China*.

In 1984, Cundey began another intense collaboration, this time with Robert Zemeckis, as director of photography on *Romancing the Stone*, the *Back to the Future* trilogy, *Who Framed Roger Rabbit?*, which garnered an Academy Award nomination for Cundey, and *Death Becomes Her*.

Dean Cundey has photographed two films for Steven Spielberg, *Hook* and the box office phenomenon *Jurassic Park*. For Ron Howard's *Apollo 13*, Cundey worked closely with the effects team to create a period film about the space race without one shot of stock footage. *The Flintstones* and

Casper brought the classic Toon characters to the screen, employing bright colors and a fanciful photographic style.

SELECTED FILMOGRAPHY

1974   *Where the Red Fern Grows*

1975   *Black Shampoo*
        Ilse, Harem Keeper of the Oil Sheiks

1977   *Charge of the Model-T's*

1978   *Bare Knuckles*
        Halloween

1979   *Roller Boogie*
        Rock 'n' Roll High School
        Separate Ways

1980   *The Fog*
        Galaxina
        Without Warning

1981   *Halloween II*
        Escape fom New York
        Angels Brigade
        Separate Ways

1982   *The Thing*
        Halloween III: Season of the Witch

1983   *Psycho II*
        D.C. Cab

1984   *Romancing the Stone*
        Jaws of Satan

1985   *Back to the Future*
        Warning Sign

1986   *Big Trouble in Little China*

1987   *Project X*

1988   *Big Business*
        *Who Framed Roger Rabbit?**

1989   *Road House*
        Back to the Future Part II

1990   *Back to the Future Part III*

1991   *Nothing but Trouble*
        Hook

1992   *Death Becomes Her*

1993   *Jurassic Park*

1994   *The Flintstones*

1995   *Apollo 13*
       Casper

1997   *Flubber*

1998   *Krippendorf's Tribe*
       The Parent Trap

*Academy Award nomination for best achievement in cinematography.

Q: How did you become a cinematographer?

A: As far back as I can remember I've been very interested in the film business. I helped put on the grammar school play, and in high school I was fascinated with theatrics. I was the production manager of the senior musical. I was a magician as a kid, so I've always been fascinated by the idea of creating an illusion for an audience, whether it was painted sets that looked real for a play, a musical, or magic. In eighth grade, we had to do a term paper and choose an occupation that fascinated us, so I immediately thought about television and motion picture directing. Not having access to any motion picture directors, I interviewed a couple of television directors.

In high school, I had a pretty clear idea I was going to be a production designer. I had gone to the set designers' local union and said, "How do you become a set designer?" and they said, "You have to have a degree in architecture." As I was reading about what it takes to get a degree in architecture—calculus and civil engineering and beam stressing—I didn't see exactly how it would apply to the film business. So I went to California State, Los Angeles for two and a half years. I was taking design, graphic design, history of film, and theater, aiming towards going to the UCLA Film School. I was going to specialize in scenic design. I transferred and actually got into the film school. Today, there's a very high application rate to get into USC, UCLA, and any of the film schools. I don't think I would be able to get into film school now if I applied with the background I had.

I was taking film classes at UCLA, but also continued some of my architectural classes. In my senior year, I took a class James Wong Howe (*Yankee Doodle Dandy*, *Hud*, *Seconds*) was teaching. Stephen Burum (*Mission Impossible*, *Hoffa*, *The Outsiders*), who is now a working cameraman, was the teaching assistant. The class was immediately filled. I talked to Steve and weaseled my way in as an observer, then ended up being allowed in as they increased the size of the class. To me, it was the most valuable class I had taken in film school because here was not only a working professional, but a legend who gave us insight into the techniques of real filmmaking. We had a little three blank walled set. Twice a week, James Wong Howe would show up and say, "Now we're going to light this in a particular style, today it's a seedy hotel room." He would go through the thought process of how he would create the mood and style of this hotel room with nothing in it but a table, a chair, three walls, a window, and a door. We were also his crew members, so we had to actually move the lights and set them up. He would tell us, "No, no, no, you've got to put the barn doors like this!" Not only did I gain insight into actual, creative cinematography, but we all learned how to use the real lighting equipment, the real grip equipment; flags and nets. I came away from that class with the most clear understanding of the creative process, how James Wong Howe worked, and how cinematography worked. I wanted to be dynamically involved with the process as opposed to sitting over a drawing board and working away from the set. So at that point I decided to turn to cinematography. I try to go to film schools as much as possible and give back some of that professional insight I got from James Wong Howe.

Q: Do you think your initial interest and study in production design has benefitted you as a director of photography?

A: Yes. I have always been interested in three-dimensional design, buildings, and spaces. Also, I worked as a draftsman, so I understand construction techniques and how to read drawings. I relate very much to the production designer, their job, the challenges and the problems. I evaluate the work they do based on the result they want and not just, "I want another window for lighting," or "There should be no ceiling because we won't be able to light it." So I really enjoy helping production designers solve their problems, at the same time helping them solve my problems, and helping both of us do something better than we might do if we were just doing it on our own. Film is so collaborative, you really have to understand other people's jobs. In cinematography, you have to understand the problems and challenges—the physical, visual, and optical effects in accomplishing any piece of action or creating an illusion to photograph a shot so it can be delivered to the editor and they can use the piece. You have to understand what it is an editor needs to put together a sequence. If you're always thinking, always being creative and everybody's collaborating, it makes the job we do a lot of fun.

Q: Halloween employs a very effective use of the camera frame. Throughout the film, the viewer's eyes are constantly darting at the edges of the frame waiting for Michael Myers, a murderer who has escaped from a mental institution and is stalking the Jamie Lee Curtis character, to jump in and scare us. How did this concept come about?

A: Before *Halloween*, I had worked on about twenty low-budget films, action adventure films—projector fodder for the drive-in circuit. The learning process was, "How do you get the day's work done? How do you light a set with the least number of lights because you don't have much to power them? How do you shoot a car chase so it's effective?" It was a lesson in efficiency. I got to watch directors and got an understanding of the storytelling technique. So, prior to *Halloween*, a lot of good work I'd done was just learning how to get a movie shot. What was interesting to me about *Halloween* was John Carpenter's definite aesthetic sensibilities as far as composition. He was a very good collaborator. I realized I had learned how to work as effectively or efficiently as I could. Here was an opportunity to explore other things.

Halloween was a film about composition of the frame. How do you create tension, expectation, or suspense just by framing a shot? Certainly the audience has become conditioned to understand a moment in a film by the music and sound effects, but sometimes blatantly or just subconsciously, the frame is creating an emotional response. A lot of times it's a simple, nicely composed close-up, but other times, by placing the character off to one side and composing for the door that's back there, you can imply something is going to happen. Somebody is going to come through the door. Sometimes you're just doing it to artificially build the tension because you're now going to surprise them by having the character come from the other side of the frame. We would work on that kind of blocking or composition of the scene. For me, *Halloween* was a great step in learning how to manipulate the audience—to create an intended response from them, or to fool the audience so you can really catch them the next time. John Carpenter wanted to do *Halloween* with no blood, no gruesome, grisly violence. He wanted very psychological suspense and not blatant slashing. One of John's great strengths is understanding the filmmaking process, the psychological, emotional response an audience has to a particular technique or scene in a film. *Halloween* started or restarted a trend because horror films had been around for years. One of the satisfactions is we made a very low-budget film, on a very short schedule with a minuscule crew and equipment, and it did become a classic of the genre. *Halloween* started a lot of people making films, some successfully and others not so successfully because they did go for the gore and didn't necessarily understand you could do it a lot more effectively just with mood, composition, music, and sound.

Q: What films did you and John Carpenter screen while you were preparing to shoot *Halloween*?

A: We screened several Howard Hawks films. John was a great fan of how Hawks told a story and used the camera. Sometimes John would deliberately choose not to move the camera, and other times we would. The Steadicam had recently been developed and John immediately saw it as a tool for moving the camera and moving the audience through a scene. So we would screen a Hawks film and John would say, "But we're going to use contemporary equipment in order to do it." The opening of *Halloween*, which is a long, continuous moving shot, was done with the Steadicam. I had heard about the Steadicam and used it a little bit prior to *Halloween*. At that time, almost nobody knew how to use it. My camera operator, Ray Stella, and I traded off doing the opening shot because it was so long and tiring. We did the one shot for an entire night. When I worked in low-budget filmmaking, I always looked for some new piece of equipment or lighting technique I hadn't had a chance to experiment with, that I could learn to use or try out no matter how low the budget or how silly the script. That was one of the great benefits about *Halloween* and working with John Carpenter. He was willing to experiment with the Steadicam to see what was possible.

Q: Your first film with Director Robert Zemeckis was *Romancing the Stone*. When you read the script, how did you conceive the film visually?

A: My agent said that Michael Douglas was producing a film and there was a relatively new young guy directing. They sent me the script. It was interesting because Diane Thomas had never really written a script before. It read very much like a paperback novel. It had the stage directions a reader would read, but the audience wouldn't necessarily see—little descriptives like, "The door smashes open and the most gruesome man we've ever seen steps in," "In the rafters, a spider faints." That's nòt something you normally see in a script. The rule of thumb is you just describe only what the audience will see because you're trying to create an impression of the film. So in reading I thought, "This could be very interesting because if this Zemeckis guy, whoever he is, can create this kind of feeling for this action/adventure, romantic/adventure, comedy film, it might be a lot of fun." Then I met Zemeckis, and he obviously had a vision for the film. He was constantly rewriting the script more for storytelling with film. It had a lot of really interesting romantic visuals. I scouted locations in Mexico with Bob, and he was very open to my input. Logistically, it became the most difficult film I had ever done because we were shooting in really muddy groves in remote areas of Mexico on rainy days where it was very difficult to get equipment in and out of the country. We had an excellent Mexican crew who had done all of the big John Wayne Westerns. They had great stories about all of these old films they had worked on and they were extremely experienced, which really helped us.

The story was the classic guy and a girl who seem at odds at first, but develop a relationship over a period of time. It was taking the Kathleen Turner character, a mousey woman who still is appealing, but always out of place, tentative, and unsure of herself, and helping her develop this self-assured attitude. That was partly make-up and wardrobe, but also in how we photographed her. She becomes a little warmer. When she first arrives in Colombia, or Mexico as it really was, we worked with overcast, very cool light, cool colors, and finally moved towards the warmer scenes where it was candles and firelight. Her flesh tones become warmer and more appealing. You develop a feeling as you watch a scene rehearsed and say, "Oh, I see, now she's going to make a turnaround where she becomes intrigued by the guy. So now she should become a little more appealing to him and to us. Okay, why don't we have her stand over here next to this table lamp for when she turns and tells him that line." Those are things you do instinctively. You do them consciously to a certain degree, but hopefully you are reacting as the audience reacts (or you understand how you want the audience to react) at a particular time. You start to build in this grammar, a vocabulary they are used to.

Q: So you apply these instincts while you are actually watching the rehearsal as opposed to intellectually imposing it when you first read the script.

A: Yes, I used to go through a script and start to mark out things. I would do little sketches of shots I thought would be effective. I would make notes about filters and start to preplan. Then you discover it isn't at all how you had envisioned it. The location isn't the same, or the director has a different approach, or the actors are taking a whole different attitude. So, now I read a script for the story content, an understanding of the characters, where the locations might be, but because those change so drastically, or they decide to build a set, or they don't have the budget to build a set, I don't invest a lot of pre-thought into a script. When I prep a film for four or six weeks, I'll talk to the production designer. I look at the set drawings and we'll scout locations. I'll talk to the director and maybe we'll look at a couple of films. He'll talk about how he sees a scene. Then I start to coordinate. The production designer will say, "We need to put a sky backing outside this window, how big should it be?" You start to solve the technical things. Then you begin to get involved and say, "I was thinking about the time of day in the script, how about a nice sunset backing?" You start to contribute more towards the end of the prep period. Hopefully, you've lined up a lot of the elements when you start filming. You go to a location and it's not sunny, it's rainy. So someone will say, "Let's change this to a rainy day," and that alters what you were going to do, or you find some way to make it look like it's a sunny day and that changes how you shoot—you can't look out the windows. So I'm reacting in a way that coordinates all of the other elements and serves the story, the director, and all the people involved.

Q: Have you ever had an editor on the set to talk about coverage or shots that may be necessary to make a sequence work?

A: Yes, it's fairly common. Sometimes we get down to the end of the day and we're missing a particular shot. The director and I will say, "What if we do a shot that combines two or three shots?" Then the film goes off to the editor and they start to cut it together. Most of the time, editors are working very much up to you. So it's not uncommon for the editor to come back three days later or in dailies and say, "The sequence worked perfectly," or "I'm sorry, it didn't cut together." The editor explaining what worked and didn't work is part of the learning process and one of the ways we can make the film effective. Video assist is extremely valuable. We have the film on the set all the time.

Q: How is video assist employed during filming?

A: On all of my early low-budget films, we never dreamed of affording video assist. Often I was the operator, so I was actually able to look through the camera. As films got more complicated and I was able to have an operator, he would watch. The director and I would stand next to the camera and watch the action, but we never really saw through the camera. The advent of video assist has made a huge impact. There was trepidation at first that it would be a committee process and would slow the process down. In my experience, that never really occurred. It became a great tool and time saver. The prop guy didn't have to ask, "Was that prop in-frame? Do we need to have this table dressed?" Even though they had been able to look at the direction the camera was pointing in and had been told there was a 50mm lens, there are people who don't understand how big the frame of a 50mm lens is. Now they can look at rehearsal on video assist and see exactly what is in the frame. The assistant directors know whether they have to get extras in the background. People can make their own evaluations. Video assist has speeded up the process considerably. The director can instantly assess whether the actor entered frame exactly on his line or whether he was partly in or out of frame and any of the things you normally had to quiz the operator about. Sometimes the camera operator was just worrying about keeping sandbags or lights out of the shot and wasn't watching the performance. It has become a very valuable tool for that reason.

Q: How often do you record video assist during shooting?

A: All of the time, and most of the time we don't play it back. A third of the time we'll play a shot back to evaluate whether the dolly move was correct or whether we captured all of the stunt work, but often we file it away. It becomes a reference for matching continuity, for how big the close-up we shot last week was, so we can match sizes. It hasn't taken creative control out of anybody's hands. People who respect a director allow him creative control without sitting and critiquing. Effective directors realize the crew is the first audience. Many times, the crew is a very productive film audience because they're in tune to films and the process.

Q: You have worked with your camera operator, Ray Stella, for over twenty-five years. What attributes does he bring to the job?

A: What makes Ray Stella one of the best camera operators in the business is his innate instinct for good composition. It is something you can learn, but it's really part of an artistic sensibility. You either have it or you don't. He's a very effective people person. He relates to directors. Spielberg goes through operators constantly because he's very demanding. Steven enjoys operating himself, he's very critical about composition, and Ray doesn't take it personally. He can separate the personal and the demand for a good film. Ray relates well to actors, the difficult actor doesn't annoy him. He works well with people. Film schools teach you technique and the mechanics of filmmaking, but they don't always teach you to deal with a lot of creative people, egos, personalities, the politics and protocol of working with a big crew or a small crew. Ray goes between the personalities and the technique—operating the camera, the composition, moving the dolly, and all of the things which are part of capturing the image with the camera. He's interested in the shot. Ray can be tenacious when he thinks it's important to do one more take or that the shot would be improved by a slightly wider angle. He will move the camera back, even if it means we have to clear part of the set, but if the director says, "Let's make the shot wider," he doesn't immediately say, "No problem," because he realizes now we have to move all of this stuff. If it won't improve the shot, he'll say, "I don't think it will help." So he's able to evaluate the important aspects of a particular shot and deal with a lot of the elements.

Q: In terms of protocol, does Steven Spielberg talk directly to Ray Stella or will he talk to you and then you'll talk to Ray?

A: All of those. If I have to do additional lighting or we need to change something on the set, Steven will start with me and then it will filter down. If it's slightly moving the camera, panning faster or slower, Steven will address Ray directly. Again that's one of the valuable aspects of video assist.

Q: How did you get the assignment to shoot *Project X*?

A: Typically, on a film I have anywhere from four to eight or more weeks of prep. *Project X* is the shortest prep I ever had, it was about three or four days. I had been working on *Big Trouble in Little China* and the art department was right across from the *Project X* art department. I ran into the production designer, Lawrence G. Paull (*Blade Runner, Back to the Future* trilogy). I'm always interested in design, so I went over and looked at his drawings and plans, and he said, "We're building this big vivarium." I said, "Who's shooting it?" It was the English cameraman, John Alcott (*Barry Lyndon, The Shining*). As we were shooting, I would drift by. They were building the set. Larry talked about the floor because they wanted to try to do dolly moves without putting down tracks. I talked to John Alcott about the skylights and how they were lighting the vivarium. Then, just before we were wrapping *Big Trouble in Little China*, the production manager, producer, and Larry Paull came by the set and said, "John Alcott just died . . . so we're wondering if you would be available. You would be the logical choice because you've followed this whole thing." It was to start the week after we finished. At lunch, I would go over and talk to the director of *Project X*, Jonathan Kaplan (*Heart Like a Wheel, The Accused*). I walked the set with Larry, started prepping, and ended up having a week to rig the lighting and to prepare the show. Prep is really good, but if you have good people who are preparing the show, you can just walk in and do it. I was fortunate I had worked with Larry and had met Jonathan Kaplan a couple of times. He was another Corman graduate. They had done a little bit of second unit, they had shot tests of some of the chimps and had worked with the trainers. Learning about the social structure of the chimps was interesting. One of the things I enjoy about filmmaking is we get to learn and experience a lot of things that people in their usual walks of life don't get to do.

Q: Did the chimpanzees have to hit marks for the camera like actors do?

A: Yes, if they could. Some chimps are very quick learners, others are not. Some are very willful—it's all part of their structure. They all aim for dominance. They were able to hit marks and understand English, something like, "Put your feet down," the chimp would immediately sit very calmly. They would put a big red dot on the floor and say, "Go to your mark," and the chimp would go and stand there. Eventually, they'd go to a smaller mark and then a tape mark. So after the process of learning, the chimp was rewarded by friendliness, grooming, and affection if he followed the orders.

Most animal training is looking for a trait that is natural, rewarding it so it becomes repeatable, and then adapting that trait to something we find cute, effective, or part of the storytelling.

Q: Did you employ multiple cameras on *Project X* in an effort to capture a full performance from the chimps?

A: Yes, working with animals you learn getting them to repeat is very rare. Any time you want to do a close-up and a wider shot or a medium shot and get any action to match, you end up shooting multiple cameras to cover it.

Q: How did you light the vivarium set?

A: It was designed with a large skylight. One of the things Jonathan Kaplan and Larry Paull talked about was to create different times of day—early morning, late afternoon, nighttime. The set was restricting because it was so large. It went up to the permanent parts of the stage. It was very difficult to move the lights around up there and to get shafts of sunlight to hit different parts of the wall. So we devised a system with a lot of overhead lights, all aimed at different parts of the walls. They were on switches so we could get the different times of day with light hitting different walls just by turning these switches on and off. The lights were preset. We had a whole series of switches on the wall with a map of the set. For nighttime, we had blue moonlight overhead. We had the practical lights on switches so we could change the mood pretty quickly without doing a huge relight—it was a series of flicking switches. As you get into a complicated film, there are considerations that build in layers of complication. You've got special effects, on top of that you have chimpanzees, and on top of that you have different times of day. All of these are variables you have to factor into any one particular shot or scene. You're always looking for ways to make it as flexible as possible.

Q: Who Framed Roger Rabbit? is a landmark film in its presentation of live action and animation. What were the challenges in photographing a film where many of the main characters were to be added later during the animation process?

A: What made it such an interesting challenge was we had been told by Disney there were certain ways to do these animation/live action films. They said, "We've done *Mary Poppins*, we've done *Pete's Dragon*. You lock down the frame and let the animator move the character around in it." So they laid out rules they considered to be hard and fast. Of course, there's nothing that intrigues Bob Zemeckis more than an opportunity to push the edge of the envelope. Richard Williams [*A Christmas Carol* (1971), *Raggedy Ann & Andy* (1977)], the head of animation, was very much in tune and had done all kinds of moving perspective animation. We were going to absolutely arbitrarily violate every rule we'd been given—just to see if we could. We shot a test that had a whole list of don'ts that we did. Richard began animating to it, and we realized it was possible to move the camera, to have the character move in and out of light, to do dolly and crane moves, as long as the animators knew where the camera was at any particular time. We built floor and wall patterns into the set that were all clues and cues to the animators as to how the perspective was changing, how fast the camera was panning, and all the things they would need to be able to animate effectively to moving cameras. The focal length of the lens you use alters the apparent change of perspective. A wide lens will allow a character to become very small in the background to very large in the foreground faster than if you were to use a long lens, which tends to compress.

In order to see how animated characters would change size according to perspective, we developed rubber figures to stage the action so that anybody involved with the shot knew where this character was. It was one thing for Bob and myself to stand back and say, "We see the rabbit doing this and this," but it's tough for the actors, effects people, and the camera operator to visualize where the animated characters were at any time—it was almost impossible. The rubber figures were sculpted to full size. We would then rehearse with them. Having Charles Fleischer, the voice of Roger, and other actors performing voices on the set meant we could time the performances. The camera operator could then compose. During the rehearsals, either myself or Bob Zemeckis would manipulate the rabbit or whatever characters there were in the frame. Bob Hoskins would follow and learn his eyelines. The camera operator would learn when to pan and when to tilt on what dialogue he was hearing off-camera. Then we would photograph one of those takes, so the animators would be able to look at where the figure moved, how large he was when he stood back by the door and then when he came up over to the desk. What was the relative size change? We would usually do one reference take. If something went wrong or we got a better idea in that rehearsal, then we would do another take. Then the editor, Arthur Schmidt (*Coal Miner's Daughter*, *Forrest Gump*), would be able to understand the intent of the scene, so when they cut together the footage that didn't have animation in it, they would understand where the character was standing at a particular time. Somewhere there exists a strange film of Bob and myself moving these rubber rabbits around and there's enough reference footage that they could cut together a whole version of *Who Framed Roger Rabbit?* with just the two of us bouncing these rubber rabbits.

Q: Was there a sculpted rubber figure for every character?

A: There was one for Roger. We had two or three of the weasels. We had a Baby Herman figure. We had two women who were approximately the right height who stood in for Jessica. We also had a human figure for Judge Doom, Chris Lloyd would actually do the reference for him.

Q: Did you and Zemeckis approach the film as a film noir?

A: Yes, we spoke about early detective films, Sam Spade, forties, and film noir. It was an interesting challenge for me. At the time, we didn't know how well they would be able to do the shadowing, tone-matting, and modeling on the characters because up until then, live action and animation films just had flat characters. We accepted flat characters in animation for years. It was amazing when once in a while in *Snow White* or *Alice in Wonderland* a character would move in and out of shadow, but at the time, they were always painted very flat. In order to get the characters to look like they were three-dimensional, they were trying to develop a shadowing process. One of my concerns was how effective will that look if we light to very high contrast with the humans and then we put an animated character in? The shadowing and contrast had to match. The lighting process became a fine line between a film noir look, a high-contrast and stylized lighting, and a not so contrasty look so the animated characters wouldn't stand out as not being part of a three-dimensional world. When we started working, we had not seen the tone-matting process. It wasn't until towards the end when we started to get animated material back that they were developing a process. Then we began to see how much they could do shadows and highlights on the animated characters. So it was a real tricky process to pre-visualize how much they could move in and out of shadow and how much shadow and contrast you could build into a shot and still not be too much for the animation process that was coming later.

Now, the techniques developed for *Who Framed Roger Rabbit?* carry through as you watch animated features like *Beauty and the Beast* and *The Lion King*. Animators don't animate flat anymore, there are tremendous perspective changes. Now, they computer generate backgrounds so the apparent camera moves through the animated landscape and the characters all have highlights, shadows, tone-matting, and all of the things *Who Framed Roger Rabbit?* started. It was pushing the envelope, creating something the audience now accepts as part of animation language and grammar. Now, if it isn't there, then it becomes something that's missing and looks false to an audience.

Q: The ship sequences in *Hook* were shot in the studio. How were you able to create daylight on the stage using artificial light?

A: Steven Spielberg and I had initial conversations. They were going to build a ship and the town on an island in the Caribbean. Then Steven realized it might look too real. What he wanted was something between a theatrical fantasy and a real look. The decision was to build everything on stages which would give us more control, but also the challenge of creating the illusion they were outside.

Steven and I screened *Greystoke: The Legend of Tarzan, Lord of the Apes*, which had effective jungle sequences. They had shot some of it exterior and some of it on the stage. We analyzed what made it look real. In the early days of Hollywood, they often would build a set on a stage that was supposed to be an exterior. They had control over all the lighting and could make everything perfect. They made exposures of the contrast ratios from the shade and the shadows so the sunlight fit the film, especially in color films. The early Technicolor days were dictated by contrast ratios. So audiences got used to seeing two kinds of exteriors. The ones on the stage looked phoney, but in reality everything was very controlled. When you go out in the desert, it's very bright sunlight and very dark shadows. So you have to compromise. A lot of times you expose more for the shadow areas, and the sunlight and the highlights get very hot. Sunlight is brighter than film can accept, so the audience is seeing burned out highlights and overexposure in certain areas, and the shadows are darker. Steven and I decided the sunlight coming through would be overexposed, hotter than what the film would want to see, and also tried to build in a single source. Often, to get as much light, you have a lot of lights on the stage and you get multiple shadows on the ground which the audience interprets as being incorrect. The trick was to find ways to create the illusion it was just the sunlight creating the light. The rest of it comes from the normal process, which is the ambient skylight, by using a very soft fill light. So we built a very hot sunlight into lighting of the sets and on the deck of the ship. One of the difficulties was, anytime we tried to get a wide shot, we always ended up seeing the limitations of the stage; where the sky ended and where there was no ocean past the ship. We accepted that as part of the theatrical, fantasy feeling. They were in a land that didn't have all of the same rules we do.

Q: How do you and Steven Spielberg work with the camera?

A: Spielberg is a visual storyteller more so than directors who deal strictly with performance. So his eye is really trained for that kind of visual evaluation of the frame and composition in addition to performance. He has said he feels the film is being made within the frame lines in the camera. Over a period of time, I've worked more and more with a remote head. It's a process of putting the camera on a motor servo-controlled head. Then, instead of physically looking through the camera on the dolly and operating the head there, you are looking at a video image and operating the head remotely at a video monitor. A long cable runs down to the end of the crane arm or wherever the camera is. The image is larger. Instead of looking at a very small image through the camera, you are actually looking at a pretty good size image in front of you. There's just something about the effectiveness of being able to watch with two eyes on a monitor as opposed to one eye, squinting. You can evaluate, your eye can click around the frame and watch what's happening. You can actually do much more complicated moves than if there was a guy looking through the camera. You can do 360 degree pans and complicated dolly moves. Spielberg used remote heads to a certain extent on the *Indiana Jones* pictures. Bob Zemeckis uses it constantly. I would say half of the film is shot with a remote head when I work with Bob Zemeckis. Steven tends to design complicated shots like low angles that sweep along the floor, then up over the table and across the room—shots that are most effectively done with a remote head. On the past several films Steven and I have worked on, the majority is done with these heads. Spielberg's reflexes are good. He's operated for many years, and has developed those reflexes. Steven is one of the few directors I have worked with who operates. Ray Stella still operates most of the time. In the case of Bob Zemeckis or with Ron Howard on *Apollo 13*, the operator operates the camera because they have all these reflexes they've developed over the years, but Steven is actually able to adapt very quickly to operating. We recently gave Steven an honorary operator's card because he has so frequently operated and has so much respect for the operator. Steven feels the film is made *by* the operator. A lot of directors don't feel comfortable operating because it really takes a very trained set of reflexes to look for little visual cues of reacting in advance of when an actor is going to move. There are all kinds of reflexes an operator has, and an instinct of when to stop the camera because the shot is properly composed. How much headroom do you give an actor and where do you place them in the frame which balances visually without putting them right in the center? Most of the time, the operator is ignoring the dialogue or the performance because they have other things to evaluate. Most directors prefer to evaluate the performance rather than being worried about panning too far. Wisely, most directors don't fool with that. I know if I operate the camera, I suddenly have to shift into operator mode and watch for the sandbags, lights, and composition. Sometimes I don't get to watch if the actor landed in his light properly. My job as director of photography is somewhere between evaluating as a director and as an operator.

Q: How did you photograph the sequence in *Jurassic Park* where the two children, played by Joseph Mazzello and Ariana Richards, are trapped in a kitchen by the dinosaurs?

A: The kitchen scene is the most effective use of storytelling and the dinosaurs in the whole movie. Instead of the dinosaurs just being in the background, they are an integral part of the action and the drama. Steven Spielberg was very concerned with controlling the cost and schedule on *Jurassic Park*, especially since we were dealing with a lot of unknowns in the effects work. They storyboarded the film, principally the action sequences, but not just in the conventional way of a storyboard artist drawing sketches. They made a computer-generated video storyboard. They went to the trouble to construct a T-Rex and the Rapters, and they were able to move the camera and actually do the shots in a very crude, primitive way to see how effectively they would work. They also intercut static shots of the drawn storyboards so we would end up with an animatic of whole sequences. We could look at the timing and at how effectively the scene worked. When we actually shot the sequences, we would run the animatic to see how the script had dictated and interpreted the action. Steven had a great deal of input on the animatic, and it became the very serious guidelines we followed. There were times where we said, "This worked pretty well, but a really good angle would be down here," because now we had the real set, we could see a really interesting, dynamic angle. So we would modify as we felt was necessary, but there were particular shots that worked real well in the animatic. If there had been two or three iterations, they would find a very effective one and we would as much as possible do those shots. There were some really effective moving shots for that kitchen sequence. One of them was a very low angle on Joseph Mazzello, and the camera dollies around as the Rapters come around behind him. Then it becomes a real low angle, looking up, and the Rapter lifts his head up and hears Ariana at the other end. We had been doing other shots typically with the heads of Stan Winston's (*Edward Scissorhands*, *Terminator 2: Judgment Day*) creature puppets, but this particular shot required a movement, the head turn, and stepping forward that could only be done by the computer. So that was a case of analyzing the move which would allow the space to put in the computer-generated creature, and understanding the timing of when you would hear Ariana. Then the creature would raise his head and we would have to tilt up with him. Ray Stella had so effectively learned to frame for things that weren't there with *Who Framed Roger Rabbit?*, he was able to visualize in the frame when he had to move and how high he had to move. We would rehearse, again taking the *Who Framed Roger Rabbit?* reference technique. We had full-sized rubber Rapters and other creatures we would rehearse with, so everybody knew how much room to allow for a creature that size at that distance. Again, we would frequently shoot one take with these rubber Rapters with someone just walking along behind them in order to have the reference material for the animators, even though they were going to be using a computer to do it with reflective changes.

There are times when you have to do a moving camera shot with a motion control camera and a computer because the information rate of panning and tilting the camera and of the dolly move will then get recorded by the computer for it to generate the movement of the creatures. With the computer, we're less and less restricted by what we had to do in the past by putting in frame reference points like little fluorescent dots on the floor, the set, the props, and on furniture pieces and using a motion control camera. Now, those have all become reference points for the computer. We measure from the camera to the dots, then we'll make a chart of which ones they are and the angles. So that becomes information between the animators input into the computer for reference of the camera moves. On that shot in the kitchen, it was a case of rehearsing and visualizing what was there, then just shooting empty space and air. The animators very effectively put in the dinosaurs later.

Q: You have worked on so many complex special effects driven films. How have you learned about the technology involved in special effects photography?

A: One of the things that's so fascinating is there are no courses for what we do. We can give them after the fact, but at the time when somebody goes up to make a film, everybody's just out there learning how to do it. When we started *Jurassic Park*, the intention was to use all stop-motion dinosaurs and conventional effects. So at that point, yes, any of us could have taken a course in stop-motion dinosaurs from anybody who had done *King Kong* (1933), all the way up to contemporary times. It came down to somebody who said, "I wonder if we could do this with computers?" They did a couple of tests and showed it to Steven. Just before we started, Steven said, "Do you think you really can do this?" and everybody said, "Yes, we can," not knowing whether they could or not. So Steven had the courage and confidence, having worked in the past with these guys who had said they could do something and then delivered. He also fortunately had the clout to be able to go to the studio and say, "We're going to dedicate millions of dollars to do something that nobody has ever done before and nobody knows if they can do it," and the studio said, "Okay." So, we started the film not knowing if any of the special effects could be done, and throughout the film they developed the technique.

One of the satisfactions I've had is to know that so often the techniques and the effects have not all been done. They build on techniques that have been done, but by being able to take them just a little bit further, you develop new techniques. I can trace very clearly in my mind the progression of the films I've been involved with, from the original *Back to the Future* through *Who Framed Roger Rabbit?* and the other *Back to the Future* films to *Jurassic Park*, to *The Flintstones*, to *Casper*, and now *Apollo 13*.

Q: Often, the director of photography is responsible for creating the background plate used in a special effects shot. What is involved in the process of working with the special effects team?

A: The usual process is working out beforehand with the director, the storyboard people, and the special effects people the intention of a particular special effect shot. What you want it to look like, what it's suppose to accomplish, how the action is supposed to go. You work out the techniques they either know or think they will use. Then my job is to provide them with the materials they need to accomplish it. Most of the time, it's a background plate. It can be much more. Typically, a plate is a shot you shot on a location which is the background and something is going to be put in front of it. The plate may be used in the rear screen process or blue screen. Later they have to do the part of the shot that is put in front of this plate. The plate could be a simple locked-down camera shot going behind action. It can be as simple as panning and tilting. It can be two or three passes with a motion control camera over the same scene. It can be all of the action of an entire scene with the exception of the characters being flown on wires, cable, or a rig that's going to be removed later. Sometimes it's a lot more complicated. So the plate is the term for the raw material that is then going to be processed in some way by the effects people. The effects people used to shoot most of their own material. If they were going to put the castle on the hill, they would go off and shoot the plate of the hill, then go back and put the castle on. Often, the first unit didn't even know about it. They might have been part of it, but it was all shot by the special effects people. Now, more and more the visual effects people will be on the set and will be part of the collaborative effort. It will still be my jurisdiction to light and shoot the scene, but it is all done with the input and information the effects people will provide when you're on the set. It's gotten complicated, but also a lot more interesting. The effects are less and less something that are added to the movie or cut into it. Now it's becoming a much more integral part of the action. The computer is going to allow us to do so much to first-unit work. To enhance the sky, to remove wires and telephone poles is not necessarily considered an effects shot, but it is an enhancement to the first-unit work. That work is becoming an exciting aspect of visual effects because now it becomes a tool we can use to enhance what we do and not just some kind of a special shot that gets cut into the picture. So what lies ahead is very exciting.

Q: Do you feel it's important for a director of photography on features to also shoot commercials, television, and documentaries?

A: The audience now is a great deal more sophisticated than they were when this business first started. We are so used to all kinds of visual information. You go home and watch television, there's everything from old movies to contemporary movies and sit-coms to commercials and MTV. Every kind of visual storytelling possible is there. It's now getting to the point where it's going to be interactive, a whole other era of visual storytelling and audience involvement. In the early silent days, filmmakers felt they had to be photographing a stage play. You had to see the actor full-figured because producers would say, "The audience won't understand if they don't have feet and we can't cut to a close-up because there's no body!" The audience learns pretty quickly. Now, there's almost nothing we can try that an audience can't learn to understand. As a director of photography, it's important to understand all of the visual storytelling techniques being done. So I shoot and direct commercials. You learn to pay attention to all kinds of documentaries, television, and commercials. You don't want the audience to become smarter than you are and understand more about the language than you. You always have to stay with the visual vernacular being spoken by all of the filmmakers and how you can use it as part of your storytelling.

Q: You started in low-budget filmmaking and have worked on big-budget films which utilize state-of-the-art technology. As we near the next century, where do you think the filmmaking process is headed?

A: Things always run in cycles. As the pendulum swings, we develop a technique—the computer and digital technology, for instance—and it's used in a very dramatic, dynamic way like creating the dinosaurs for *Jurassic Park* in such a way that it is obvious we are being shown a special effect. There's no way you can believe that there's really a dinosaur. So as an audience you know it's a trick, but it's done so well you don't know how they did it. People begin to use the techniques for great, impressive effects, but then we also realize it can be used to put in a sunset instead of a bald sky, so the audience isn't aware of it as an impressive special effect. It just becomes part of the techniques we use, just like the first person who dollied a camera. That very first close-up in *The Great Train Robbery* where the cowboy shoots the gun was a striking visual image. Everybody became aware of it, and now when we see a close-up we think nothing of it—it's just part of the process. Effects will always be used for impressive and unusual films, the *Stargate* kind of movies, but I think also as they become economically feasible, we'll start to use effects for just everyday enhancements and as another tool. The same way with interactive. It's going to go off into some very strange directions for a while. It will become real showy to the extent they play video games now. My son is just out of USC, and he is exploring computers, interactive, and filmmaking from that standpoint. People are going to look very hard for some way to make an interactive story, but over a period of time it may become just another technique. It won't be just sitting in front of a television and going off in all kinds of directions, but it will be just something we haven't thought of yet, just another way of intriguing an audience to following a story and becoming involved. It's hard to say what that will be—it's all part of this evolutionary process.

8

Edward Lachman

Edward Lachman, ASC, is an explorer of images. A cinematographer who has worked worldwide, Lachman discovers his images in photographs, paintings, movies, screenplays, as well as in life.

Lachman's grandfather owned vaudeville theaters, which evolved into the first American movie houses. His father was a film exhibitor and distributor. Lachman first became interested in painting while studying art in Europe, and during the seventies he completed a film appreciation course at Harvard. He began shooting a wide range of documentaries which investigated political, social, and aesthetic themes through a myriad of photographic styles. In 1974, he shot his first fictional feature film, *The Lords of Flatbush*. Lachman was a camera operator and second unit director of photography for Robby Muller, Sven Nykvist, and Vittorio Storaro, and is one of a select cadre to work with four of the most influential German directors of the seventies: Werner Herzog, Rainer Werner Fassbinder, Wim Wenders, and Volker Schlöndorff. This international experience has influenced Lachman's cinematography on uniquely American projects such as *Desperately Seeking Susan* and *Light Sleeper*, as well as international works like *Stroszek*, *London Kills Me*, and *Mississippi Masala*.

Edward Lachman's documentaries and films include: *Christo's Valley Curtain*; *Say Amen, Somebody*; *The World of Mother Teresa*; *Stripper*; *Tokyo-Ga*; *Chuck Berry, Hail! Hail! Rock 'n' Roll*; *Ornette: Made in America*; and *Passion: The Script*. Lachman has worked as director and cinematographer on *A Family Affair, Route 66, Blue Train, Report from*

Hollywood, *Songs for Drella*, *Red Hot and Blue*, and *A Day in the Life of Country Music*.

Edward Lachman has worked with a diverse group of directors, including: Gregory Nava, Paul Schrader, Mira Nair, Hanif Kureishi, Dennis Hopper, Susan Seidelman, Shirley Clarke, Jean-Luc Godard, Bernardo Bertolucci, Nicholas Ray, and the Maysles brothers.

An independent craftsman and artist, Lachman's New York home is a spacious loft which serves as his base of operations in a life filled with constant travel and filmmaking. He owns his own camera equipment, which he employs in a career that defies classification. His versatile camerawork expresses a voracious interest in images and the world. Edward Lachman described himself to *Sight and Sound* magazine as "a visual gypsy," a phrase which translates to a provocative and aesthetic experience for audiences viewing films which bear his name.

SELECTED FILMOGRAPHY

1974   *The Lords of Flatbush* (with Joseph Mangine)

1977   *The American Friend* (with Robby Muller)
       Stroszek (codirector of photography with Thomas Mauch)

1980   *Union City*

1982   *The Day You Loved Me*

1985   *Desperately Seeking Susan*

1986   *True Stories*
       Little Wars

1987   *Making Mr. Right*
       A Gathering of Old Men
       Less Than Zero

1989   *Backtrack*

1991   *Mississippi Masala*

1992   *My New Gun*
       Light Sleeper
       London Kills Me

1995   *My Family/Mi Familia*

1997   *Touch*
       Selena

1998   *Why Do Fools Fall in Love?*

1999   *Virgin Suicides*

Q: Throughout the development of your career, paintings, still photographs, and movies have influenced your visual sensibilities. What images influenced you to become a cinematographer?

A: I studied painting before photography. I was interested in German expressionism because there was a visceral need to get an emotional quality and feelings towards the subject matter on the canvas. German expressionism was an outgrowth of impending doom between the wars. It was a very emotional approach to painting, abandoning academic conventions to create an expressionistic realism. Then I got interested in photography and had taken a film appreciation course at Harvard. I became cognizant that images didn't just appear on the screen. Italian director Vittorio De Sica's *Umberto D* greatly influenced me, as it relied heavily on images to create the story of a lonely pensioner. How De Sica told a story in just image and mood was a revelation. In the Dadaist period, Duchamp and Man Ray took commonplace objects from the real world and made a statement that this could be art too. Our perception of what we see creates it as a form of art. I've always liked what the found image could represent. So all of this attributed to the idea I could take a camera and create stories. Being frustrated learning the technique as a painter, film was a more immediate way for me to respond to images. I made my own films, and people always seemed to connect to the imagery. I approached a story by drawing back to painters and other visual references in photography as ideas to a story line. People then asked me if I would be interested in shooting their films. I thought this would be an inexpensive way to learn how to make films for myself, and I ended up becoming a cameraman.

Q: Is it the cinematographer's role to capture the director's vision or to express their own visual ideas?

A: Some directors are more visual than others. So I've always felt my job was to read the script and then bring forth visual ideas to contribute to whatever ideas the director has. Some directors formulate an idea and others don't. It is always that marriage between the director, production designer, and the cinematographer to create a visual world, but it has to emanate from the story. Every script should find its own filmic language, its own visual grammar, and the discovery of that grammar has always been an important aspect for me. It's something that evolves. You bring in a lot of visual ideas and references. They could come from books, films, or paintings. Whatever the visual references are, it's important to play that game with each other to then find what's unique about that script, that story.

Q: Is there a protocol for how that process unfolds? When you read a script, do you share your visual ideas with the director right away or do you want to hear their visual ideas first?

A: It depends, when you read the script you might know the director's work, you know what kind of world they inhabit. Sometimes with first-time directors, it's more of an involved process in finding it together. I'll ask the director what their visual idea is towards the script, then I can come in with many ideas of my own, but it's essential to hear what's important to the director and what their visual interests are in the story line.

Q: There is a strong international sensibility in your work. How did European influences affect your approach to cinematography?

A: While in art school in France, I met Werner Herzog at the Berlin Film Festival. He really gave me my first start by working on documentaries, *La Soufriere, How Much Wood Could a Woodchuck Chuck*, and *Huie's Sermon*. That led to working with Wim Wenders on *Lightning Over Water* and *Tokyo-Ga*, then with Fassbinder on *Blue Train*, and then Volker Schlöndorff on *A Gathering of Old Men*. I think I was the only cameraman who worked with all of the formidable directors that came out of Germany in the seventies. Their visual styles emanated from a philosophical and a political context. I learned through each director's perspective that one could find their own language to tell their stories.

Q: How do you develop visual ideas out of a story?

A: On *True Stories*, I worked with David Byrne, who has a highly visual context to his ideas. The reference there was literally the shopping mall Photomat, how Americans see themselves through themselves. Another reference was the style of William Eggleston, who is recognized as the father of American contemporary color art photography. His work is a seeming amateur style of fragmented snapshots depicting everyday life. David Byrne and I tried to actually break convention of what would be considered good cinematography, for instance, a balanced frame by the use of color, light, or composition. When the average person takes a photograph of themselves, they're more interested in the content than a formalistic approach to the image. I tried to actually photograph things in a certain randomness, like cutting off buildings, cars, or people in awkward compositions like a home movie. When the film was finished, I realized it didn't bother people as I thought it would, but created its own aesthetic. *Desperately Seeking Susan* was shot in two separate styles. The first style was derived from the German expressionistic school, where the colors were more primary and saturated in the dark and foreboding Lower East Side world of Madonna. The world for Rosanna Arquette was more naturalistic, embodying a suburban pastel and opaque palette. On *Making Mr. Right*, the director, Susan Seidelman, and I were searching for a style and we finally approached it as if it were a Roger

Corman film. It was a take on B-movie science fiction films, where the style would be flat and have a pop quality to it.

Q: Does this process of developing the visual style have to be complete by the time you start shooting?

A: Not always. You go in with certain ideas, then you try to ascertain how to achieve these ideas technically. A lot of it comes intuitively, and it happens during the process. You don't always see it in the first week or two of dailies, but if you're true to what you are doing, you start to see a certain style emerging. One of the most important roles of the cinematographer is to be stylistically visually consistent in your approach to the story—not one day doing Max Ophuls camera moves, and the next doing Yasujiro Ozu tableaus. What the aesthetic is and how you approach the story line is very important. You work very closely with the director about whose point of view the story is being told by and why. The photography is about the point of view in the storytelling, and that gives you reasons for what you do with the camera. In the American studio system, you are expected to shoot multiple coverage to be able to select a point of view in the editing room. The difference between the European and independent cinema and the American studio system is you don't have the time and money to film extensive multiple coverage of a particular scene. You have to rely more on the strength of the camera to convey the story. Then, out of necessity, that locks you into a certain approach.

Q: How does the approach of working in long takes affect a film?

A: When actors know they're going to play a scene in a long take, there's an energy that can happen in real time between the camera and the performance. You can't create the same tension in cuts. American films are getting better and better visually. The audience has become more sophisticated about filmic language through music videos and commercials. Today, with film stocks, lenses, and the labs being so good, it's almost what you don't do that creates the image. It's knowing what not to do, trusting what you're doing in the storytelling, and trusting that images can tell a story. Part of the problem in the States is that we have relied so heavily on dialogue, having come out of a culture of literature and television. We rely so heavily on the written word to translate an idea and we don't trust how images can express an idea. Look at *Red* or any of Kieslowski's films, or the films of the Hong Kong filmmaker Wong Kar Wai, who directed *Fallen Angels* and *Days of Being Wild*. They have an understanding of images that threads the emotional context to the story line. Words are an intellectualization of an idea, but images are the emotional fabric of the story. There's an intelligence there, we don't always have to be force-fed. I can go back to a Robert Frank image, time and time again, and learn something about myself through it because it's not always an easy read. There's more happening to express the idea that I'm supposed to get. It's about the interrelationship between an image and elements within an image. I'm always searching for images that are contradictive and play off of each other—elements that allow the audience to participate and be challenged. That's what you would expect from a painting or a photograph. I greatly admire Conrad Hall's work. He is always creating a world for his characters within an emotional context, as in the scene in *Searching for Bobby Fischer* where the little boy goes behind a stained glass window and you see him as a silhouette. It says everything about the ambiguous nature of childhood, about who that child was going to be, and it was also a mirror for the child—something we couldn't see. I get an emotional feeling from open-ended images that have something to say within the context of the story line.

Q: Many American directors like Martin Scorsese, Brian DePalma, and Quentin Tarantino utilize images in their work from films they admire. You have worked with many European directors who were equally inspired by other films, but incorporate images in a different context. How do they manage to bring an original visual style to their work?

A: I worked with Godard, but he never talked to me about an image. He talked to me about the idea of the image. So that creates a different framework. If people just talk to you about the aesthetic of an image, that's not really getting to the meaning of why you do something.

Q: The use of visual references seems to be an element of the filmmaking process that is going to be with us as we approach the next century.

A: It's part of our culture. Visually, in the art world we're always building on our own history. So the aesthetics become part of former aesthetics—things repeat themselves. Certain styles in the sixties are becoming in fashion now, like the cinéma vérité school of Jean Rouch and Chris Marker in France, and D. A. Pennebaker and the Maysles brothers in the United States. The idea of taking a handheld camera, a small tape recorder, and capturing life became a reaction to the cinema's ability to falsify the world with commercialized gloss and stylized cliches. The audience is more willing to see things about themselves that they can believe in.

Q: How does technology affect cinematic concepts?

A: Technology goes hand in hand with aesthetics. For example, in the fifties the black-and-white television show *Naked City* was shot outside of a studio on actual locations—on the streets where the reality became more important to the stories and the lighting was more naturalistic and rougher. *On the Waterfront*, shot by Boris Kaufman, was also important in this semidocumentary style, where the camera and lighting became motivated by the actions and the performance. They were abandoning the black-and-white stylized studio lighting approach of Hollywood for the stories and streets of New York.

Q: You have photographed many documentaries. Has it had an effect on your work?

A: All films are really in a sense documentaries. Everything comes together for that one moment, happens in that one moment, and cannot be reproduced. No performance is exactly the same. The movement of the camera, the light, how the actors hit their marks isn't exactly the same as in a former take. The director and cameraman are really the first audience, and I love to respond to those moments. That's why I like to operate the camera. Films live in real time.

Q: During the 1980s, you were on the forefront of the postmodernist film style. How did you develop the visual style of *Desperately Seeking Susan*, a film largely responsible for defining this movement?

A: The script was a kind of a 1940s screwball comedy. The director, Susan Seidelman, Production Designer Santo Loquasto, and myself wanted to convey the underground post-punk scene, which had developed more of a sixties sensibility. I was trying to interpret where the New York scene was in the eighties. I always admired *Midnight Cowboy*, shot by Adam Holender, which became a statement of the New York attitude in the late sixties—a sense of alienation. I really thought about how *Midnight Cowboy* affected me as a viewer, and how people saw New York through the eyes of Ratso Rizzo and Joe Buck, the cowboy.

Q: How did you utilize color in *Desperately Seeking Susan* to create that downtown New York look?

A: I referred back to German expressionism by pushing the colors. I made the mercury-vapor fluorescent lights greener and the natural tungsten sources in the street warmer by enhancing those colors motivated from the practical sources. Also, I used contrasting colors, something one learns about in pop or op painting. A lot of the sets were only in two colors. They were contrasting because one recedes, one advances. So that could give depth, shape, and form to the image. For instance, using yellow against blue—one's a warm color, the other a cool color. Those would be contrasting colors versus complementary colors which would be yellow, orange, and red that would blend together. So by using those colors and working with the production designer, Santo Loquasto, we reenforced that visual idea. The sets, the wardrobe, everything attempted to have an abstract expressionistic feeling in the storytelling. A director like Ingmar Bergman had already utilized similar techniques in the films *Cries and Whispers* and *The Passion of Anna*, where he used sets in one color palette to create a psychological setting for the viewer. Claude Chabrol had also used color as a symbolic and psychological framework for his films. In art school, I studied Josef Albers, a painter and theorist who experimented with color and how people psychologically reacted to certain colors and combinations. So all those things went into it.

Later, in *Less Than Zero*, I played with two complementary colors versus a contrasting color. In regard to lighting, I wanted to invert day and night because the characters lived in a world at night. So even the day became more of a night existence for them. Also, there was a heightened, drug-related experience. The light was very sharp, very hard, very crisp, and the camera movements were more kinetic.

In *Mississippi Masala*, the color was more naturalistic, except for certain scenes in the Asian world, where certain colors had symbolic meaning in the context of their culture.

Q: Did you use gels on *Desperately Seeking Susan* to achieve the color effects?

A: Yes, by using gels on the lights I could mix and separate the colors to give depth and contrast in the frame. If a wall was painted a very warm color like orange, I lit the wall with a complementary gel to that color.

Q: Light Sleeper also had a complex color approach to the lighting. What was the concept behind it? At times you had two different colors going in different rooms.

A: In the days of black-and-white, a cinematographer had to see shades of grey, black, and white the way the film saw it, through the wardrobe of the particular set. In the same way, you have to see color and color temperature the way the film sees it, not just the way it looks to the eye. In *Light Sleeper*, I was trying to create two worlds: the world of the Upper East Side, which was more designed, lush, and homogenized; versus the street, which was about mixed lighting with different color temperatures, fluorescent, mercury-vapor all colliding. In the scene where Willem Dafoe goes back with his old girlfriend to the Paramount Hotel to make love, I created the ambience of Vermeer's northern light replicating the Vermeer painting hanging over the bed. After making love to his old girlfriend, played by Dana Delany, she tells Willem, "Never call me. Never write to me," as she is dressing and leaving him in bed. I wanted to leave him visually in the sensation of being rejected, abandoned, and cold. I came up with the idea of a neon sign out the window. When I did tests, the color I felt could best evoke that feeling was green. So I used the deepest emerald green, and as the contrast or opposite of green is magenta, it enhanced the viewer's perception of the color. I motivated the magenta by the tungsten lights left on in the room. So mixing the magenta against the green, for me emotionally, gave a very eerie feeling of his loss. I'm always looking at colors, not for decorative reasons, but for reasons I feel can work emotionally to the portrayal of that character's situation.

Q: In *Light Sleeper*, the characters lived by night. In the interiors, you were never sure whether it was day or night. What was the concept behind this?

A: That's what we were trying to create. We were saying their world was nocturnal. It was always lit from practical sources, and you only knew if it was day or night when you saw Willem Dafoe outside the apartment. The director, Paul Schrader, also wanted to create a sense of paranoia and isolation by using the camera to follow Willem's character through the streets from above—creating a feeling of oppression or being pursued. Those were all psychological elements we tried to search for in the storytelling that would create the atmosphere. Paul Schrader and I looked at early Antonioni films that we greatly admired, *La Notte*, *Eclipse*, and *L'avventura*. We studied how he created a psychological state through architectural space. Antonioni is a master of framing and composition, moving the camera to depict the alienation of his characters in their worlds. Antonioni also uses the device of unconventionally breaking screen direction to create the effect of his characters emotional displacement through editing. Schrader understood this, and liked the device. He felt it could work in the cafeteria scene between Dana Delany and Willem Dafoe, where the camera jumps the line between their cuts and jars the audience so it visually conveys the separation between the two characters who cannot resolve why they are not together.

Q: What was it like to work with Dennis Hopper on *Backtrack*?

A: I had a great experience working with him. Dennis always knew where he wanted to put the camera because of the actor's point of view in the scene. Thirty-five or 40 percent of that film was shot on a Steadicam. He never wanted to interrupt the mise-en-scène; the movement of the performance in the scene. It made it much more difficult for me to be lighting so many different rooms and areas and still create a look. He never once looked through the camera, he knew in his mind's eye where the camera should be to tell the story. He said *Backtrack* was "A gangster film about the art world." Dennis is a big art collector and a painter himself, he understood the different sensibilities about art and images. When I first met with Dennis to talk about *Backtrack*, without saying too much he showed me *On the Water-*

front. I realized what Dennis was conveying to me was the simplicity of telling the story and that the camera should be motivated by the performance.

Q: What is the visual style of *Backtrack*?

A: We were doing a version of the film noir classic *Out of the Past* by the director Jacques Tourneur, within an eighties art world. The film took place in Los Angeles, Seattle and New Mexico so I picked different artists who were emblematic of those worlds. I referred to Georgia O'Keefe for New Mexico. One of her prominent paintings was of a church in Taos we used as a backdrop in the film. In Los Angeles, we used references to Ed Ruscha, those were all games we played to create these different worlds. Jodie Foster's character was based on the artist Jenny Holtzer, in which you see her truisms in Liquid Crystal Display (LCD) signs that became a very Godardian element.

Q: Mississippi Masala was photographed in a much different style from the films we have been discussing. What was the photographic approach here?

A: Mississippi Masala, which I did in the early nineties, was created in a naturalistic style. We were documenting the expulsion of East Indians from Uganda by Idi Amin in the early seventies. The film's context was really about the loss of your roots and cultural identity. It's also an interracial love story between Denzel Washington and an immigrant girl, played by Sarita Choudhury. We went for a period documentary style, contrasting Uganda in the seventies to a contemporary American South.

Q: What was the nature of the light you were trying to capture in Uganda versus Mississippi for *Mississippi Masala*?

A: For the Mississippi scenes, we went with a more saturated primary color palette. I shot tests on different film stocks and went with the newly introduced ASA 50 Daylight Kodak film 5245, a very fine-grain saturated rendition that created what I call juke box colors. In Africa, we found Fuji stock to complement the use of greens, umbers, and naturalistic colors against the Asian and black flesh tones. At the time, Fuji seemed to have a lower contrast and a softer feeling, to differentiate the seventies time period in Africa against contemporary Mississippi, which we wanted to be more of an American commercialized perspective.

Q: When you print the release prints on Kodak stock, do you still get the qualities of the Fuji negative?

A: You still get similar qualities from Fuji because the actual colors respond to the Kodak stock. The color rendition and subtleties of Fuji would be more enhanced making it on Fuji intermediate negative and printing it on Fuji print stock than on Kodak at that time. Today, Kodak has such a fine interpositive and internegative stock in 5244 that if I were to use Fuji, I would prefer to print Fuji on Kodak stock for release prints.

I shot different parts of *Mississippi Masala* with different makes of lenses to lend itself to different styles. After having done many tests, I found different makes of lenses have different characteristics in relation to color, contrast, and sharpness and could affect the image much like filters. In Africa, I used Cooke Speed Pancros, which are softer, warmer, and more forgiving. They have a certain roundness of shape to the image due to their older style optics. Those lenses were designed over thirty years ago, the elements were hand-grounded. They are not as precise as newer Zeiss lenses, which have a very flat feel and are critically sharp in a very clinical way. I used those lenses for the Mississippi portion to contrast America and Africa. So for me, it was the combination of using different film stocks and different sets of lenses that created the different looks and feelings in the film.

Q: Why do films produced in other countries look different than American films?

A: If there are contributing differences between Hollywood studio films versus American independent and smaller European sized productions, then it becomes more of an attitude and point of view to the storytelling. Not to say there aren't European-style productions that don't emulate American sensibilities, like *Subway* and *Le Femme Nikita* by French director Luc Besson. In my experience and perception, European directors search for a visual language of their own, while in Hollywood one is expected to create many possible options in coverage and multiple angles to tell the story in the editing room. In smaller budget films, one does not have the time or the resources to create these options, and sometimes these limitations can be a strength. For example, a performance can be played between two actors in an orchestrated two-shot, which can have the advantage of creating the performance in real time. Different countries seem also to perceive colors differently in their films. Many contemporary French films seem to have a cooler bluish look to them. In part, it's the quality of the light they use and the way they print their films. German films seem to have an analytical, microscopic look to them, partly due to Zeiss lenses that have a very sharp and unforgiving crisp look to them. The English filmmakers like Ridley Scott, Tony Scott, and Alan Parker, who came out of commercials, created their own stylized three-quarter-edge light look with smoke or rain. Only when I photographed *London Kills Me* in England did I understand why they created their own photographic look in films. England, during the winter months, has five or six hours of daylight if you are lucky, so you are always put in a situation where you have to create your own supplementary light, which in turn creates an aesthetic. Even when you're on real locations in England, you're sometimes forced to create your own daylight, which becomes a clean daylight three-quarter-highlight-edge source. This exterior hard-edged look influenced the interior look of sets, a chiaroscuro effect of light and dark on the actors and settings. It's a look that many talented British cinematographers like Peter Suschitzky (*Privilege*, *The Empire Strikes Back*), Peter Biziou (*Pink Floyd—The Wall*, *Mississippi Burning*), and Michael Seresin (*Fame*, *Birdy*) created.

Q: How do you approach photographing an actor's face?

A: People say the face is a landscape. No face takes light the same. So I like to look at a person in life and see how they look under different lighting situations, and light the environment in relation to that specific face. I create a world for the actors and then capture the face in that environment. There are actors and actresses who like to make demands on the cameraman to create their own image. Barbra Streisand, for instance, always looks like she's in a different movie than everybody else because she has requirements about the way she wants to be photographed, whether it serves the emotional visual context of the story or not.

Q: How do you know how much light it takes to photograph an actor's face properly?

A: I use a spot meter for most of my interiors, then evaluate different people's complexions against the set for exposure, mood, or feeling for the scene. You finally get into the zone where you get to know the film stock and light you're using, and with trust and experience you can see by eye what it's going to look like on the film. I used to think of it as a calculated risk, but it's really previsualizing. If I knew exactly how everything was going to look, it would be boring. One has to take risks and place yourself where you are able to take chances. You need a director and crew to take that risk with you, or you just take it upon yourself.

Q: You used the term "zone" in discussing how you light. This is a method developed by the great still photographer Ansel Adams. How does it apply to lighting for motion pictures?

A: You figure out the exposure range of the negative from your highlights to shadow detail, your film stock, the light meter, and the lab. What you are doing when you're lighting a set is really creating a type of zone system, a range to the negative that creates your desirable look or mood to the scene. The high-speed film stocks have become so good today that the film can see what your eye sees in low-light situations. I worked with the French director Jean-Luc Godard, who doesn't like to use any lights, or very minimal amounts to augment the practical lights on the set. It's where you put the camera and the understanding of how to control what you see. Any cinematographer is going to understand how to use an exposure meter, but it is how you interpret the light to create an image. Eventually, you get to a point where you don't rely on your light meter as much as on your eye. The light meter might be a disadvantage because it might make you fall back on a certain look you're trying to get past. Falling back purely on a technical aspect of exposure and contrast, you might lose the happy accidents that happen. It's not to say you don't use those things, you do use them, but there's a certain place where your intuition and experience takes over—that's what we're all working towards.

Q: How does a cinematographer develop an eye?

A: When I started out, I walked around and saw everything in a frame. I looked at how light fell, then later tried to understand how I could recreate that. It's important to become aware of what's around in your own environment. Another way to develop your visual awareness is to study films. You become sophisticated enough to look at a film and analyze it visually, and you are left with how you're affected by the images in the context of the story. That's what we're talking about. I don't think it's good photography if people walk away from a film more aware of the photography than the story. There are many well-photographed films that aren't good films, and there can be a great film that's not well photographed. It's when you have both elements working together, in films like *Searching for Bobby Fischer,* directed by Steven Zaillian; Kieslowski's trilogy *Red, White,* and *Blue*; and Wong Kar Wai's *Fallen Angels* and *Days of Being Wild* that it is such a revelation.

Q: Do you feel the technology and technique on a period film has to complement the time period? On *Barry Lyndon*, Stanley Kubrick and his cinematographer, John Alcott, used the zoom lens extensively. How do you feel about using the Steadicam and other technology on a period film?

A: Cinema didn't exist when *Barry Lyndon* took place, so that gives you license to do anything. I looked at the use of zooms in *Barry Lyndon* with Gregory Nava when we did *My Family/Mi Familia*, which takes place in three different periods—the twenties, fifties, and the seventies. Most cinematographers don't like zooms because it's a mechanical way of bringing the audience into something. The zoom in *Barry Lyndon* has a whole other visual context, it was used as more of a literary device. It was like the page turning or the chapter changing. I saw it more indicative of an eighteenth-century novel, where the landscape comes upon you. You can use any tool you want—there's no rules. The application of techniques take your story further. Look at the way a great stylist like Nick Roeg uses a zoom. I worked on *Insignificance*, and he'd use three cameras always shooting in different angles. He uses it in a very evocative way. He's always looking for a point of view that gives some kind of an emotional context to the character. Roeg uses a zoom in a different way than Luchino Visconti would, as in *Death in Venice* which he did in a baroque, sweeping aesthetic, or the way that Peckinpah used the zoom which had a visceral violence to it. In all honesty, I try not to use zooms because it draws too much attention, except in documentaries where I have to respond to the image very spontaneously.

Q: How did you achieve the sense of period on *My Family/Mi Familia*?

A: There were three different periods—the twenties, fifties, and the seventies. For the twenties, we looked at silent films of that period and old photographs of family albums. For the fifties, we looked at periodicals like *Life* magazines and fifties album covers. Then, for the seventies, we worked with a Chicana artist that lives in the community where we shot, and interpreted our story through renderings of her paintings. Gabriel Figueroa, the renowned Mexican cinematographer, and Jose Clemente Orozco, the great Mexican artist and muralist, served as an overall inspiration for all the different styles of our periods.

Q: What films do you consider to be landmarks in cinematography?

A: It always changes. Gabriel Figueroa's films *The Pearl,* and *Los Olvidados*—he is somebody whose work I've always respected and greatly admired. Of course, Orson Welles and his cinematographer, Gregg Toland and Russell Metty. Toland's work on *Citizen Kane* is certainly a landmark film, and Metty's black-and-white photography on *The Magnificent Ambersons* (Metty worked uncredited on the film, as did Harry J. Wild. Stanley Cortez is the credited cinematographer) and *Touch of Evil. I Am Cuba*, by Russian director Mikhail Kalatozov, is a brilliantly conceived and photographed black-and-white film created with long, extended, innovative handheld camerawork. The Hungarian film *Time Stands Still*, photographed by Lajos Koltai, created an expressionistic, political world of the fifties in Hungary through the eyes of teenagers coming of age. Other landmarks are the intricate visual poetry of Russian director Tarkovsky. The approach of each film by the Polish director Krzysztof Kieslowski had a totally different visceral style. The young Czech director Ivan Fila made a remarkable first feature film, *Lea*. It is a beautifully ethereal film that is an unconventional love story. The Hong Kong director Wong Kar War and Cinematographer Chris Doyle are creating the most contemporary and provocative imagery today with *Chungking Express*, *Days of Being Wild*, and *Fallen Angels*. Images in film are always evolving and reinventing themselves, which in turn will inspire new film language.

Q: You've done so much in your career, working in so many different forms—features, documentaries, commercials, and music videos. What haven't you've done that you would like to do?

A: Just to work with inspired people. I was very lucky from an early age to work with the people I most admired. I was on a set with Bernardo Berto-lucci and Vittorio Storaro as second unit director of photography on *La Luna*. I worked with Jean-Luc Godard, with Werner Herzog, Wim Wenders, Rainer Fassbinder, and Volker Schlöndorff. I would like to continue work-ing with inspired and passionate artists, young and old.

Q: What advice do you give to students who ask how to become a cine-matographer?

A: Just pick up a camera and start telling stories with images. If you want to be a cinematographer, learn about editing. It's not enough just to take pretty pictures, it's important to understand how these images are constructed to tell a story. Editing is as important as shooting. Cinematography might be an additive process and editing is a subtractive process, not necessarily in a pejorative way; it will help you become a better cameraman. Seek out the artist whose work you most admire, and they'll know and respect you if you understand their work in the context of what is important to them. If you are true to them, those are the people who will help you because they'll find a familiarity with you. I was fortunate enough to work with the people I most admired. You have to make whatever sacrifices it takes to afford you the possibilities to succeed.

9

Garrett Brown

Since the invention of motion pictures, filmmakers have longed to free the camera from its shackles. Every imaginable technique and method of suspending, carrying, floating, throwing, and pushing the motion picture camera was attempted, but not until the 1970s did anyone really develop a viable way of stabilizing the camera itself to give complete, maneuverable control to the operator. Cinematographer and inventor Garrett Brown shared the dream of Abel Gance, Jean Rouch, D. A. Pennebaker, Max Ophuls, Stanley Kubrick, Stan Brakhage, and John Cassavettes to empower the camera to see with the responsiveness of the human eye, and with his creation of the Steadicam he freed the motion picture camera.

The story of how Garrett Brown, ASC, came to invent the Steadicam, a camera stabilizing device, is captivating, hilarious, deeply serious, and a bit miraculous.

Brown has navigated his Steadicam on over two hundred films and has captured many magical moments—the triumphant Rocky Balboa soaring up the steps of the Philadelphia Museum of Art in *Rocky*, Woody Guthrie wandering through a grim migrant farm camp during the Great Depression in *Bound for Glory*, and Danny Torrance whizzing around the haunted Overlook Hotel on his Big Wheel in *The Shining*.

Garrett Brown currently holds over forty patents worldwide for camera devices, including the Steadicam JR, a miniature version of the Steadicam for camcorders; the Skycam, which flies on wires over sporting events; and the Mobycams, Gocams, and Divecams that pursued Olympic swimmers, runners, and divers from Barcelona to Atlanta.

Garrett Brown is a cinematic Thomas Edison, an autodidact, and an American original—a man who has changed the moving image forever.

SELECTED FILMOGRAPHY

1976   *Bound for Glory*
        Rocky
        Marathon Man

1977   *Exorcist II: The Heretic*

1978   *The Buddy Holly Story*

1979   *Rocky II*

1980   *The Shining*
        The Formula
        Altered States
        Willie and Phil
        Can't Stop the Music
        Xanadu
        Fame
        No Nukes

1981   *True Confessions*
        Blow Out
        Fort Apache, the Bronx
        Wolfen
        Deathtrap
        Reds
        Sharkey's Machine
        Prince of the City
        Taps
        Stripes
        Four Friends

1982   *One from the Heart*
        Let's Spend the Night Together
        Annie
        A Little Sex
        Tootsie
        Lookin' to Get Out
        The Toy

1983   *Twilight Zone—The Movie* (George Miller segment, *Nightmare at 20,000 Feet*)
        Return of the Jedi
        A Night in Heaven

The Man Who Loved Women
The King of Comedy
Baby, It's You
Yentl
The Hunger

1984   *Greystoke: The Legend of Tarzan, Lord of the Apes*
Indiana Jones and the Temple of Doom
Falling in Love
Hard to Hold
Give My Regards to Broad Street
The Muppets Take Manhattan

1985   *The Slugger's Wife*

1986   *Legal Eagles*
Hannah and Her Sisters
Sweet Liberty

1990   *Rocky V*

1993   *Philadelphia*

1994   *Wolf*
Love Affair

1995   *Casino*

1998   *Bulworth*

Q: How did you first become interested in filmmaking?

A: When I was a kid, I had no idea what I wanted to do when I grew up. My father was an inventor, a chemist for Dupont, and he invented the material that binds paperback books together. I was sick in bed with nephritis for six months when I was in the fourth grade, and I read through the World Book and filled notebooks with drawings of inventions—including some gadgets that would still be quite revolutionary, like a matter transporter. Regrettably, I neglected to include enough detail to allow my adult self to cash in. I was a ham operator and an extremely fast Morse code sender; as an eleven-year-old, I could send forty or forty-five words a minute and used to love editing audiotape to humorously alter conversations. I was enthralled when a neighbor wrote a book on trick photography, but I never specifically thought about the movie business.

When it came time for college, I had a full navy scholarship to Tufts; I was bright enough, but very lazy when it came right down to it. I was also an extremely fast banjo player, always a good organizer, and I had energy—enough to round up five adolescent buffalo, turn them into a folk group, and get everybody all enthused. In the early sixties, a folk act was just an entertainment, all polish. We wore blazers, sang laundered pop folk songs, and told jokes. I wanted to be an entertainer, and I quit my navy scholarship in order to sing full time. "Brown & Dana" recorded for MGM and sang at colleges and folk clubs for the next three years. But we didn't write any of our own songs, so when blazer-wearing buffalos fell out of fashion, we were in trouble and Brown & Dana split up. I was just married and I had to earn a living, so I hung on as a solo act for about five months, but that didn't bring in enough money to live on. Finally, I had to take a job—selling Volkswagens—and I began to cast about for my next career.

I was a real movie buff, and the thought of a job in the film business had great appeal. To prepare myself, given my ignorance about the practical aspects, I read the entire section on film at the Philadelphia Public Library, literally thirty linear feet of books, while my wife worked at the phone company. She paid the bills while I read. It took four months, after which I headed off very confidently to get a job.

Q: How did you become a cinematographer?

A: It took me much longer than I expected. No film company would hire me. When they asked if I had ever A and B rolled, I would tell them no, but I was sure I could (Hey, I was a fast banjo player!). The Philadelphia Yellow Pages listed thirty local motion picture production companies, but I couldn't even get a job sweeping floors.

Finally, an adventuresome ad agency hired me as a writer on the basis of a brochure I had made for myself, along with some dummy ads. When the agency's producer quit, I got the job by default. We actually won a lot of awards, but just when I was becoming valuable to the agency, I realized where I really wanted to be was on the other side, in production. So, I left to start my own production company and promptly starved. I eventually took a job as director with one of my former suppliers, and after eight months of recovery I restarted my own company. Now I was both director and cameraman, making commercials and beginning to win awards for novel special effects.

Q: What led you to invent the Steadicam?

A: I started contriving gadgets to help me do impossible shots, like shooting people moving backwards, but speaking forwards. For instance, I made a rig that held a camera with a primitive video assist in a ball suspended thirty feet below a helicopter. With this, we could move the camera alongside automobiles at ground level, fly up over the hood to look in the windows and then fly away into a wide shot.

Generally, I loved moving the camera, and I liked the resulting three-dimensionality of the film medium. To me, the moving camera lets you break into the medium itself—the screen stops being a wall and becomes a space you can play in. At that point, I shot a lot with my Bolex, which weighed all of eight pounds, but in order to move with that eight-pound camera, I had to lug around an eight hundred-pound Fearless-Panaram dolly, the old one with the crank and the jib-arm. I broke my heart lifting that thing in and out of pick-up trucks.

I would stare at that pin-headed dolly with my tiny little camera perched on it and my rusty rails laid down, all for a crummy ten-foot move—it just seemed ridiculous. It seemed to me there had to be some way to isolate a human being from a camera without all the rest of the paraphernalia. I needed something I could use to shoot with every day. I didn't think of the Steadicam as an invention as much as a gadget or a rig. An invention is more of an intellectual property, a rig is a contraption you figure out to make something specific possible. But the rigs I devised got more and more expensive and more and more different from anything that had been done before.

I took one early variation as far as I could. Eventually, I had so much money in it that I realized it couldn't be just a rig—I had to make it into a product. Then, of course, patenting became an issue, so I acquired patent attorneys. We actually wrote up one of these early concepts, but it proved to be a dead end—it was too heavy, it required too much skill, and it wasn't very flexible. So I had to start all over again.

In those days, I would go into a motel room for a week at a time, primarily to get away from the phone and to give myself the chance to think about nothing else from morning until night. I wouldn't leave my room; my only contact would be with room service, there was no stimulation of any kind except the project itself. That first time, I emerged with only a few minor improvements. Then I went through this isolation process a second time, and realized I could get further if I relaxed my requirements. All right, maybe the thing doesn't have to be able to take the lens from the floor to over one's head. I finally realized it didn't necessarily have to do everything, that there was no possible rig a human could lug around with cameras worth using that would provide that much vertical range. There would have to be some compromises.

I sketched variations of the current design, pages full of them, so I could flip through them to see what caught my eye, what insights emerged. In the end, I went back through it all, and there it was, sitting there in a drawing that already existed. This time, the compression process had worked—I came out with a drawing of the Steadicam as we now know it.

As it happened, I had a friend, an old fellow named Jack Hauser, a former navy machinist. He was so good, he could think with a milling machine! He built my prototype and it worked immediately, just as I had imagined.

Q: How did you sell the idea of the Steadicam to the film industry?

A: I made a 35mm demo in the suburbs of Philadelphia with about twenty-four shots that had never been seen or done before. By then, I was under pressure. I hadn't paid my lab bill and things felt a little desperate, but I knew this demo was good. The shots were all impossible, with no clue on-screen as to how they had been done. One of them happened to be a sequence I shot while running down and then back up the steps of the Philadelphia Museum of Art chasing my wife, Ellen; others were filmed leaping off ledges or rushing straight ahead through narrow openings. We basically winged twenty-four amazing shots in a single day.

Once we were done, I took the unprocessed negative off to Los Angeles. My lab account was closed, and I knew I had to score fast. I had already shown a similar 16mm demo made with an earlier version of the Steadicam to Panavision and they had given me the proverbial, "We'll get back to you." They never did. Instead, as I learned, Panavision started a program aimed at knocking this "Brown Stabilizer" thing off, doing it in-house instead of buying it from me. I didn't know this at the time, but as luck would have it, when I couldn't get to them the second time around, I went to Cinema Products. I had an appointment for the next day with Ed Di Giulio.

Quickly, I went to Deluxe General, who hadn't yet gotten word that I was a deadbeat, and they processed the film. When I showed up for it the next morning, they wouldn't give it to me—they had gotten word that I owed the East Coast lab money, and they weren't going to turn the print over to me until I paid it. I pleaded with them, "Guys, you've got to help me—just take a look at this film. If you don't think it's worth a million bucks then keep it, but if you do, let me show it so I can get the money to pay the bill." They were skeptical to say the least, but they took the film into the screening room and ran it at high speed—and then they ran it again for the executives in the big screening room. When it was over, they just handed over the can with a breezy, "No problem!" So Di Giulio saw the demo, and I came home knowing I had a deal for what was at that time a fantastic amount of money—I could pay my bills and buy the little sailboat that I had coveted for years.

Things moved very quickly once that demo got around because that same day Di Giulio took it over to Universal and showed it to a producer who immediately tried to buy it out from under him. That in itself was a pretty clear indication to Ed that this was a good thing. He, incidentally, came up with the name "Steadicam" which, at the time, was a disappointment (I wanted it to be called the "Brown Stabilizer"), but now Steadicam seems like a perfectly proper noun.

Q: What were some of the early approaches to viewing what the Steadicam saw as it was moving?

A: Initially, I had approached American Optical and persuaded them to give me a coherent fiber optic bundle, six feet long, through which I could see what I was shooting. The bundle, in effect, produced a flexible remote reflex viewfinder that extended out of the camera and up over my head. All of a sudden, I could walk around and see with one eye directly through the lens three hundred thousand pixels of perfect color at f1, which is optically "faster" than any normal viewfinder. I had a brighter image from six feet away than I would have had with my eye right on the eyepiece of the Arriflex. The optic bundle was worth $10,000—American Optical gave me one in hopes that this idea would take off and they would sell a bundle of bundles. It would not really have been commercially practical to have such an expensive component ($20,000 today) in the rig, but it was incredibly exciting to be the first cameraman ever to be able to look through a Steadicam with this magic eye. I did nothing but wander around with this combination for days. I didn't roll film, I just walked for hours in and around my house with the then lightweight prototype. On top of the rig sat my old World War II Rommel-era Arri, with the optic bundle poking out of its side and up over my shoulder. I just walked or ran wherever I wanted, looking and watching what happened, experimenting—doing things that couldn't be done any other way. It really was like moving into another dimension.

Q: What are the basic components of the Steadicam?

A: If you combine the following four things, you have a Steadicam. Number one, the camera has to be expanded and made more inert, otherwise it is too compact and you have no access to its center of gravity. Second, the camera has to be supported without affecting its angle. The handheld camera requires too much contact with the ever-moving cameraman. A gimbal, which consists of a series of attached concentric rings, each mounted on bearings, can keep the camera isolated while you shoot. Third, there has to be an exoskeletal arm that will take the weight of the camera and reach as far as the operator's arm—the whole rig is too heavy for a human arm to hold up for long unaided. That exoskeletal arm is more or less analogous to the human arm, complete with shoulder joint, but it is tireless because its titanium springs neutralize the camera's weight, so the camera basically just floats. That arm, of course, has to be attached to a harness you wear on your body. Finally, the operator has to be able to see through the camera to make it do what he wants. The original patent cites either the fiber optic viewfinder or the video assist, which was very new at the time the Steadicam came into being. Fortunately, I threw the bit about the video assist into the patent—at that time you couldn't find one, but that's what we depend on now. So if you combine all four of these things correctly, you have a Steadicam—and it works.

Q: After you built the prototype, how did you proceed to work with the Steadicam?

A: The first people I showed it to said I should just continue to do what I had been doing—using the prototypes on jobs. I did go shoot commercials with them, but I realized I would have to get everybody to sign an agreement of secrecy if I wanted to protect my invention. So there was a spectacle—agencies full of people, clients, actors, extras, and anybody who would be attending any of the shots, all signing disclosure agreements. I had to have a sheaf of them to do every single job. Then, with black cloth draped over the various parts and pieces, very ineffectively, too, I can assure you, we would shoot and there (in some otherwise routine commercial from the early seventies) would be a shot that was theoretically impossible. I loved having those rigs because they let me get the shots I wanted without having to lug the goddamn dolly around.

We finally hit a wall regarding disclosure agreements while shooting an Arnold Palmer spot in Latrobe, Pennsylvania. Palmer's manager, Jules Rosenthal, was sharp, but he ultimately outsharped himself. He took a look at our very harmless agreement and said, "We ain't signing this. What's in it for Arnie? What would you do, sue him in a couple of years from now if you think he talked about your gizmo?" I told him the only thing in it for Arnie was a better commercial, that I didn't care whether he signed it or not. I would use the gizmo if he was willing to keep it secret, but otherwise I would shoot it the way anyone else would. So, on Arnold's own gold course in Latrobe we shot a very routine, static commercial using a tripod. Then at twilight, as soon as Arnie went home, out came the prototype which had been lurking in my motor home. We zipped it out and I made some shots while running around on the golf course, while my assistant used the second camera to film me in action. I was always careful to document whatever we did, and we added that shot to the demo along with other shots taken while galloping on the greens and running between pine trees.

People who had only seen the prototype draped in black and had no idea how it worked advised me to keep this unique rig for myself, charge $20,000 a week, and do high-end jobs only. I thought it over, but I guess that if the stakes were that high, someone would peek under the curtain before long, like the great Oz. I couldn't sleep with it, after all. Somebody would eventually bust it if I made it too precious, if I didn't patent it, and disseminate it, and make it available.

Q: What led you to realize you had to train more people to use this new technology?

A: Even when I had the only one in the world, before we began to sell it and I had done *Bound for Glory*, *Rocky*, and *Marathon Man*, people still weren't beating a path to my door. As it turns out, only the boldest cameramen and directors—hotshots like Connie Hall, Haskell Wexler, John Avildsen, and a few other early starters—would dare to try anything this radical. The rest tended to play it safe. I was amazed. I had the only item in the world that could do these things, and yet there were many days when I didn't have a job and waited for the phone to ring. This changed once the Steadicam was featured in *American Cinematographer*. Everyone knew about it, but to my astonishment, I still was not called for every movie being made. Moviemaking is a very traditional business.

Finally, I decided the only way to get rolling was to teach other operators. This was just before 1980. I had come back from *The Shining* and realized there weren't enough people out there using it. In the States, I had taught Kyle Rudolf, Dan Lerner, Larry McConkey, and a few others. The nicks in the door frames of my townhouse, formerly initialed by the initiates, are still visible. These early starters were worried about losing business if we let anyone else in. I argued that if you're among the best at what you do and a lot of other people also do it, you'll remain at the top of a very much higher, more important pyramid. So I called up David Lyman of the Maine workshops and told him I had something he ought to have in his catalogue. The late Ted Churchill and his brother, Jack, took the first workshop in 1980. We concluded that the way to make the Steadicam a success was to have a big constituency, and we never looked back. I must have conducted a hundred workshops since then, in a dozen countries. Jerry Hallway is running his ninth workshop in Scandinavia as we speak. The knowledge and the skill have spread, and the ever-increasing client base now includes most features and a vast number of film and video projects throughout the world. The expanding ranks of operators has its own proportion of hotshots and stars.

Q: What personality traits are important for a good Steadicam operator?

A: There are probably three hundred ace Steadicam operators in the world, and of that group, probably a hundred are the godlike beings we jokingly call "Living Masters." These are people you could drop in by parachute anywhere on earth and know they would bring back amazing shots. They are an amazing, close-knit group, entrepreneurs and artists willing to put everything on the line for the sake of a great shot. The people who have gravitated to the Steadicam are people with nerve who trust themselves, physically and artistically. This Steadicam culture has permeated the planet and it's still spreading, as those who know teach the skill to others.

Q: Do dancers and people involved in the martial arts make good Steadicam operators?

A: They certainly have a head start—as well as people who are good at wind surfing, fencing, etc. However, I think specific skills are less important than personality. Operating a camera is as political a job as there could possibly be. A good operator has to have a filmmaker's sensibilities—able to collaborate, able to organize a shot, and make it happen. The Steadicam operator needs the innate ability to communicate effectively and is frequently encumbered with longer sequences which require real feats of memory and concentration. The Steadicam operator is something of an auteur and has a lot more pieces to put together. To deliver a world-class, spectacular, four-minute uncut extravaganza of the sort increasingly seen at the movies, one needs the whole kit of camera operator's skills relating to the politics, art, and science of filmmaking and to everything that has to do with the script, the style, and the editing of the specific picture, not to mention a solid feel for the history and potential of film, a healthy regard for flares, uneven steps, erratic extras, and the etiquette of the catering line.

When you start tallying what this job requires—it's big! It takes everything you've got and then some. Ted Churchill referred to himself as an "arty pack mule," which is somewhat less grand. Certainly after you sort out all the things that will make a shot work, you have to have the physical wherewithal to get through the required number of takes. That's where you share the skill of dancers and martial artists.

On the other hand, you can take somebody who had tremendous heart, drive, and determination, but who is the most uncoordinated, weakest, flabbiest klutz in history, and they can still become good at the Steadicam. They may not be able to operate with the same degree of endurance, but if all the other qualities are there, they can be successful.

Q: How is a shot communicated to you? Through storyboards? Video? Are models of a set ever presented to you?

A: Yes, all of the above. Francis Coppola, on *One from the Heart*, is the only person who ever used video to show me a proposed shot. Storyboards are common, but it usually boils down to somebody saying, "This is what we want to do. . . ." We talk it through and walk it through, and all the while the brain is going a hundred miles an hour, "Can I do it? Can I get through here? How do I get over to there?" Of course, directorial styles vary widely. Some just describe the action and tell me to make it work and they're off to their trailer. Frequently, I just work for the director of photography in the American system, or on a British film they may hand me the responsibility for the design aspects. In that case, I work it out with the crew and the stand-ins and whistle when we're ready. From a Steadicam operator's point of view, it's much more fun to work in the British system as far as the mechanics of a shot are concerned. In the American style, I've been given either a little detail or a lot, as in, "All right, it's a lo-mode shot and you go here." A knowledgeable and experienced director may already have in mind exactly how he wants a Steadicam shot to work. He's the same guy who might draw a line for the dolly, call for a specific lens, and tell the grip when to boom up or down. That's a particular breed of filmmaker that I also enjoy working for.

Q: Bound for Glory was the first feature film to utilize the Steadicam. The film contains an extraordinary shot that follows David Carradine, playing Woody Guthrie, as he walks through a crowded migrant farm camp. How did you and the Steadicam become involved in this film?

A: It was due entirely to Haskell Wexler (*Who's Afraid of Virginia Woolf?*, *Matewan*). Haskell had used me with the prototype for a Keds commercial. He was a friend of Ed Di Giulio's, became a friend of mine, and he loved the idea of the Steadicam. So he was on the lookout for a big way to use the Steadicam. His innovation was the combination shot: ride down onto the crane, step off and walk, shooting all the time. As it turned out, I arrived with only one film magazine. Between takes, I had to get off and reload our solitary mag. They all went mad, but in fact I'd be back by the time everything was reset, replaced, and dusted down. They brought the camera truck up as close to the set as they could, so we didn't have far to walk. A loader was standing by and it was—zip!—into the darkroom and right back up onto the crane. Don Thorin was the regular camera operator and he was very helpful to me, especially since I had never been up on a Titan crane before.

The shot was very well rehearsed. There were nine hundred extras picked up in Stockton, California, and not a single one looked at the camera—except for one poor guy, a professional extra who had been knocking around for years. He thought he knew what a camera was, all right. However, I appeared to be somebody strolling along with a sewing machine, so he had no clue that we were rolling film. At one point, as I was following David Carradine, he walked right up to him and asked when they were going to break for lunch. Everyone was horrified—he just talked on, and everybody jumped on him. He felt bad, needless to say, and he apologized, but how was he to know? No one had ever seen anything like this gadget before. It was very funny.

Q: How many takes were done of that scene?

A: Three. The next night was the first time I had ever gone to dailies on a feature. I couldn't wait for news of the shot, so I asked a guy standing there if he was the projectionist, thinking I could find out in advance how it looked. The guy turned, looked at me coldly and said, "I'm the producer." I felt completely humiliated and just sat there quietly and watched Haskell's amazing footage. It was all great stuff. He was shooting at three and four footcandles, using fire in barrels for the light source. Then came my shot. They only printed one take—the one used in the film. It was bloody good—I was very excited. There was a standing ovation right there in the screening room—everybody literally stood up, turned around, and clapped. Life can hardly offer a better moment—what a thrill! They were hugging Haskell, they were hugging me. It was absolutely amazing, because we all felt this was historic.

Q: How did you shoot the sequence in *Rocky* where the Steadicam follows Sylvester Stallone up the steps of the Philadelphia Art Museum?

A: That shot is in the film because on our initial demo I had chased my wife Ellen down the stairs and back up. The director, John Avildsen, saw our demo and recognized my assistant, Ralph Hotchiss, in the background. He called Ralph, asked for details, and got my name and phone number in Philly. He reached Ellen, who said, "Hold on, I can call Garrett." At that very moment, I was on stage 15 at Burbank, showing John Boorman the Steadicam because he was prepping *Exorcist II: The Heretic*. Ellen asked Avildsen where he was so I could call him back, and it turned out he was on stage 16, also in Burbank. Ellen didn't let on, but called me on the other line, "Avildsen's on the next stage and he wants to get together with you." I told her to have him step outside the entrance and just stand there, but not to tell him anything else. He stepped out of stage 16 and stood there, looking around. I came out of studio 15 with the rig on and walked right up behind him.

After being revived, he wanted to know where the place with the steps was, and that's how it got into the movie.

Q: How was that shot executed?

A: *Rocky* actually started as a little, nonunion B-picture in Philly. John Avildsen was basically operating, and Ralf Bode was director of photography. All of us fit into one motor home—this was a tiny little crew. My wife, Ellen, did wardrobe and script. The weather was amazingly cold. It was barely dawn and the camera wouldn't run because we had dropped it the day before. The motor shaft ran right up the center post. In those days, the motor was down below the camera so once the shaft got bent, it rubbed and the motor wouldn't run. In order to make the camera go, we had to hook it to two car batteries. So poor Ralf ran next to me, carrying both a twelve-volt and a six-volt car battery, wired in series. My running speed was restricted by Ralf's, as he chugged along with those batteries.

Q: What was it like to shoot scenes of Rocky running through the streets of Philadelphia?

A: During the film, I made the first vehicle shots with the Steadicam. We pioneered shooting out of the back of a van in the Italian market, so nobody would know what we were up to. We shot on some very bumpy roads, but the Steadicam smoothed them all out. Stallone was charging up the middle of the street, wearing that gray sweatshirt, yelling at everybody, "Yo, how ya doin'?" People started yelling back, "Yo, how ya doin'?" There was a strange and wonderful emotional quality to the stillness of those frame edges, as if you were flying through the market in a dirigible. What appeals to me is the way the perspective lines flow away—you're perpetually leaving everything except Stallone, who is the only consistent moving element in the frame.

Q: As Stallone is running, sometimes you move with him in dead sync, sometimes you move faster or slower.

A: I learned quickly that the Steadicam is facile enough to become boring if you don't vary the distances. A bust shot can be so stable that it looks like rear projection—you have to force yourself to let the frame have some life.

Q: How did you execute the shots where you were running behind Stallone with the Steadicam?

A: I had the first Akai one quarter-inch reel-to-reel video recorder, and I had a little video viewfinder on the Steadicam. So I ran a coaxial cable from myself to John Avildsen, who held the recorder and was running after me. Stallone is fast, and I was also very fast in those days—I had the legs for it. The Steadicam didn't weigh much, so I could keep up with Sly at his absolute top speed, but of course, Avildsen has shorter legs. At one point, he was behind me holding the recorder and we took off across a junkyard in south Philly. I got involved in not falling down in all the junk—the speed was phenomenal—and I forgot about Avildsen. Poor John was yelling at us and we couldn't even hear him. He had run out of cord and was stretching his arms out as far as he could. Finally, the coax broke right out of the back of the recorder, and John went down. A little yelp and a crash finally stopped us—poor John had fallen down in the junk trying to save my recorder.

Q: You spent a year with Stanley Kubrick on *The Shining*, which proved to be a landmark film for the Steadicam. How did you come to work on this film?

A: It certainly was a watershed event. I was in London with Ed Di Giulio for Film '77. While we were there, we arranged to go out and show Stanley the prototype of the Steadicam—he had seen the demo, and now he wanted to see the real thing. By this time, it was on the market for sale commercially. We went out to Elstree Studios at Boreham Wood, where set construction had just begun in late winter of 1977. The big question was whether or not we could do shots at knee height, and we immediately devised the gear for lo-mode shooting with the camera hung on the bottom of the Steadicam. Production finally commenced in late 1978, and Stanley had built all the sets so they were interconnected—the entire hotel was laid out between a number of stages. Up the stairs from the lounge were all the second-floor corridors with hotel-room doors, and the individual rooms that he needed were actually there behind the doors, propped and dressed. If you went laterally from the lounge, there were the kitchen corridors, some of which went right on through the stage doors to the adjacent soundstage—itself dressed as a kitchen. There were two huge lobbies, next to which were respectively, seven hundred thousand and one million watts of Par lights, giving him that wonderful effect of daylight all flooding in from one side. Off in other directions were corridors that looped around and made all those continuous-action scenes possible.

Q: Did the script indicate precise camera movement throughout the film?

A: Certainly a lot of camera movement was indicated, but the Steadicam wasn't particularly specified. The camera was just to move, or truck, or dolly here or there. Stanley may have had me in mind from the beginning, however, because the floors were not constructed smooth enough to dolly on at the speeds at which he wanted to move. I was originally supposed to be his wild card for the maze sequences, but I ended up shooting virtually every moving shot in the film because of the floors and because of the supernatural serenity of the moving Steadicam frame. The only conventional dolly shots used were a couple of exteriors parallel to the hotel, when Shelly Duvall ran off to check the Sno-Cat, and one shot that went into the ballroom from the corridor where the wall hid the rails. They laid some rail for those shots, but the rest of it was Steadicam.

The shot of little Danny Lloyd on the Big Wheel became an inspiration after the fact. Everyone, perhaps including Stanley, failed to realize how impressive the soundtrack would be—and that's what made the shot so exciting. It hadn't occurred to us the wheels would make that loud grinding noise on bare wood and that contrasting silence on the carpets. We discovered it in the dailies because we had put a mike on the camera while we made the shot, but we were too involved in the pursuit of Danny to pay attention to the sound—all these people with their muffled sneakers and muffled curses, trying to keep the damn idiotic wheelchair rig moving fast enough to stay behind him. So we were caught up in avoiding death and destruction and re-placing the grips who were knackered with fresh guys lurking along the way who could leap in and start pushing. I was at the apex of this carnival, trying desperately not to roll over in the wheelchair going around corners. We were caught up so completely in what was going on that when we finally settled back and looked at the shot in the dailies we were all stunned. It was great.

Look at that lens height! Even an Arriflex with a conventional motor sticks down four or five inches. I shot that with a BL, and there was not even half an inch between the camera and the rug. The BL had an 18mm lens, which had to stay essentially level in the set or it would distort all the walls. But if you raise the lens even three inches above the rug, all of a sudden it be-comes a completely different shot. The fact that we were below the kid and the vanishing point toward which we were moving was hidden behind *him* gave this whole sequence a fantastic quality.

Q: How did you work with little Danny Lloyd as he drove his Big Wheel through the hotel?

A: It was so easy for him and so hard for us. It was useless to try to slow him down—he just had to go at his own fantastic tireless speed. We just tried to keep up and hoped he would go where he was told. It was like pursuing a miniature locomotive—he was amazing.

Q: How do you focus the Steadicam on a shot like this?

A: All by wireless. On that shot, Doug Milsome, who has since become a well-known director of photography (*Full Metal Jacket*, *Breakdown*), was with me controlling one of the early wireless focus units.

Q: Were you in the wheelchair rig for the kitchen tour sequence?

A: No, I was walking backwards.

Q: How difficult is it to shoot with the Steadicam while walking back-wards?

A: In a place like that, it isn't very difficult because there a lot of clues to tell you where you are, but in a high-speed shot on flat, open terrain I walk forward and shoot to the rear—the so-called "Don Juan" position.

Q: Did Kubrick have any preferences about the style of composition?

A: We had a lot of discussions about the location of the cross hairs. An audience adrift in a big movie screen is not going to know whether or not

Shelly Duvall's nose is centered. Kubrick likes centered compositions because they have a certain Palladian quality that he admires. I hated it at first, and then I got to like it. My "eye" had to be reprogrammed to work on that film, and then it had to be reprogrammed afterward to shoot more conventional compositions.

Q: Stanley Kubrick is known as a director with a high take ratio. How did that impact on your work?

A: That's where I really learned to control the Steadicam. I got to the point where I could put the frame lines or the cross hairs anywhere I wanted at any time, like a dance. I loved doing fifty or seventy takes, he could not have done too many takes for me because under the circumstances it wasn't very tiring. After each take, there was an equivalent time spent playing it back and frequently a lengthy discussion about the exact position of the cross hairs, so I got a chance to recover. It provided an unparalleled opportunity to bear down and concentrate on technique. Normally, half the work is lugging the gear to the job, through airports in most cases, and the other half is trying to catch up with events and then make a shot based on your own native abilities. If you get three takes, you're lucky, but you never get this kind of opportunity to do a take and see it and do it again and see it again, and to realize that if you keep this shoulder here—this works. If you put that foot there—that works. You cultivate a muscle memory, so you realize that if your hand is just at your belt *now*, and just at your breastbone *now*, that you have exactly the boom height you need. I was able to take this wild-haired, wing-it machine and make it into an instrument of real precision, a refined instrument instead of a gadget. A lot of things happen when you have a seminal opportunity like this. Look back at the zoom lens. For all the excesses committed with that tool, the early shooters with zooms had a chance to do something that had never before been done, for good or ill. They had the chance to combine moves and zooms, drifting the focal length in and out. We had similar opportunities to experiment and refine.

Q: What areas of innovation did you achieve with the Steadicam on *The Shining*?

A: We experimented with variations in the technique of tracking shots—particularly in the maze, and during those tours through the kitchen. A camera on a dolly had never been able to take an optimum line around a corner the way a race car driver will. The race car's line is the largest radius you can cut, the closest to a straight line you can get, and therefore comes extremely close to the actual corner. As I backed around through the kitchen, I tried to produce the least disruption to the course of the lens. I needed to maintain a smooth flow of background so the actors would not

ever be violently swept across it. The result was a shot with a wonderful serenity, and the compositions blended into one another without sudden rota-
tions. The same thing happened in the maze. When we cut those corners
with a 9.8mm lens, the shot took on the quality that those aerial shots used to
have in early Cinerama movies when they were flying the viewer up a canyon. They flew as if the plane were a race car and the shot had that same
magisterial quality.

Q: Is there any improvisation in the daytime maze sequence when the
Steadicam follows Shelly Duvall and Danny Lloyd?

A: Yes, quite a lot. The actors didn't know where they were going. We
were all always lost in the maze, totally lost. The daytime maze sequence is
the great example of those slow-motion race car turns. There was no dislo-
cation, the frame stayed aimed at the actors and the radius of the maze corners had nothing to do with the radius of the camera's motion. The key with
the 9.8mm was to keep the camera level, fore and aft. I had to put bubble levels on it to make sure because if I tilted at all, there was hideous keystone
distortion.

Q: You shot the background plates for the speed bike chase through the
forest in *Return of the Jedi*. Why was the Steadicam chosen to do this?

A: That was an interesting use of the Steadicam. There were three possible choices, and ultimately it came down to an accountant's decision. The
traditional choice for shots going through the woods would have been to lay
rails through the woods. Only in this case, it would have meant laying thousands of feet in several locations—very expensive and very uneven terrain
to work with. Then they would have had to cover the rails with leaves, which
would have to be brushed off as they moved along. They would have had to
make the shots going forward with a sweeper hiding beneath the lens. They
would dolly at max speed along the rails and undercrank the whole time to
end up with the desired screen speed. Of course, the rails would have to be
bloody good, smooth enough to allow them to speed up the action, because
speeding it up would accentuate any flaw in the track.

Choice number two was to build a model of the forest and then to push
through that on a motion-control camera. Huge.

Choice number three was suggested by a random phone call from Dennis
Muren asking me if I thought I *could* do the shot. I don't think either of us
comprehended how tricky it would be when he made that call, because although you can make a respectable shot going through the forest, you can't
speed the shot up thirty times and not expect to see the long-term variations
show up looking like bumps. Any slight dip or rise that might take thirty seconds in real time shows up as a wild lurch. So my thought originally was to

eliminate those possibilities for error one by one. I would have to give my-self long-term stability and not worry so much about the short term. I had al-ready tested an approach in an ecology film I had written that was made by a foundation in Virginia. I drove all around the country for eight weeks, shooting locations from a motor home. I wrote into the film a shot going down various highways all over America taken at two frames a second that I would then cut into a montage. The only narration in the whole film would be over this eight hundred-mile-an-hour rush down roads. When I shot that sequence, I learned that all the normal bumps average out. When you're shooting at one or two frames per second, the little stuff may slightly affect the sharpness of certain frames, but the frequency is way too high for them to appear as bumps. The average point that you aim at on any straight road is always absolutely at the vanishing point, which makes the shot look quite good on average and quite stable.

Well, I didn't have a straight road as a reference out there in the woods. However, I knew I had to keep the camera aimed at a consistent point. We came up with one technique that relied on a telephoto finder looking at a particular sunlit leaf in the distance. In addition, I followed invisible thread stretched through the woods to keep myself from long-term dips and rises. It got rather arduous, but in the end we delivered the plate that they used for those brilliant mattes. They did a wonderful job on the foreground action, and the whole thing cost a third of what it would have cost for plan A or B, dolly or model. It was just me and Dennis Muren operating a slow-motion, motorized roll-cage on the camera for a banking effect—just schlepping through the woods with a Vistavision camera, walking the thousand feet re-quired for each take, stepping over logs, rolling camera at three-quarter fps. Sped up to projection speed, it was pretty astonishing. I was stunned when I saw the completed scene.

Q: What Steadicam work did you do on *The Exorcist II: The Heretic*, the sequel to *The Exorcist*?

A: I did a shot up into James Earl Jones's mouth, where a tiger jumped out. I did one scene I would never do now and never, ever tell anyone else to do—but I was very athletic in those days. It was a running scene that ended up in a close-up of James Earl Jones's mouth, out of which jumped a matted tiger at the lens. I ran down an alley pursuing a woman through a flapping flock of chickens and wind-born debris. She was to fall in front of me and the camera was supposed to lift up over her. Well, I couldn't quite jump over her, but I ran up a set of steps on the left side of the alley so the camera ap-peared to rise in the air as I ran up the stairs. Then I changed hands and jumped to a set of stairs on the other side of the alley and ran down them, so the camera just went up and over her. We arranged for her to fall right in the middle, as I jumped from one side of the alley to the other. I never thought a thing about it—amazing shot.

I also worked on the shots in the African village, and I went to Rio to shoot the film's opening in the slums. In the video version, they restored the sequence—some amazing and, with hindsight, ridiculously dangerous shots.

Q: How do you work with the sound crew on a film?

A: Sound guys coexist with us the same way they coexist with everyone else. There have been times when I have actually helped the sound department by carrying a wireless mike because I was the object floating closest to somebody.

Q: Your vision of what the camera could do if it were unleashed from its bounds led to the development of this remarkable invention. Can you describe what you see when you look through the eye of the Steadicam?

A: Personally, I like to imagine looking into transparent space, not aware of a frame line. The human eye is not conscious of any enclosure around the space that leads away out of sight. Bumpy motion of the camera produces the illusion of vibration of the frame edge, and this makes a mechanical liar out of the moving "eye." Once the frame edge creeps into your awareness it defines an oscillation, a variation around the edges that is really inhuman to me.

Good shooting to me is content-driven, and content suggests how the viewer is to be inserted into the scene. It's based on lens placement and a still-to-be-defined art form which considers composition as a dynamic, not a static medium. All of the current rules of composition are written to static shots—I'm interested in the phenomenon in motion. As the camera starts to move, composition becomes fluid because as you move past an object, that has a diminishing weight in the frame. The rules are not of any use in this context because the moment the camera has moved past, the frame becomes unweighted and *pops* like a soap bubble into a different compositional form. Departed objects continue to have some psychological weight. You sense they are still going by, but now it's off-camera, in space somewhere. The way the frame feels changes instantly as that object becomes unweighted and then is gone. A moving shot may not be centered around the point toward which you are moving, but it may contain that point for a while—perhaps at the frame edge. To me, that's a really interesting shot. Suddenly there's a completely different dynamic to that kind of shot. That shot holds a place static, out of which things flow as you approach it. As you move, everything else, every other pixel in the frame is in radial motion. The mechanical process is not obvious to the audience, but it can have a big impact.

I also like the ephemeral quality to the Steadicam moves—it can appear to occupy virtually no space itself. Watching *ER*, for example, you have no idea where the cameraman's physical corpus is. The Steadicam operator is not necessarily at the traditional place behind the eyepiece of the camera, and so the camera moves without the necessity to reserve that clearance—it passes objects like a ghost. It's a thin little wedge that can fight it's way through holes to get a moving shot.

Q: Is there ever an improper way to use the Steadicam?

A: Like any other tool for moving the camera, if a move doesn't serve the movie, it's a bad idea. It doesn't matter whether it's done with a dolly, a handheld camera, or a Steadicam.

Q: What does the future hold for the Steadicam?

A: Steadicam is a tremendous growth industry at this point. I now believe that it's idiotic to do a movie of any size without a Steadicam operator on hand all the time. It's not a special effect to be brought in, it's as essential as a tripod, particularly on a location film. It is one of an ever-larger group of very clever ways of moving the camera, but it's a key one and one of the best. The art of Steadicam operation by now should be considered a basic survival skill for any camera operator. So I see the Steadicam remaining as one of the basic filmmaking tools.

In the early days, we always thought some solid-state little black box was going to blow us out of the water. We felt we might have five years before something else came along. I've come to believe now that no black box is going to replace the tripod and no black box is likely to redefine the very fundamental phenomena of Newtonian physics at work in the Steadicam. I think it will be with us for as long as literal film goes through literal cameras. If film continues to be 35mm wide and if motors and magazines are still needed, cameras will only be able to shrink to a certain size and there will not ever be a black box that will move the camera any better than the Steadicam does. If film is replaced by video and everything shrinks down to the sort of camera you hunt for on the floor when it gets lost, like a contact lens—then all bets are off. But if we continue to use real sets and real, nondigital people, then I think this thing has real staying power. We'll grow up to its potential and it will be used very, very well. Excess will come and go. Unmotivated camera movements which are so absolutely, counterproductively, laughable will be in and out of fashion. But the camera will move and must be elegantly pointed. It will move well or it will move stupidly—it's up to us. I think the noble "gizmo" will continue to be an important part of the process for a long time—which gives me joy.

10

Fred Elmes

Fred Elmes, ASC, first became interested in photography when his father encouraged him to use his Leica camera. Elmes took still photographs from grade school through high school. He began to make 16mm movies, borrowing his father's Bell and Howell motion picture camera. Elmes applied to the Rochester Institute of Technology to study still photography and went on to the New York University graduate film school, where he was a teaching assistant. He began to shoot films and learn the craft of cinematography.

In the seventies, Elmes drove out to Los Angeles and was accepted to the American Film Institute, where he met John Cassavetes and David Lynch. These iconoclastic directors gave Elmes the opportunity to explore significant and divergent cinematic roads. On *The Killing of a Chinese Bookie* and *Opening Night*, directed by John Cassavetes, the camera peers into the soul of the characters capturing performances honed from improvisation and constant revision. The dark and surreal black-and-white images of *Eraserhead* explore the private world of David Lynch. The seminal shot of the central character, Henry, his piled-up hair backlit and surrounded by glittering particles, defines the distinctive and disturbing tenor of the film.

Elmes's association with David Lynch on *Blue Velvet* and *Wild at Heart* produced powerful imagery which informed the director's vision. A white picket fence with brightly colored roses against the blue sky, the dim light of a voyeur's gaze, and matches exploding into fire are images that enhance the visual lexicon of contemporary filmmaking. On *Night on Earth*, directed by Jim Jarmusch, Elmes defined the expanse of five international cities, shooting inside the confines of a taxi. The body of a murdered girl in Tim Hunter's *Riv-*

er's Edge is photographed in a matter-of-fact manner which is both chilling and disturbing. On *The Ice Storm*, directed by Ang Lee, Elmes supplied the photographic metaphor which defined the self-involved characters from the 1970s with frigid blues and a pristine sense of composition.

Elmes received an Independent Spirit Award nomination for his cinematography on *Blue Velvet*, and won the award for *Wild at Heart* and *Night on Earth*. He got an Emmy award nomination for his work on *In the Gloaming*, directed by Christopher Reeve. Elmes has also worked with directors Martha Coolidge, Diane Keaton, Franc Roddam, Marisa Silver, and Norman Rene.

Fred Elmes is a gentle, intelligent man with the gift to capture the dark, offbeat, and ironic visions of cutting-edge filmmakers.

SELECTED FILMOGRAPHY

1976   *The Killing of a Chinese Bookie* (Camera operator with Michael Ferris; Mitchell Breit in charge of lighting. Note: Reedited version released in 1978).

1977   *Breakfast in Bed*

1978   *Eraserhead* (with Herbert Cardwell)
       Opening Night (Camera operator with Michael Ferris; director of photography, Al Ruban. Note: Original release withdrawn, re-released in 1991.)

1983   *Valley Girl*

1985   *Broken Rainbow*

1986   *Blue Velvet*
       River's Edge

1987   *Heaven*
       Aria (Franc Roddam segment "Liebestod" from *Tristan and Isolde*)

1988   *Permanent Record*
       Moonwalker (with John Hora)

1990   *Cold Dog Soup*
       Wild at Heart

1991   *Night on Earth*

1993   *The Saint of Fort Washington*

1994   *Trial by Jury*

1995   *Reckless*

1996   *The Empty Mirror*

1997   *The Ice Storm*

1998   *Ride with the Devil*

Q: How did you become interested in photography?

A: I started taking still pictures in grade school. My dad had a Leica camera he got after World War II. He wasn't afraid to let me just walk off and use it, which was very trusting of him since no one else's dad let them use their expensive cameras. So he just turned me loose with it and I started taking pictures of everything. I did that all through high school. I was photographer for the yearbook and the local paper. My dad also had a Bell and Howell 16mm camera, so I started to make my own movies. We learned how to do sync sound. I was the editor as well, so I got to learn it all. It was fun. I was really torn between movies and still photography.

I ended up going to the Rochester Institute of Technology to study still photography. They have several schools, one is very technical and the photo illustration program is exactly the opposite. We had to illustrate music and poetry with photography or make a short film, which seemed to be much more up my alley. I was really headed toward photojournalism. The idea of telling a story or having something that had a beginning, a middle, and an end instead of one picture really appealed to me. It was how to do something with a series of pictures. So I went through the stills program at RIT, although my thesis was a film, to New York University graduate film school for a couple of years, where I was a teaching assistant and made and shot some films.

Then I realized truly dramatic feature films were what I really wanted to do. They weren't being made in New York. One summer, I drove out to Los Angeles to say hello to anyone I could find and got into the American Film Institute, which at the time was in Beverly Hills. I was there for a couple of years. It was a great introduction to feature films. It was a way to be a student again, not to have a job for a couple more years and just to learn the ropes. Then it was a matter of finding interesting films to shoot which appealed to me. I stumbled on some good ones early on. It was a matter of being at the right place at the right time.

Q: One of the first directors you worked with was John Cassavetes. How did you meet him?

A: John Cassavetes and I met at the American Film Institute (AFI). When I first got there, there was an apprenticeship program where a filmmaker was taken into residence. John was the filmmaker. He was going to make a film and people from the American Film Institute were going to work on it. I worked on *A Woman under the Influence* just for a couple of weeks. John's relationship with the cinematographer at the time didn't work out, so I left with the cinematographer who had hired me, but John and I remained friends. John was at AFI for a couple of years cutting the film and I just stayed in touch. Then, a year later, he said, "I have this other film, *The Killing of a Chinese Bookie*, do you want to shoot it?" which was just my wildest dream. So I walked right in, did it, and had a great time.

Q: What was Cassavetes's attitude toward cinematography?

A: John had total disregard for anything technical, and at the same time he had an innate sense about where to put the camera to see the drama of the scene. At the start of the day we would rehearse the scene with the actors. If the scene wasn't working, he would throw the script out and improvise with the actors. He would have the new scene transcribed, the actors would learn it, and then in the afternoon we'd shoot it. Having seen the rehearsal, he and I would talk about where the cameras would go. Sometimes it was a couple of cameras. He seemed to know just where they belonged. He never described why, but it always seemed to make sense for the scene. I learned a great deal about drama from him because he certainly cared most about the actors, about creating a dramatic moment that fit together as a film. It was good for me that he had so little regard for technical things, because that's one of the things I was hung up on at that point. I was a perfectionist. I would say, "No, it has to be this way, the light has to be exactly like this in the camera—period." I would set up a shot. If we were making a very careful pan and John was making an entrance as an actor, he would just nudge me on the way in, and the camera would bobble during this delicate pan I was doing. He'd say, "That's what I want the scene to feel like. It has to have a new sort of energy—you are making it too pretty, too perfect." He wasn't afraid to pick up the camera, shove it in someone's face and say, "This is the feeling, this is the drama of the scene." The character becomes confrontational in the scene. It was a real education for me.

Q: Did you shoot a lot of *The Killing of a Chinese Bookie* handheld?

A: A lot of handheld. A lot of crazy things I wouldn't have tried, like mixing a handheld shot with a dolly shot, chasing somebody down the hallway with a handheld camera, then cutting back to a very wide shot and just showing the whole drama unfold as a set proscenium camera. Cassavetes seemed not to care, yet there was something else that took over when he designed the scene. He had this innate sense of how the drama would play and what gave him options in editing to make it play the most powerfully. He really considered himself a dramatic filmmaker. It was about the acting. It was about creating the moment that could be the most powerful. He certainly was a very powerful personality and a great actor himself. He could manipulate situations. He could do anything that was necessary to make an actor give the performance he needed, and actually the same was true on some level with the crew. If he needed more out of the camera operator, out of the crew for whatever reason, he had the power to do that. He would intimidate you. He would make you laugh, he would make you cry—he would rise to the occasion and make it happen—that was his style of filmmaking.

Q: So Cassavetes was directing you as the cinematographer.

A: He directed everybody. He was really in control of things, even though he acted in a crazy fashion sometimes and it appeared to be chaos. He got things he needed out of situations. He always said, "You guys are lucky, you're young filmmakers, you could do anything you want. You could take the camera out on the street and shoot anywhere you want. I used to, now I can't do that anymore. They follow me now, I can't get away with it. Now you guys have to go do that." *Shadows* and *Faces* were all on-the-fly productions. He was right, now that he was a bigger filmmaker no one would let him get away with it. He had to make a proper film and rebelled constantly against making a proper Hollywood sort of a film. He just hated it—too many strings attached.

Q: How did you light the club in *The Killing of a Chinese Bookie*?

A: We actually went into that Gazzarri's club eight or nine different times to light it because we couldn't go and stay there for the whole film since they had shows at nights. They had to take our gear out and we could only work certain days, for certain hours. So we went in there on eight or nine separate occasions during the course of the production of the film, which you just never, ever do on a film. We lit it many different ways and many times, but what we really wanted was to make it look seedy. We wanted to capture some sense of the underside of these two-bit Hollywood Boulevard gangsters who were trying to be somebody bigger than they were. It was grainy and gritty. People walk into shadows and scenes get played in shadows—this appealed to John a lot. That's the cue we took. The club had to have a seedy look. That was the home of these characters, and that felt right to me. The dressing room was a narrow, little room. We really wanted everyone to look good in there. We wanted the lighting to be seamless, and that's why there are these bulbs around the mirror. The same is true with Gena Rowlands in *Opening Night*. You have those situations like dressing rooms where the glamour is important, but out on the stage of the club in *The Killing of a Chinese Bookie*—anything goes. There was this blasting red light from one side and a blasting blue light from another side—that was the kind of glamour which belonged in that club, and that's what John really wanted.

Q: Cassavetes did not cover a scene in the classic fashion. In *The Killing of a Chinese Bookie* where the gangsters take Cosmo Vitelli, played by Ben

Gazzara, to a coffee shop, the camera is very close on the men as they talk around the table. Was there any coverage shot on this scene?

A: No, there wasn't. It was one of those situations with five or six people around a small table, and we would just let it roll. Every take was a full ten-minute camera load of film, partly because the scene tended to ramble, but also because John wanted to allow people the option to experiment. So it started with the script and it opened up from there. We'd reload, he'd talk it through again with the actors. We'd pan over and do somebody's close-up, but then run the whole take out on that person and not be afraid to do it. There was no formal coverage. John really wanted to create situations where things could happen by chance and we would be there to catch them, but it all came from the scene. It all came from what the actor did. Every last John Cassavetes movie was driven by the drama of the scene, which is why I loved him and his films. There was always the drama. He was just an original talent when it came to looking at film in a new way. There was nobody like him. There were elements of cinéma vérité, documentary, and even elements of Hollywood movies, but certainly in his own way, his own fashion, and completely with his own rules. He also used nonactors to a fair degree. He was not afraid to put people in uncomfortable situations, situations where you could see them cringe but, boy, they cringed for all the right reasons and it was so very believable.

Q: A good portion of the play within *Opening Night* was shot on stage in front of a live audience. In many of the shots, the audience is prominent in the frame. What was the concept behind this?

A: We needed an audience—that was integral. They knew they were part of it, and we just planned it all with that in mind. Certainly, there was more shooting of just the actors without the audience. John rehearsed with the actors beforehand, and they all knew the scene before we started shooting. So we just used our days with the audience wisely and got the most mileage out of them.

Q: Were those scenes shot in different venues?

A: Yes, there were two different theaters. There was one smaller theater, then one bigger theater. That was an experience because I certainly had never done anything on that scale. It was a big deal. Then there was all the backstage action that goes on.

Q: Did you try to light the scenes so they looked like theatrical stage lighting?

A: Yes, John really wanted it to feel like theatrical stage lighting. Again, he didn't want glossy Hollywood lighting. Certainly, there were shots where people had to look beautiful and look great, but he was just so opposed to the sense of a Hollywood movie that he rebelled against it. He didn't want anything to do with it. Theatrical lighting seemed to fit just fine for him.

Q: You have collaborated on several films directed by David Lynch. How did you first meet and come to work together?

A: I met him at AFI, right at the same time I met John Cassavetes. David was doing this odd film called *Eraserhead.* A cinematographer named Herb Cardwell had started the film when it seemed like it was going to be a much shorter, scheduled project. Herb had to go, and they needed somebody to come in. So Herb actually shot the first couple of months of photography and I shot the last couple of years. It went very slowly, but we were really there to get what David wanted. When I first met him, David asked me if I would be interested in picking up the photography on this film. He seemed to like me and I liked him. He said, "I'll show you some scenes from the film." I had no idea what to expect, but he started with the easy ones and then we eventually saw the baby footage at the end, which was, of course, very shocking. It was a good relationship. I enjoy it still. We're still friends.

My view of photography and filmmaking was much more akin to David's, so we saw eye-to-eye on the approach to visual style. I started *Eraserhead* and had to take a break. I went off and shot *The Killing of a Chinese Bookie* in the meanwhile, and then we came back and finished *Eraserhead.* So I have these two completely divergent styles during this same period, and it was very good for me to see these completely opposite sides of the coin. They are two very distinctive filmmakers. They're both driven to make films the way they do with the degree of detail and aesthetic that they have, but just opposite. *The Killing of a Chinese Bookie* and *Eraserhead* are both very powerful films.

Q: How did David Lynch communicate the unique visual style of *Eraserhead* to you? Did he use photographs, paintings, or films to express it?

A: We never really looked at films or photographs. We actually talked about the mood of things, about how the room looked, and how the light was. How much shadow was on his face, how much you could actually see in the background, and how much it was going to disappear. There are very few day scenes in *Eraserhead*, but they have a different character. Sunlight wasn't acceptable. We could only go out and shoot on heavy overcast days, otherwise we couldn't shoot those scenes. It's very specific language we learned along the way. We both felt out what seemed to be required. There weren't catch phrases.

Q: So many films have a seminal shot. The image that immediately comes to mind in *Eraserhead* is the close-up of Henry with his hair backlit and the particles flying in the air. How was that shot created?

A: That was an image David had in his head. When Henry goes through this change and pops out the other side, it's kind of in space, but they're not stars, they're sparkles. David always described it as "Little sparkles behind him." We just had to find a way to make them float out there and then have this wash of light come over his face. It was one of the most distinct images out of the film. David always spoke out of mood and of going to another place.

Q: How did you create the lighting atmosphere in the scene with the neighbor next door? There is an eerie effect of how her eyes registered in black-and-white.

A: The scene between her and Henry was done in very low light levels. It was meant to be extremely dark and very soft. That's really what we found worked, so we went with it.

Q: What black-and-white film stock did you use on *Eraserhead*?

A: It's Kodak Double X negative. We did some testing with make-up, with wall color, with different effects. I never shot in 35mm before. I'd shot black-and-white, but not on a big film like this, so it was a real learning experience. From the Rochester Institute of Technology, I had enough technical knowledge to come into it and be able to talk to the lab intelligently: "What I'm seeing is not what I think I should be seeing. How do we go about fixing it?" I could keep up the relationship fairly intelligently, but we all learned as we went along. There were problems, shots we wanted that we didn't know how to solve. We would get somebody's number, somebody referred us. We'd call up and say, "We're from the AFI and we're making a student movie. How do you do this effect?" and they say, "We do it this way, we buy one of these, and we assemble this . . ." Then we say, "How do you do it if you don't have any money?" and they say, "Well, back in the old days . . ." and there inevitably would be some simple solution everybody had disregarded or just discounted because it wasn't so easy or it wasn't so good anymore, but it was cheap. We just did cheap, simple solutions that the handful of us who made the film could do.

Q: What kind of cameras did you use?

A: We used several, we used an Eclair CM3 with a blimp for sound scenes. It was a little like a tank, a small car. We used an Arriflex camera for wild shooting. For some of the effects, we used a Mitchell because we needed pin registration. Most of these either came from the AFI or were borrowed. There wasn't a lot of money to go and rent extravagant amounts of equipment. The AFI was very good to us. They let us use equipment for a long time, but the strings were pretty tight and there was only so much we could do when it actually came to cash dollars. It was a long period of time because that was the way David was most comfortable. We didn't need a big crew. Most of the film is really one or two characters in a room, so it was pretty simple production-wise, and that was the best way to get the look David wanted. Nobody imagined it was going to take a couple of years. We all hung in there. Having started on it and spent so much time, we all really wanted to see it through. David was driven. He felt certain there was an audience for *Eraserhead*. It played at the Waverly Theater in New York at midnight for a long time. It opened at Filmex at a midnight screening—the audience was speechless afterwards. Then it was picked up by a distributor and *the* print went to the Waverly Theater in New York. For the longest time that was *the* print of the film—there wasn't money for more, there wasn't a need for more at the moment—so there it was.

Q: Blue Velvet had a very strong visual style. The shot of the white picket fence with the blue sky and the flowers has a very American look. We think we've seen this shot before, but there is something strangely different. How did that image come about?

A: The approach came out of the idea right from the very beginning. David and I talked a lot about how *Blue Velvet* looked and what the progression in the visual style was. It had to start out very American, a very small, ideal little town. Then it descends, and you discovered things. It got a little darker, and you discovered more things. You realized you were seeing the underside of this small town and meeting characters you didn't know existed there, knowing that in the end you were going to pop back up and be in this idealized, perfect world again. So we knew we had both ends, and we knew what we wanted in the middle. Those early scenes were shot at the end of the schedule. We had a good idea of what the middle looked like in terms of the descent, the darkness, how dark it was, what color quality it had, and then it was easy to go back and say, "This is easy, this is sunny, this is ideal." It's a matter of picking the light, using a real white fence, using really bright colored flowers, and just doing it on a bright, sunny day. There weren't really any tricks. We used a polarized filter on the camera—that's the only trick we used. They're fresh flowers and green grass and the light was right. We used what we had, but we knew that's what it needed to be. Certainly, if it was a cloudy day, it wouldn't have worked. We couldn't have shot it. We would have had to wait, so we knew the importance of those images to set up the style. Those were images in David's head, those bright colors were this transition part of the style.

Q: Dorothy's apartment in *Blue Velvet* is a very evocative setting. Where was this shot and what was the concept behind how it was photographed?

A: Luckily, we were able to build Dorothy's apartment. The only set we had was the apartment and the hallway around it. David was very specific: "In this corner of the apartment, this is where she answers the phone. This is where this action takes place and it has this kind of a feeling. Now over here is this really dark corner and she only goes there once or twice, but it has a completely different feeling than any other place in the apartment. Over here is kind of harsher, bright light." He knew that ahead of time. We talked in those terms, both when we built the set and when we talked about lighting it. We talked about how a scene played in a room, what part of the room it played in, the layout of Kyle's view out of the closet doorway when he could just barely see her go down the hallway and then she disappeared. That was carefully built so that you didn't know there was a mystery there. She walked almost out of view, then came back in a little bit, and that was the right feeling.

Q: The scenes of the Kyle MacLachlan character peering out of the closet were imaginatively done. You had profile shots of him looking, and point-of-view shots in addition to other angles.

A: Yes, we found a good combination. The visual style we found grew out of the drama of the scene. It doesn't come from a vacuum, it comes from what's happening out in front. It comes from what's written in the scene. The things that were happening out there were very scary and horrific, things nobody had ever seen before, and this seemed to be the appropriate way to bring drama to the visual style—to lift it off the page and make it come alive. It really starts with the drama and it starts with what the actors do—that's really important.

Q: Were you working with very low light levels in the apartment? You almost feel like you can barely see.

A: Yes. When we did that first scene where Kyle comes in and the place is dark, I thought we'd really gone too far. I sat there in the theater and said, "I can't see him, how is the audience supposed to see him? I know where he's supposed to be." But David loved it that dark. That was part of the drama, that was why it was scary. We'd already seen it in daylight and we knew where everything was. What you needed to see for a moment was just Kyle's head bobbing around in darkness to get a sense of what it must have felt like for him. I watched people in the audience quiver during that scene, so it seemed to work.

Q: What was the concept behind the use of the fire images in *Wild at Heart*?

A: David had an idea how important it was, but it's not something we talked about. We knew where it belonged. It was all in the script. The credit sequence was about fire. Right from the start we knew all those close-ups of matches lighting and cigarettes burning were right there in the story. That was just integral in the lives of these characters.

Q: How were those fire images described in the screenplay? Were there clues to you on how to shoot them?

A: It was really simple: "extremely large close-up of a match striking the paper," or "a match lighting a cigarette." As I read it, I didn't realize it was quite so large. When we came to film them, I lined up a shot that was an inch and a half wide and David said, "I need to see less air around the match head lighting. I need to see it bigger in frame." It works great, it just has so much visual impact. The sound that goes with it makes it kind of magical—it lifts it off the page and makes it a real dramatic moment.

Q: River's Edge, directed by Tim Hunter, is a powerful film with a strong atmosphere. How did you approach photographing the many scenes in which the dead girl's body is prominent in the frame?

A: What it really comes down to for me, is it's a good, well-written story. Tim Hunter cast very interesting characters and he really brought it to life. I was saying, "How are we going to do this? I know she's supposed to be naked, but shouldn't she be wearing something? Couldn't she be covered up a little bit?" His approach to photographing the dead body was saying, "No, that's the point, she's naked. That's what the audience is going to see, no clothes, nothing. It's an Edward Weston nude, and that's the way that we're going to approach it." And sure enough, *bonk*, that's what it was. He really wanted it that way, and that was absolutely the right way to do it.

Q: It always seems to be cloudy and overcast in the exterior scenes. Did you have to wait for that weather to shoot?

A: No, *River's Edge* was a very low-budget film. We had twenty-five days or twenty-six days to shoot, period—no more. That was when the money ran out. We were having trouble because the river we had scouted up in northern California had flooded, our location was under water. So we pushed it back and pushed it back and finally got there at the end of the film, but it was absolutely worth it because the shore had been all ravaged. It gave a whole different landscape to the location that we had chosen months before. The river was still high and very muddy. It looked great, it really became the character it should have been in the film. We knew it should feel overcast, we knew it should not be particularly sunny, but should have a cool feeling. We just played our days in such a way that we could take advantage of the overcast. If it was raining, we felt we should use it. It was southern California in January and February, which was the only saving grace. That's the time when it does rain.

Q: Night on Earth, directed by Jim Jarmusch, is comprised of five stories, each taking place inside of a cab in a different part of the world. What
was the concept behind what each sequence should look like?

A: We worked hard to talk out how they all hang together as scenes. It is
five short stories. They're going to be judged as, "I like this one best, I like
that one best," everybody's going to have their favorites—there's no way
around that. I really wanted to have a noticeably different style for each
film, subtle, but something that people did grab hold. So it was a matter of,
"Where do you put the camera?" If you use diffusion on the lens, how much
do you use? What was the quality of the light, was it harder or softer? The
color of the light certainly was part of it. Jim and I sat down and designed it.
"This city looks like this, let's go for this look, let's go for this feeling. This
city feels like this, how do we augment that?" In Paris, we chose to use color
and play off areas of the city that were colorful. So there was neon, we added
more light to the dialogue inside the cab when they were moving. In Rome,
we did the opposite, we just took it all the way and kept it all almost mono-
tone and earth tone—yellows and browns. We were working in that palette.
So that was designed in, and that was our way to follow through and make
each scene distinctive.

Q: What rigs were used for shooting inside the cab?

A: What a routine! In every city we would decide what kind of cab it was.
We'd find a car that ran and painted it up to look like a cab. We'd find one
derelict chassis that had been wrecked, pull the engine out, redo the interior
to look like the first one we'd bought, and there we would have our two cars.
So we could drive one around the city and photograph it driving by a location in a specific spot or a specific time and shoot out the front windows. We
would see it driving about, and the other cab we would tow around the city
with the actors in it. I'd be strapped in where the engine used to be, manning
the camera and photographing the action as it unfolded inside the car. That
was the pattern. We built a lighting rig to fit each cab in the style the photography seemed to demand for that city.

We went into Italy and they said, "We build our car rigs out of wood, so be
prepared." We brought material we could use instead of wood. In Helsinki,
they said, "We don't do car rigs, so you better bring everything." So every
place had a different approach. It was a wonderfully fascinating study in
cultures. There were only six of us who traveled on the film, everybody else
we had to pick up locally. So the assistant director, costume people, production manager, camera assistants, and all of the workers were at whatever
country we were in. We had to bring equipment we could count on, like the
camera and the little lighting equipment we were bringing along from the

U.S. That's all we had. Then, when we came to a big night exterior, we would hire more people. We would hire lifts or whatever was needed for those scenes, but only for a few days. The rest of it was pretty much planning. Jim knew the cities, I knew a couple of the cities. We knew what the character of the locations was to be. It was just a matter of going out, finding them, marching our cab through on cue, and doing as much lighting as we could afford.

Q: Were the city montages in each sequence of *Night on Earth* scripted? Was each shot detailed in the screenplay?

A: Yes. Jim knew this when he interviewed me to shoot the film. He said, "There's a section which is the introduction to each city, and there will always be still, very specific, locked-off images to draw the character of the city." There were neighborhoods he liked or images he wanted. Then, in the last image, the cab drives through. It stayed pretty consistently the case. Then we go into the cab and there's the scene, or you see the cab driver beforehand, or we go to the pickup scene where we know there's a passenger who's going to find a cab and somehow they're going to get together. There's the dialogue in the cab. Then, there's a drop-off scene and interspersed throughout there are some point-of-view shots outside the cab where we see a neighborhood and pertinent images out the window. Occasionally, we fall back and we see the cab drive through another very specific landscape. So Jim knew it right from the start. We knew we needed the Coliseum in Rome and the Coliseum in Los Angeles where the car drove by, so we just had to do it. It was really specific, and when we got to each city, we found those shots. We just pounded them off, there's six or seven for each city.

Q: Jarmusch's earlier films like *Stranger than Paradise* were photographed in single, locked-off shots. On *Night on Earth,* he evolved from this very rigorous style.

A: He has. He made a big leap in *Night on Earth,* because all of a sudden he decided there could be cutaways. So you could actually see somebody roll the window down and toss a cigarette out, like Roberto Benigni does, or you could see somebody adjusting the radio. That was alright for him and he loved having them, but it's still a proscenium sort of film. Each one of those cabs is just this little bitty room. One of the reasons he went to cabs is he figured there would be a great deal of control. He would have the actors captive, they're not going anywhere, but he didn't quite count on the production end and the difficulties involved. Certainly, there's a great deal of control for him with the forced situation of two people in a car who don't know each other and he just loved it.

We did the same thing in every city: we'd come into town, we'd go off and start to scout locations. We had the cast set, but we'd cast the minor characters, and then we'd be building the cab having found the locations. He would do a couple days of rehearsing in every city and then we'd start shooting. That was just the way it had to be—it's a very low-budget, very little film.

Q: As a cinematographer, what is your relationship with the actors on a film?

A: It's a matter of learning what the actors need. It's a matter of learning their style and giving them the room to perform, to make it easy for them so the director gets the most out of them. It's a matter of being ready, not taxing them anymore than you have to, being ready to go again right away. Those things are very important because it's a matter of momentum. It's a matter of building, getting a scene going, building it up, and then stepping back and letting it play itself. You're just incidently the photographer who's watching it all unfold. You're not intervening, you're there watching what's been set up and worked out beforehand. It's really important to me to do all this work ahead of time, but not to prevent it from happening. You're there just to augment it and help it along.

Q: What do you look for in a project?

A: I don't think there's a genre better than another. I love them all. I admire so many directors, from Martin Scorsese to Stanley Kubrick—there are just so many. I love watching films. I grew up on foreign films, they were my mainstay because I was the projectionist in a film program. I saw them all in the sixties and seventies, so it was a great education for me. I need to find projects that are fascinating, that make me think. I like doing films that are compelling, that transport me to somewhere else, where we get a chance to try something new, to visit a place I haven't seen before.

I've been fortunate that many of the filmmakers I've worked with have these desires. They're driven to make films that take people to a different place, that move people in a different direction, or are different than they've seen before. Certainly, David Lynch, John Cassavetes, Tim Hunter, and Jim Jarmusch have that. Cinematography is a job that can be either boringly technical or magical. I was never trained to be that technical, so I guess it couldn't be boring for me. It has to be magical. The quality of the light has to do something for the drama that makes it arrive and live. I've been lucky to meet directors who have that same desire, who are able to communicate to me so I have all of the clues, because I realize as I go along, I don't do it by myself. The chemistry that has to happen just doesn't happen every time. Most of the ideas in the films I have shot are not my ideas—they're collaborative. They're the director's ideas translated through me to the crew, who have their own way of solving problems, who add their part to it, too, and it all gets mixed together. So it's the people I communicate and deal with on the crew who help to lift it off. It's my relationship with the actors and how comfortable I can make them feel in a dramatic situation that helps elevate it above a mundane scene and makes it a little bit magical. All of that mixes in to get not just one person's vision—it's everybody together.

11

Sandi Sissel

Sandi Sissel, ASC, was raised in Paris, Texas, a proper cinematic location for a cinematographer. She became enthralled with photography watching her father, a freelance news photographer, develop his pictures in the dark-room. Sissel worked on her high school newspaper as a photographer. The politicized atmosphere of the sixties inspired her to study journalism and television. In college, she received an internship with an ABC-TV Dallas affiliate, which provided her the opportunity to gain experience working on a film crew.

Sissel moved to New York and established herself in the documentary film community, working on Ira Wohl's Oscar-winning *Best Boy,* and with filmmaker Jill Godmilow. After getting into the cameraman's union, she worked for the NBC and ABC networks shooting news stories on a variety of investigative and social issues. Her participation in a series of important political documentaries—*The Wobblies*, *Seeing Red*, *Witness to War*, *Americans in Transition*, *Before Stonewall*, and *Chicken Ranch*—and her experience as a camera operator for Robby Muller, Frederick Elmes, and Haskell Wexler informed her later work as director of photography in fic-tional feature films. In 1998, Sissel recieved the Women in Film Crystal Award for Cinematography and a Kodak Vision Award for excellence in cinematography and support for other women pursuing a career in her field.

Sandi Sissel demonstrates great range in her work in documentaries, television, commercials, and theatrical films. Her resume includes the mini-series *The Drug Wars: The Camarena Story*, the TV series *The Flash*, and reportage on *20/20* and *60 Minutes*. She has been a camera operator on *No*

Nukes and *The Believers*, and has contributed to the documentary *Paul Jacobs and the Nuclear Gang* and a segment for NBC's *Saturday Night Live*. From the relentless, unblinking camera eye probing the underside of legalized prostitution in Las Vegas in *Chicken Ranch*, to a Pogocam whizzing through the claustrophobic tunnel of *The People Under the Stairs*, to the golden light of India in *Salaam Bombay!*, Sandi Sissel is a seeker of truth, a storyteller, and a filmmaker.

SELECTED FILMOGRAPHY

1979   *Curse of the Killer Tomato*

1988   *Salaam Bombay!*
        Calling the Shots
        Heavy Petting

1990   *No Secrets*
        Rising Son

1991   *The People Under the Stairs*

1993   *Full Eclipse*
        Double Switch

1994   *Camp Nowhere*

1996   *Soul of the Game*

1997   *The Reef*

1998   *Barney's Great Adventure*

Q: How did you become a director of photography?

A: When I was born, my father was a still photographer who freelanced for the UPI (United Press International) and AP (Associated Press). He had photographs in *Look* and *Life* magazines. He covered the homefront during World War II and took a lot of Rosey the Riveter photographs. As a kid, I would go with him to the darkroom. I had a real fascination with photography from a very young age. I always got cameras for Christmas. In high school, I was a photojournalist for the school newspaper. I went off and started college in 1967. It was a politically active period. I was a tremendous fan of live television broadcasts. I loved people like Sander Vanocur and all of the journalists in those days. I was addicted to the Democratic and Republican conventions and any kind of civil rights activity. My desire was to become a reporter, so I started studying journalism and television. By the end of my freshman year, I realized I still really liked the camera better than anything else, so I got an internship with the local ABC affiliate in Dallas. I would go out with news crews and shoot film. I had majored in what was called "film art." By the time I got out of college, I had done lots of small films, but my real desire was still in journalism. So even though I loved dramatic films, my aim was certainly much more to get involved in documentaries. In 1970, the idea of being in the film business was still tough and remote. The fact I was a woman was really not that big of a factor. There were not that many people doing it. My husband and I moved to Wisconsin where I got a job teaching beginning film production, made educational films for the University of Wisconsin system, and went to graduate school because I felt the way to make it in the business was through education. I finished my graduate degree and taught for three years—I was really ready to do more hands-on work. In the early seventies, New York was really the center of documentary work, so I moved to New York and spent about a year freelancing. I worked for free on a lot of films that ultimately did very well. I worked on *Best Boy* with director Ira Wohl, which won an Oscar, and with Jill Godmilow (*Antonia: Portrait of a Woman, Waiting for the Moon*)—I helped her on a few films. Sometimes I shot, sometimes I was an assistant. I got a job transferring sound at DuArt. That first year in New York, I did whatever I could to get by. ABC, NBC, and CBS networks in New York suddenly were being sued because they had no minority people whatsoever in their technical departments. The union put the word on the street they were looking for blacks, Hispanics, and women to come in and show reels to consider membership. I made an appointment. I was twenty-four, and it was overwhelming. The IA (IATSE—International Alliance of Theatrical Stage Employees) was the hallowed halls. I went in. Guys like Sol Negrin were there. They looked at my work, and at the end of the screening they said, "Your work is very good, we would be interested in you coming in as a member." I was walking on the clouds when I walked out the door. Of course, it cost a thousand dollars down, but I borrowed some money, went back, and did it.

My career has parallelled the women's movement. Two, three years previous to that, I could have knocked on that door endlessly and it would have made no difference. Most of the people who were getting into the IA in those days were the sons and nephews of members.

By the end of the week, I got a phone call from NBC: Would I come in and work as vacation replacement? I was completely excited and terrified. I called cameraman Tom McDonough (*Enormous Changes at the Last Minute, The Day after Trinity*)—we were doing *Best Boy* together at the time—and I said, "They have CP 16s and Frezzolini's, I've never used these cameras. Will you show me how to load them? I have to go to work at seven o'clock tomorrow morning." NBC employed me six days a week for the next three months solid. I made more money than I had ever dreamed of, enough money to make a down payment on my own NPR camera. I got a call from ABC, who said, "We'd like to put you on staff." That was the year they hired people like Geraldo Rivera, Felipe Luciano, John Johnson, Melba Toliver, Joan Lunden, and Rosanna Scarmadella. We did a lot of wonderful stories together. I went with Geraldo to Willowbrook. Shooting network news was a way to work every single day, to stop using a light meter and to just really run with a camera. We were still shooting film. I became one of the original virtual staff members on *20/20* and did a lot of stories with Geraldo Rivera, then I did a lot of *60 Minutes*. Because I had my own camera, I suddenly became very sought after by independent documentary people. If you own your own equipment, you can do it for a better rate. You become much more interesting to people when you can donate your equipment. I did this up to 1982. I became more interested in manipulating the image and telling stories. Ed Bianchi, a very well-respected commercial director, called me and said, "I have this director of photography coming over from Germany named Robby Muller (*The American Friend*, *Dead Man*) and he's looking for an operator. Since you're in the IA and he's not, if you came in and worked as the standby director of photography, he would love for you to operate for him. Then he can come into New York and work through the IA." So, I worked with Robby for two weeks on this commercial. He loved my work and said, "Wow, you can really follow action." I said, "Maybe it's from documentaries, I've just been used to doing it." Eddie had a real fancy for European directors of photography, so he brought in one after another—*great* directors of photography. So, intermixed with directing a documentary called *Chicken Ranch* and shooting a documentary about Mother Teresa, which lasted for about four years, I worked as an operator for various directors of photography on commercials and learned a lot about lighting. I learned a lot about 35mm cameras, even how to use the wheels, which was something terrifying to me in those days. Ultimately, I even got a chance to shoot a couple of commercials with Eddie. Then Robby did *The Believers*, and he hired me to operate. I got to work with Director John Schlesinger. Then Fred Elmes hired me to operate for him. Haskell Wexler directed some commercials and hired me to shoot, which, of course, was very challenging and a huge responsibility. So all of this led up to my reading several low-budget scripts, but they weren't really interesting enough visually to do until *Salaam Bombay!* came along. I thought, "I spent my whole life doing documentaries—I can do this film." So, I went off to India for seven months, made ten thousand dollars, and shot a film that really opened up a whole new world for me in terms of being a director of photography.

Q: Salaam Bombay! is a powerful fictional film about street children in India which is directly influenced by reality. How did you work on location in India?

A: We ended up having principal photography delayed a couple of months because of monsoons and money problems. The director, Mira Nair, and I took time to break the script down and do storyboards. We didn't have a storyboard artist. I drew stick figures, but in thinking the script through visually, it helped me to show the entirely Indian crew, who didn't speak my language, what we were doing. Being in the streets of Bombay without the luxury of money, we followed that blueprint almost exclusively. It also made us really aware we were doing a simple story through a child's point of view and not to get caught up with India at large.

Q: The light in India has a remarkable quality to it. Can you describe it?

A: India has a very specific kind of light. When you work in Los Angeles, New York, Ohio, Toronto, Vancouver, or England, you're always going to get a certain kind of light which has to do with where you are compared to the equator, pollution, clouds—all kinds of things affect the kind of light you get. The two most obvious times I've noticed light are in Moscow and India. You can take a lens with absolutely no filtration and point it, and you'll get footage back from Moscow that will be grayish blue, and you will get footage back from India that will be golden. In India, you're quite close to the equator, but you've got so much red dust in the air, ground that is basically red dirt, and buildings that are basically saffron. You have these beautiful golden brown skin tones, and everywhere you look, everything is getting bounced off by something that's in a red hue. So your footage comes back that way. When you're in India, you almost have to work in the opposite direction if you want to go away from a golden color. It's the same as the way the brown smog in Los Angeles affects the light. You have this dust in the air in India that affects the light.

Q: Are you very conscious of the specific color and texture qualities of the light where you shoot and how you are going to deal with it?

A: Oh, absolutely. I just finished doing a pilot up in Toronto. It was supposed to be Chicago in the winter. I said to the director, "My ideal would be to have footage that was gray. Neither blue nor warm, but absolutely gray, as close to black-and-white as you could make it." We were lucky because we had overcast snow. The few times the sun came out, I put blue on the lens and got away from the warm color. Wherever you go, the light affects what you are doing. If it's bouncing off green grass or brown buildings or gray buildings, or if it's bouncing off all of the glass in New York City, you get a different kind of reflection. I was getting very frustrated for a while because I was shooting Pennsylvania in Los Angeles, Chicago in Los Angeles. I'd be doing L.A. for anything but L.A. If you're doing exteriors, you really have to work very hard to make L.A. look like anything other than L.A. Part of the joy as a director of photography is to get to experience all that different kind of light. You can go to a small town in Ohio and make beautiful footage because you're inspired by the difference in the environment. If you are in Los Angeles, and you're constantly going to the Valley, Burbank, or Malibu trying to make it something other than what it is, you have to work doubly hard. If you're in a studio, you can make it whatever you want. You've got a window, it can be sunrise, sunset, midday, overcast, raining, night, you can just play, but when you're dealing with nature, you're not only photographing nature, you're manipulating nature—it can be both exciting and frustrating.

Q: The director of photography really has to be a student of light. Are you constantly studying the quality of light wherever you go?

A: Very much so. I've done films that are entirely night or 90 percent night, and you can't help looking at the way light comes in windows at night without the lights on. You start looking at how the moon shadows are. I can't tell you how many scripts I've read that start out with "moonless night" and you go, "What is this, a moonless night in the woods?" You become a complete student of light. Recently, I was doing a lighting workshop, and Allen Daviau talked about how everywhere he goes he's become a complete student of the way light falls on the face, the way ambient light or practical light affects people. If you're lucky enough to work on films where you can truly play with natural light—it's great fun. You also become a student of lenses and film stocks, so you know exactly how to re-create something the way you saw it. If I were to take a lens and shoot you right now, it might not come back the way it looks to my eyes. So you have to learn how to add just enough fill light or just enough key light to make it look like it looks to the eye, and in turn will look very natural to the audience.

Q: How did you come to work with contemporary horror master Wes Craven on *The People Under the Stairs*?

A: Wes had asked me to work with him before, but our schedules had not clicked. I admired him as a filmmaker tremendously. I'm not particularly a fan of horror films, but when I read the original script for *The People Under the Stairs* it was the story of a little black kid from a poor family who discovered a little white girl who was being kept captive. He saves the kids from the evil parents and gets money for his family. It was a modern-day fairy tale. It didn't have that much of a horror element involved in it. As we started shooting, Wes couldn't help himself. He had to add a disembowelment scene and many other horror elements. One day, I was looking through the lens and said, "We need more blood here," and he said, "See, even *you* got involved in this." I made it very clear to him I knew nothing about horror films. I was very involved in telling the story and shooting it in a style that Wes said was very different from any way he had worked before. He had worked in a slightly more garish horror style, and we lit *The People Under the Stairs* differently. It didn't necessarily have the look of a horror film. Wes wanted a really, really dark movie. The Universal executives were looking at dailies, and I felt an automatic need to be able to see things within the darkness, which is very difficult to light. One day, when we were doing all the scenes in the basement, Wes said, "I SAID DARK! I WANT IT DARK AND I MEANT DARK!" So we really had to come to an agreement as to what level of darkness Universal would accept and Wes would accept. It was fun to be able to work as dark as possible and still be able to see an image.

Q: The area where the people under the stairs live was lit in a dramatic and visually exciting way. What was it like to work on these sequences? It looks like there was barely room enough for the camera to move.

A: There barely was. We designed it to be only wide enough to get a human body through. We couldn't even get a Steadicam through there. We used the AbyssCam camera that was designed by Clairmont Camera for *The Abyss*. Basically, it was an Arri 2C mounted on a Pogocam with an element from the Steadicam to help stabilize it and a video monitor on top so that you didn't look through the lens. You looked at a tiny video camera, and you could run through there at high pace so that we could actually create this sense of things being very narrow. If it had been any wider to be able to accommodate a Steadicam, you wouldn't believe you were actually in between the walls of a set.

Q: Who was the camera operator on these sequences, and what is a Pogocam?

A: I was the operator on the film, so I did most of it. A Pogocam is a stabilizing rod you put on the base of a camera so it is not bending back and forth. The camera is stabilized in an upward/downward motion. You can mount whatever camera on top of it you want. You can either put the camera on the bottom or the top, and then you just hold the rod and run with the camera. I've used it in several films, *Drug Wars: The Camarena Story* and *Full Eclipse*. Sometimes I didn't want it to be completely stable like a Steadicam, I wanted that little edge that you get from running full out, but if you don't use something like a Pogocam, the camera jerks too much. So the Pogocam is actually a wonderful in-between. On *The Abyss* sometimes they did Steadicam, sometimes they ran through the submarine with just the Pogocam.

Q: In *The People Under the Stairs*, there's a reaction shot of the evil brother where a forward and backward movement of the lens is occurring at the same time. How did you execute this shot?

A: This is the shot that Alfred Hitchcock developed for *Vertigo*. You zoom and dolly at the same time. This is something Wes uses in every film. It's actually very tough to do. You design a shot so you're either zooming in or zooming out, depending on what works, and dollying in the opposite direction. If you're going to zoom in to get tighter, then you dolly back simultaneously. You must end your dolly and end your zoom at exactly the same time. The image stays exactly the same size, but your background changes. Wes loves this shot. Everyone calls it the *Vertigo* shot.

Q: What was your approach to the action sequences in *Full Eclipse*?

A: We shot the opening nightclub sequence with five cameras. My basic theory is to be organized, know what you want, and hire a bunch of great operators who are really into it, because they find great shots for you. My real job as a director of photography in action/adventure is to light it in a loose enough fashion for the actors to be able to move within the sets and to know exactly how much smoke, gunpowder, or whatever it is you need to accomplish the shot. You're going to have to use a lot more light than you're used to because you're going to do ultra slow motion. You have to listen to the stunt men to find the right angles to pick. From the angles they are shooting from, camera operators often have really good ideas of how to shoot something. You'd be surprised how many directors get lost when action scenes come up. So they turn it over to the stunt coordinator. As a director of photography, you may love doing the drama or the love scenes, then suddenly you have three days of guts and glory and it's, "Let's get through this one way or the other." I fall somewhere in the middle. It's fun to do all that fast action, but if it's car chases or gunfights, usually the stunt men who design the shots have very good ideas about how to cover it. If I'm working with a director who doesn't particularly want to storyboard, I almost always insist we at least storyboard the action sequences because it can become awesome on the day you are doing it. It's really good to think it out and say, "We need a wide shot, then we need a close-up, then we need the gun, then we need the face, then we need the reaction, then we need . . ." That way you go into it knowing what you need and you can then have a pep rally with your camera operators and say, "I need you to cover this." You get it all done that way, mixing in a bit of handheld to give it rough edges.

Q: Is there video assist on each camera?

A: Not always. Usually you'll have video assist on your main camera, but not always, it depends.

Q: So, when you don't have video assist, you don't really know exactly what you've gotten until you see the dailies?

A: No, but you have a pretty good idea. I'll look through every camera to check every angle to make sure what I'm getting.

Q: Using the tools of your trade—lighting, lenses, and framing—how did you make a low-budget film such as *No Secrets* look richer than it's meager bank account?

A: As a general rule, from the budget of $1 million to $7 million, my tools are basically the same. I might be able to afford a more experienced crew with $7 million than I can with $1 million, but generally in terms of the camera, the lenses, and the lights, your tools are roughly the same. You get more time with more money, but on a low-budget film, there's a lot of care taken in choosing the locations you're using. I've often tried to get big shots on low-budget films by saying very clearly in preproduction, "We need to shoot this at a certain time of day or else we're not going to get the shot." If you're in a great big room that has three huge windows, and you see the sun is going to come up in the East in the morning and the windows face east, you must do that scene at nine o'clock in the morning or you cannot do the scene, because if you wait until afternoon, it's going to be too dark and there's no possibility of getting a couple of Musco lights and doing the shot. We did it that way on *Salaam Bombay!* and *No Secrets*. Certainly, your actors very often are working for scale. On a $10 million film, you've got a $7 million above-the-line project because your actors are getting a lot of money, production is getting a lot of money, the script may have been in turnaround two or three times—it's amazing how the money gets eaten up. Sometimes I'll think, "Oh, great! I get a lot of money so I can go in here and do something." In fact, I end up with a $1 million below-the-line budget to go out and do that film. Whereas, on a $2 million film, you probably also have a $1 million below-the-line budget because you're working with actors on scale, producers who are working for percentages, and directors are less experienced and not getting very much salary. So, you actually have to really get to a considerably bigger budget before a director of photography feels more money. There is, however, a tremendous difference between a twenty-day shooting schedule, a thirty-day shooting schedule, or a fifty-day shooting schedule in terms of what you as a director of photography can actually accomplish because you have much more time to light. Again, that isn't necessarily dependent on budget because a lot of independent films offer less money to the crews, but the crews do them because of the subject matter. I've done $14 million films that had forty-day shooting schedules. I've done $800,000 films that had fifty-day shooting schedules, and I've done a whole lot of $2 million to $4 million projects that had twenty-day shooting schedules. *The People Under the Stairs* had a relatively decent budget and shooting schedule, but we had enormous special effects, so a lot of the budget got eaten up in special effects.

On low-budget films, you often only shoot what you need to shoot. Unless you have a very secure director who has a certain degree of autonomy, the bigger the budget, you end up having to do an awful lot of coverage. A lot of people's hands get mixed in the pot, it isn't necessarily the director's cut in the end, and people judge you by the number of set-ups you do per day. In the independent film world, you do one or two set-ups in a day if you have that luxury because you feel you can do the whole scene in one set-up, whereas one wouldn't even consider doing that on most studio films. Just in looking at the dailies, they'd want to know where the close-ups and medium shots are—where all the coverage is. On *No Secrets*, we had a nineteen-day shooting schedule, which one often does on television movies. I always think of a television movie as showing on a little square box and you only have to light and execute something in a little square box, whereas when you're doing something for the movies that is 1.85:1 or 2.35:1—you've got twice the amount of size. So, to do that size frame in a short shooting schedule is very tough. You have to be really organized about how many shots you're going to do and how to tell a story.

On a low budget, if we're going to have big daylight-dependent interiors, we have to shoot them at a certain time of day. If you're going to do a great big night exterior, since you can't afford a lot of big lights and a huge set-up time, I do what I call "dusk-for-night." You do a great big vista at night, but you do it during that magic hour and then you slightly underexpose, put blue on the lens, and make it look like night, so it looks like you have a huge night exterior which in fact is really dusk-for-night.

Q: How long is magic hour?

A: It depends on where you are. In Canada in the winter, it's about four minutes. In Los Angeles in the summer, it can be an hour. It also depends on what you think of as magic hour. I think of it as that time between sunset and nightfall. I was in Canada once. I had flown in to replace a director of photography on a film. The director and I had both taken over the film, started shooting that day, and he wanted to do a scene at magic hour. I got the crew all organized. We were at an airport, we wanted to see the planes in the background. The director and I we were on a balcony getting ready, and I noticed the crew was snickering. We said, "Okay, we're ready, let's do it!" I would say, if we had five minutes before it became too dark to shoot, it was a lot. It was amazing. It just went like *that*.

Q: What are your fiscal responsibilities, and how do you manage the time schedule on a project?

A: I've begun to see my role as more from the business aspect of show business. Now, when I go in for interviews, I even ask what the gaffer's going to make because budgets are changing. It's less and less obvious what your crew's salaries are going to be and what money is going to be allocated for equipment as you go in for a job. It used to be I would go in and they would say, "You have a forty-day shooting schedule, do you like the script? We like you, do you want the job?" and that was it. Then I pretty much put in an equipment order, gave the names of the crew, and we'd move on. Nowadays, crew salaries vary so much that I often even get involved in how much they're going to pay the crew and when overtime kicks in, because I am as good as the crew I hire and therefore I want to know if I'm going to be able to afford the crew I want when I go out. I never make demands on crews. I want them to be happy when they're working. I also want to know if I call up Panavision, I'm going to have enough money to get the kind of equipment I want. Once I find out from the producer that money is available, then they usually will be pretty clear with me. I've had producers say, "Look Sandi, we have enough money to do X number of twelve-hour days, and I only have five or six days with two or three hours of overtime—this is how tight this budget is." You feel a responsibility to make sure that happens, because as a director of photography, if you start taking the film way over in overtime, whether it's your fault or not, people are going to look at you and say, "What's wrong here?" It is the same way that I look at a gaffer and say, "This is our lighting set-up. Do you think we can do this set-up in forty-five minutes?" If a gaffer comes in to me at forty-three minutes and says, "It's going to take another thirty minutes to get this lighting set-up done," at a certain point I begin to lose faith in the crew. If I agree to do a film in forty days, and in fact it's forty-eight days and the director really hasn't dillydallied a lot or the actor hasn't thrown a lot of temper tantrums, then in fact maybe I should have been a little bit quicker or should have made certain decisions, or I should have said to the director, "I don't think we can do that big a shot, but how would you feel if we did this?" Sometimes you have to negotiate with directors so that you can give the director their shot, and at the same time do it for the producer in the time that you agreed. It's a drag to have to think in such a business fashion, but in many ways that is a director of photography's job. More and more producers expect you as a director of photography not to help a director organize the shots in such a way that rather than shoot to your left down a block of streets that goes for eight blocks, maybe if you shoot off to the right, you see a block and a half. You can make a choice to do something that gives you the same idea, but you can do it in half the time and save a lot of money. It's tough. I don't ever enjoy not giving a director their fantasy. So you have to constantly strike a bargain to do something that makes a director happy, do something that makes a producer happy, and hopefully do something that makes you happy at the same time. Ideally, it is a collaboration.

I've never had a luxurious schedule, so I have to be very careful. You have to be organized, ideally you've had the time in preproduction to do storyboards and if not storyboards, shot lists. In most features, you end up doing storyboards. In television, that's a luxury, so you end up doing shot lists. Sometimes I do all of that, sometimes the director does all of that, and sometimes it's collaborative. It's different collaborating with each director, but ideally you know going into a day, if not a week, what it is that you're trying to do. Often you don't meet that goal, but if you've got a planned-out shot list or storyboards, then by lunch you can say, "It went so well in the master that I don't think we need this shot," or "We did this close-up and then panned over and picked up something else, so we don't need this shot." You can cross things off as you go, or maybe the weather changed. Maybe an actor got weird on you and you've lost some time, or maybe some equipment went down. For whatever reason, you can adjust as you go, but certainly, if I know that I'm doing an involved choreographed master and I'm going to cover three pages with one shot, then we might bite the bullet and say, "Okay, this is a three-hour lighting set-up with rehearsals," but then we might do twenty-five takes. This is the only shot we're doing, so we're going to spend this much time doing it. You might even spend the whole day. Whereas, if you have a scene you are going to do in a master, two or three dolly shots and then five close-ups, then you know you are not going to use that whole master. If you spend all morning lighting, it's a waste of time because in television especially, they'll go to close-ups. So I've learned to allocate time according to what is going to really be used in the finished product. Ideally, you are in sync with your director, so we try and work it out accordingly, but what's frustrating is you spend so much time on a master that when you get to the close-ups you don't have time to really mold and work the light around the actor's face, knowing full well that close-up is probably going to be used more than the master. I try to make sure I have plenty of time to do that shot. The time you have to be most organized is when you're working with children in terms of how much time you spend lighting and executing, because you're going to lose that kid in five hours every day. By the time you get to your fourth hour, the entire set starts to panic. So the best lesson as a director of photography is to learn to organize work—on children's films, you learn real fast.

Q: How do you balance lighting actors with different skin tones?

A: I happened to have worked a lot with mixed racial casts, it's very hard. My biggest challenge ever was a commercial I did with Whoopi Goldberg and Helen Hayes, arm and arm. Black actors require more light. There's nothing worse than to watch a film where all you can see of a minority actor is their eyes, it's an injustice to the actor not to be able to see their expressions. I meter in a grey scale. I assign various skin tones on my grey scale and make sure I have each actor in a certain place on that spectrum. You basically assign seven stops. I try and make everything fall within those stops. It's tough. I've had to limit the black actor as to where they could go. I hate to say, "You have to hit this X." But when you add an additional key light for the black actor within a scene where all the other white actors are, the actor must hit that spot to be able to get into that key light—it's always a real challenge. You try to do it subtly, as to not make people feel you're having to do something special for them. Most actors who are experienced are real aware of getting into the key light and what will happen if they don't cooperate with you—you just learn as you go.

Q: Do most actors really have a good side of their face to photograph?

A: Oh, it's very real. I've had actors come up to me and absolutely say they will only be shot from one side, or that they want the lens at a certain eye level. They want it above their eyes, they want it below their eyes. I like actors very much. I would only work very hard to make them look good because if they look good, I look good. It's hard to work with an uncooperative actor. Very often, the ones who need the most help are the ones who are the least cooperative, but I think it's because they might be insecure. Most actors are extremely appreciative of your help if you explain things to them. When you work with young actors, you have to teach them how to stand, how to walk, how to keep their chins up, and how to look, but if you put too many limitations on them, they'll often get upset with you. They fear it interferes with their acting, but people absorb light differently. They need diffusion on different levels. You end up with actresses who are older than the actors and therefore you need to give the actresses a bit of help—it's part of the challenge.

Q: During the studio era, cinematographers used heavy diffusion on a close-up to make an actor look younger, and often the shots did not match with the close-up of the other actor in the scene, which wasn't utilizing diffusion. What tools are available today to defuse a shot and at the same time have it match?

A: In the old days, people only worked with hard light and there was no diffusion on the lights. They put diffusion on the lens. These days, the lenses have gotten so crisp. You see so clearly that we put diffusion on the lenses just to soften the look of the lens itself. We go out and test lenses and get the sharpest lens available and then we put on diffusion to make it softer and more appealing to the eye. If I feel an actress or actor is a little bit older, or a person has pock-marked skin or deep lines or dark circles under their eyes, I add a bit of warmth to the light. There's all kinds of reasons, not necessarily age. Some actors, for example, have blue-black skin, others have red-black skin, so you add a bit of warmth to the light. You can put one single piece of diffusion in front of a light, you can put two to three pieces of diffusion in front of a light, and the light gets softer as you go. You can bounce the light and it will be softer. You can bounce the light and put a piece of diffusion in front of it, it's softer yet. So the softer the light, the softer the look on the face. If the light is very soft, then it wraps the face and you rarely have to add very much diffusion. So, in the old days, where they might have put a Mitchell C on for the woman and a Mitchell A on for the man, nowadays you can put one piece of diffusion on for a twenty-year-old actor, three pieces of diffusion on the light for a fifty-year-old actor, and accomplish keeping the same level of diffusion on the lens. If you're going to go up only one step, like a ProMist $\frac{1}{8}$ to a ProMist $\frac{1}{4}$, you're not going to notice that much difference when you look at it on the image. You can also take a light around to the side of someone with no diffusion on it. I don't care how old that actor is, it's going to be harsh and they're going to have lines on their face. You bring that same light slightly around to the front a little bit high and put two or three pieces of diffusion in front of it in varying distances, and it's going to be a very soft, wrap light and it makes all the difference in the world.

Q: What is the responsibility of a second-unit crew?

A: Second unit is photography without principal actors because, technically, anytime you have a principal actor in a scene, you must have the first-unit director. Second unit might mean sunrise/sunset shots, the action sequences of a film, additional photography, reshoots—all kinds of things. I've worked second unit on shows where you work right alongside first unit. When David Watkin accepted the Oscar for *Out of Africa*, he said, "Thank you. So much of the footage you have seen was not shot by me, but was shot by the second-unit director of photography"—which was all of the beautiful aerial footage of Africa. So, doing second unit is a fabulous job. I used to joke and say I wanted to start a company called Second Unit Inc., because you get to go out and do all the beauty shots, have a long lunch, not have the stress of the first unit, and have a good time. It's really an important part of the film because it's the cohesive thread between all the acting sequences.

Your job as a second-unit director of photography is to imitate the photography of the first unit so that it's a seamless picture. You talk to the director of photography, find out what kind of filtration, what kind of lighting, what stock they used, whatever you can possibly find out because, in fact, this is not your movie, this is the first-unit director of photography's movie and you're there to supplement what they do.

Q: Is the credit, additional photography, similar to second-unit work?

A: It could be, or it could mean the director of photography had another commitment and they had to leave early and you were brought in to finish the show. It could mean you shot four weeks out of a ten-week schedule, so the person that shot six weeks got the main credit. It can mean anywhere from eight weeks to one day of shooting. It means that you were an additional cinematographer on the film.

Q: What cinematographers do you admire?

A: James Wong Howe was just a tremendous influence. By the time I was getting in college, I started admiring Sven Nykvist (*Fanny and Alexander*, *The Unbearable Lightness of Being*) tremendously, and Nestor Almendros (*My Night at Maud's*, *Days of Heaven*). Then I got very much into Robby Muller and Haskell Wexler, and I became lucky enough to operate for them and got to know them very well. I just run out to see whatever Bob Richardson, John Seale, and Vittorio Storaro (*The Conformist*, *Apocalypse Now*) shoot. There are so many good directors of photography out there now that I'm just floored by. I'm just amazed, really, at the work that people do. My work and my style tend to be rooted in reality. The directors of photography I admire are the ones who even though they have tremendous technique, you don't notice it and their photography doesn't get in the way of the story. I'm not a real fan of cinematography for cinematography's sake. I like to see a movie that's seamless and where the photography is an element which tells the story but doesn't stand out on it's own.

Q: Where do you see your personal future headed? Are you going to work strictly in features or will you return to documentaries at times?

A: The business has changed a lot. In the not-so-distant past, people reached a certain plateau and they could stay there. I find it very sad when I go to ASC meetings and I'm sitting there having dinner with some of the greatest directors of photography in history, many of whom haven't worked in many, many years because they can't get a job. The business is so much a business. When we were editing *Chicken Ranch*, I remember having dinner with a young woman in London. She was twenty-five years old and she was going on and on about this director who was going overbudget. She was the associate producer. She just couldn't believe it. Later, I found out she was talking about Bernardo Bertolucci. As a director of photography, you're truly just a commodity in the Hollywood mentality. I have a lot of European friends who, even though they came to Hollywood and could make a lot of money, they chose to go home because in Europe they could work on low-budget films, but they were artists. They were respected and could have their families, their lives, and could just keep working. Here, so much has to do with money and the flavor of the month. What I think is hard these days with having an agent and having desires to keep working is you do tend to go back and forth between television, features, and commercials. If I had my druthers, I would just do features, but that's a luxury very few of us are afforded and we end up doing what we do for all kinds of reasons. I try to at least have some scruples about the work I do and to choose the work properly. I just recently went off and did a television movie because I thought it was a wonderful story about a schoolteacher who in midlife decided to go back to teach in a ghetto high school and try and keep kids out of gangs because his younger brother was murdered. It was a wonderful story; it was better than any scripts I've read for features in a long time. Nowadays, so many of the feature scripts I read are action/adventure and a lot of times, television movies are dealing with women's issues or stories that affect people's lives more. I would love to think I could just do one feature after another—that's the ideal. For what I do, it offers the best rewards, but I'm going to keep working. I love to work. When you are a director of photography, you can only do your job when people have millions of dollars and they ask you to come along for the ride.

12

Allen Daviau

Allen Daviau, ASC, has been nominated for the best achievement in cinematography Oscar five times, for *E.T.—The Extra-Terrestrial*, *The Color Purple*, *Empire of the Sun*, *Avalon*, and *Bugsy*. He has worked on many projects with Steven Spielberg, two films with Barry Levinson, and a film each with John Schlesinger, Albert Brooks, Peter Weir, Frank Marshall, and George Miller. Daviau is a prominent member of the Artist's Rights Foundation and has an encyclopedic knowledge of all things historic, technical, and aesthetic as they relate to the cinema. He is smart, funny, a cinematic goodwill ambassador, and an artist with the camera—but he was not an overnight success.

Daviau's story of becoming a cameraman is harrowing and inspiring. His decade-long struggle to become a working union cinematographer ended in 1978, and international film audiences were in awe at the sight of his work on Spielberg's classic, *E.T.* Daviau's odyssey is a testament to commitment and a passion for the movies.

From the epic spectacle of a forever-gone Shanghai in *Empire of the Sun*, to the magic glow of E.T.'s miraculous finger, through several time-machine journeys during the 1940s to the turbulent hell of airline passengers in *Nightmare at 20,000 Feet* and the serenity of a plane crash survivor in *Fearless*, to an American sky filled with fireworks as it welcomes its newest son in *Avalon*, Allen Daviau is a cinematographer who expands the parameters of his medium each trip out.

SELECTED FILMOGRAPHY

1982   *E.T.—The Extra-Terrestrial**
        Harry Tracy, Desperado

1983   *Twilight Zone—The Movie* (Steven Spielberg segment, *Kick the Can*,
        George Miller segment, *Nightmare at 20,000 Feet*)

1985   *The Falcon and the Snowman*
        *The Color Purple**

1987   *Harry and the Hendersons*
        *Empire of the Sun**

1990   *Avalon**

1991   *Defending Your Life*
        *Bugsy**

1993   *Fearless*

1995   *Congo*

1999   *The Astronaut's Wife*

*Academy Award nomination for best achievement in cinematography.

Q: How did you become a cinematographer?

A: In 1967, I was involved in rock 'n' roll promo films, which now we call music videos. Forms of the musical short existed going back to the beginning of sound. Nat King Cole made a musical short in 3D. If anybody gets the credit for creating the modern music video in the rock 'n' roll era, it is Richard Lester in *A Hard Day's Night—The Monkees* TV show was created wholly out of that. I had worked as a freelancer for Don Berrigan at KHJ radio before he became the promotion director for *The Monkees*. He got me on the show, shooting stills. I went on tour with them. At the time they started doing the television show, I was working in labs and camera stores. I had no family connections in show business at all. I had no way to become a film loader, so I figured the only way I was going to get in was to become a director of photography immediately. It was a good idea, because I probably would have been a lousy film loader. I used the technique of the kid who owns the football and gets to be the quarterback. I started saving money to buy a 16mm camera. I thought I was going to buy a Bolex. I was working in Studio City Camera Exchange in the Valley and a sales rep came through and showed me the Beaulieu G, which was a 16mm wind-up camera like the Bolex, but with an *incredibly* great viewfinder and all these easily changed speeds. I said, "I want to get one of those," and he said, "No, wait." A few months later, he came back and showed me the prototype of the E, which was the first electric Beaulieu. It ran off a battery. The Beaulieu was a small camera that had many big-time professional features and it sold for the same price as the Bolex. The people who owned the camera store were Swiss and, of course, Bolex loyalists. I said to Milt, the sales rep, "I'll get them to carry the Beaulieu line if you'll sell me one." So I got him to sell me the camera body at half price and I kept my camera in the store. I sold a lot of cameras from that.

I had a camera and was looking for ways to get started. A guy named Doug Schwartz and a group of young kids were trying to form a teenage film company. I said, "Hey, I've got the camera, I'll shoot the film." There was a lot of discussion, a lot of meetings, then it all fell apart. They didn't get the backing, but there was a guy there named Peter Deyell, who today is an assistant director. Peter was a friend of Ralph Burris, who was Steven Spielberg's producer. Ralph got a small inheritance and was financing this short film Steven wanted to make in 35mm. Steven was Universal's young talent mascot. He would show people 16mm movies he made, and everybody would pat him on the head and say, "Yes, Steven, someday you're going to be a real director," but nobody would give him a job. He realized he was showing this little square 16mm image in the center of the big screen in the Universal screening rooms, and to get taken seriously he had to fill that screen. That's when he knew that he had to work in 35mm. So he came up with a concept for *Slipstream*, which was a European-style bicycle racing film. Tony Bill and Roger Ernst were cast. He got all of these people in the L.A. area European bicycle racing clubs excited. Steven said, "I have to have a cameraman for this." So Peter Deyell gave him my name, and they came over to our little editing room in the Sherman Grinberg film library and I showed him some of the rock 'n' roll promo films we were doing. It was 1967. Steven was 21. We talked a lot, but I said, "I really don't know 35mm equipment, but I know a French cameraman, Serge Haignere, who shot a lot of 35mm." I sold him Serge as a director of photography and me as B camera operator. I found out shooting 35mm is easier than shooting good 16mm because it's a much more forgiving medium. We would go out to these distant locations every weekend in the dark and be there to get the long telephoto shots of them riding over the hill, coming out of the sunrise. We would shoot every available moment of light, from sunrise to sunset. We just kept shooting more and more film. Universal was giving Steven short ends. There really weren't any assistants on the film. I would be on the back of a van, reloading ninety-foot short ends into these two-hundred-foot Arri magazines. Ninety feet is like one minute of film. Then you'd have to run back and reload. Everything was too short in supply. We didn't have money. We didn't have time. We didn't have the equipment, but Steven was shooting and getting some remarkable material. If you look at that footage, you can really see him trying to evolve movement and blocking that are recognizably Spielberg.

We ran out of time on *Slipstream*. Steven bet everything on one weekend—we would shoot the whole beginning and end of the race in a little town square in Santa Monica. He went for it. We got a Mitchell camera, a Chapman Crane, and it rained liked a monsoon. We're not talking about sprinkling. It started raining Saturday morning at dawn and we had two hours of sun at sunset on Sunday. We didn't get the beginning or the end, and that was it. The money was gone, he lost the bet. *Slipstream* remains to this day an unfinished Spielberg project.

So Steven tried to do another short film, but it didn't work out. Then Denis Hoffman, who was only in his mid-thirties and one of the founding fathers of the optical house Cinefx, said, "Do I want to be in special effects or would I like to be a producer?" Cinefx had been bought out by Filmways, so they were all paper millionaires. Denis decided to try and make a short film as a producer. He figured out a way of financing it. They had put in a 16mm to 35mm blow-up printer in the lab. So, he said, "I'll get some young filmmaker to do a short film in 16mm and we'll blow it up to 35mm. I'll be the producer and it will also be a demonstration of our printing facilities." So Denis puts out the word he's looking for young creative filmmakers who want to do a short film. Steven told him an idea for a film called *Amblin'*. I call it an idyll of the "Summer of Love." Two kids meet hitchhiking in the desert, the girl more experienced, the boy more naive. They're together a few days, they have this little affair, and they part at the seashore. Steven called me up about shooting the picture and it was very, very exciting. We talked Denis Hoffman into letting us shoot in 35mm. We were, of course, to restrict the amount of film we exposed, and on the first day we almost blew the whole project. Poor Ralph Burris was standing there saying, "You guys have got to stop shooting fifteen takes of everything." It calmed down. We started the picture on the Fourth of July in 1968. We did ten straight shooting days. We shot the sunrise every morning and the sunset every night. Then we'd traipse into Technicolor, see our dailies, go back, get up at predawn, go out and shoot a sunrise, and drag everybody through. It was July. It was 105 degrees out there. I was loading my own magazines because I didn't have a real assistant. We had a bunch of volunteers. We were out there shooting this short film and there was no surprise to anybody that Steven is who he is today. You just knew it immediately when you met him. He had the vision, the passion, and the ability to be a very practical producer on one hand and a sensitive artist on the other. You just don't get those personalities packed into one person like they are in him. It was just an extraordinary experience. That got him launched at Universal.

Steven tried to bring me along, and Universal tried to sign me with all good intentions. It was a dead year in production and the union said, "What? You want him as a director of photography—no way!" Somebody at Universal may have pushed a little too hard and it wound up getting my file red flagged at the union, which basically meant, "Everybody in the world gets in, but he *never* gets in." That was the start of a long, long battle. So I said to Steven at the time, "Don't worry I've got *Amblin'*. I've got a 35mm film to show. I'm going to get one of the commercial houses to get me in the union." I did—it just took eleven more years of battling and lawsuits and things that just give you a heartache, because here's Steven rising to the stars and I couldn't get near the entrance to the union. The union was an absolute father/son, uncle/nephew, closed—*bam*—don't even think about it. I worked in everything you could work in film—educationals, industrials, I did documentaries through David L. Wolper, I got into commercials. I didn't really believe in myself as a cinematographer until I finally got into the IA. It was so discouraging. They want you to get discouraged, the whole business was set up to make you just walk away in despair. You were rewarded for continually trying all the doors and finding the day one of them happens to be open. Between 1965 and 1972, I did nine calling-card films, just freebies for people. You will do a lot of work for free to get a chance to shoot a film. I had a nighttime job working in a friend's photo lab that kept me going when I was trying to break through, and times were really tough. It was the way you survived and paid the rent. If I hadn't had a 65-dollar-a-month apartment and some other ways of keeping the overhead low, I would never have made it. It's very much a matter of the spark striking in the right place, and sometimes it takes a long time. People always say, "Gee, your first Hollywood feature was *E.T.*, that was lucky." I say, "Yes, where were you on the Fourth of July 1968, you weren't out chasing after Spielberg." You pay your dues one way or another and then when you get the break, you have to be able to deliver.

That whole decade, I stayed in touch with Steven. One of the key things you do is form alliances with people who are as obsessed and as passionate as you are about film, then you all go out and try to make your way. Somebody is going to get there first. Somebody is going to make a big leap up. Whatever you do, don't be all over them asking for jobs and favors right away because they won't be able to do anything for you the first time they get a big break to do an important picture. The people who have hired them are going to make sure that person is surrounded by very experienced brand-name people. You're going to have to wait out this person and hope later on down the line they can give you the break. I'd just call Steven up and say, "How's it going, what's happening?" because there really wasn't anything he could do for me until I cracked the union. I called him up every Sunday on *Jaws*. I stayed in touch. I talked to him about his films as they happened.

The only time I asked Steven for something was when we filed our class action lawsuit against the union in 1975. I asked him to sign our petition on behalf of all of the cinematographers. That was key because different lawsuits had been filed in the past against the union, but they were always on individual merit. Ours was different because Andrew Davis, now known as the director of *The Fugitive*, was a really fine cinematographer from Chicago who had actually gotten into the union. They gave him a card in San Francisco, which meant he couldn't work in L.A. So he went out and found a labor lawyer who said, "It's totally unconstitutional. What you should do is file class action suit and don't just sue the union, sue the Producers Association and the Industry Experience Roster Contract Services Administration. Name them both as parties to a conspiracy for restraint of trade." Andy called up a bunch of us who were in the same boat—Caleb Deschanel, Tak Fujimoto (*Badlands*, *Philadelphia*), Bob Steadman (*Executive Action*, *Return to the Blue Lagoon*), Michael Murphy (*Coach*, *Krull*)—and we got some assistants and still photographers in on this. Lo and behold, we couldn't have known how perfect our timing was because the same week we filed our suit, George Dibie, who's now the president of Local 659, filed a suit from inside 659 on behalf of the membership that held E Cards. E Cards were Electronic Cards. This meant you were segregated. You could work on anything with electronic cameras, but you couldn't work on film. Simultaneously, the whole minority program had just gone in and they had to let minorities in on the Group One level. A year later, on around November 11, 1976, they announced open season. People who can prove they worked thirty or more days for one company, ninety or more days for a group of companies, union or signator or non-signator, this time can count. Burden of proof on the applicant. You have to be able to come in with your pay stubs and call sheets. Well, it took me two more years of shuffling paperwork to get it all together. I got accountants from commercial companies driving out to warehouses in Van Nuys to pull out dusty old paycheck stubs. We'd get the paperwork in and they'd reject it or they'd lose it, and then I'd have to get more. I learned all the tricks. Contract services were nasty to the end, but finally in the fall of 1978, I got on the roster.

Q: What is the importance of being in the union today?

A: On nonunion films, you only use one-third of your energy as director of photography, two-thirds of it you use as labor negotiator and trying to get working conditions for the crew. There's a reason why there are unions. People say, "I work on nonunion productions, it's not bad." Yes, when there is a union, nonunion productions are a totally different matter than when there are nonunion productions and there's no more union, because then you're going to see what nonunion really means. I am on the executive board of the very union that kept me out for all those years, but it's a different place. The whole Catch-22 thing got thrown out many years ago. Now, anybody who works one hundred days—union, nonunion, it doesn't matter—can come join the union. We are going to keep the union going, now that we have all areas of the country working together to organize production everywhere.

Q: How did you get the assignment to photograph *E.T.*?

A: In 1979, my friend, Jerry Friedman, gave me my first TV movie, *The Boy Who Drank Too Much*, because the cameraman he had hired got a feature. I had done some commercials under the IA, but this was my first real union feature film. We had a twenty-day schedule and tried to make it look like a feature because television movies then were like television. I had John Toll (*Legends of the Fall*, *Braveheart*) as my camera operator. Abby Singer was in charge of production for MTM Productions. He hired me and made my first deal. I didn't have an agent. *The Boy Who Drank Too Much* turned out so well they sold it to GE Theater.

In the spring of 1980, Spielberg, who had run into Jerry Friedman and heard I had done these TV movies, called up and said, "I've got a sequence to do for the new edition of *Close Encounters of the Third Kind* from the original script that I didn't get to do. It's supposed to be the Gobi Desert, and helicopters and dune buggies come out and find an oil tanker ship on its side in the middle of the desert. We're going to do it with a miniature and I promise I can do it in two days." So we did it. It was great just to be by the camera with him again. Then I went off and did *Rage*, a TV movie directed by Billy Graham for the Chuck Fries Company, which led to a little picture which I dearly love called *Harry Tracy* that very few people have ever seen. We had the great misfortune to be wrapping production on a Western movie in December of 1980, the day that *Heaven's Gate* opened in New York.

So Steven went off to do *Raiders of the Lost Ark*, and I went to Canada and did *Harry Tracy*. Eight six-day weeks and we shot all over western Canada. Sometimes cinematographers talk about getting zoned in with weather. The most important rule is never try to out-wait Mother Nature. If you stand there and say, "I will not shoot in this light," you are going to get had. You've got to go with the flow and find a way to do it, particularly on a shorter schedule, and we really had some marvelous things happen in our favor with the weather. So there's some light and some scenic moments in there I dearly love. The ending of *Harry Tracy* is still just one of the best things I have ever done on any film. It was a great experience.

I came back from *Harry Tracy* in December of 1980. Columbia had passed on *E.T.* It was then called *E.T. and Me*. They had research which said nobody over twelve years old will be interested in seeing this movie. So Steven took it over to Universal and they said, "How much is it going to cost?" He said, "$10 million." They went, "Sure, with effects and spaceships. Now tell me, Steven, what's it really going to cost?" He said, "$10 million." Steven immediately contracted Carlo Rambaldi, who had done Puck, the little creature at the end of *Close Encounters*. By this time, I had a young agent, Randy Herron, over at the Herb Tobias office. This was late in 1979. I am still with the same agency to this day. I'm with the Skouras Agency, which came out of the Tobias Agency when Herb's stepson, Spiro Skouras, took over after Herb's death. They've always appreciated the fact I wasn't out to make money fast, I was building my career and making good choices. Kathy Kennedy, the producer, had been Steven's personal assistant. Steven had two films going into production, *Poltergeist*, directed by Tobe Hooper, and *E.T. and Me*. Kathy wound up producing *E.T.* and Frank Marshall got *Poltergeist*. Steven started thinking about a cinematographer for *E.T. and Me*, and he wanted to look at the work of a bunch of different people. So Kathy Kennedy calls the Tobias Agency and asks Randy about the work of a cinematographer. He said, "Yes, I'll give you that, but Steven knows Allen Daviau, and he has just been doing some really wonderful television movies. I'm sure you'd love to see what he has been doing." It's the end of January 1981. I'm in Phoenix, Arizona shooting a Lawn Boy commercial. I check my answering machine at lunchtime, and it's Randy, my agent. I call him back and he asks, "If you could show Steven Spielberg any film you've done, what would it be?" I said, "Gee, I'd love to show him *Harry Tracy*, but it's in postproduction, and I can't just show him dailies. Show him *The Boy Who Drank Too Much* because it has a whole variety of photographic styles in it and it's about kids, so I know he'll watch it." So Randy calls up Mary Tyler Moore Enterprises and says, "I'd like to get the 35mm print." "Ah, the 35mm print is in New York," they said. This is on a Thursday. So he's calling and calling, and he couldn't even get the cassette, everything's missing. Randy puts in a call to a gal he knew at CBS who owed him one, who finally calls him back on Friday. In the meantime, I am flying from Phoenix to San Francisco because I'm taking over a United Airline commercial for a cameraman who had to leave because they had gotten weathered-out too much. I'm going down to shoot on a Saturday. I'm completely ignorant of what's going on. Randy is calling this lady at CBS and says, "I have to have a print of *The Boy Who Drank Too Much* this weekend." She says, "All we have here is the air print." Randy actually drove over to the parking lot at CBS TV City. She came out the door carrying these boxes and put them in the trunk of his car. He had to go get them mounted on reels. What can I tell you about a great agent? So then he puts in a call to Kathy Kennedy, "When would Steven like to see these films?" She says, "Sunday at his house." The reel from the other cinematographer had already gone over to Steven. So, on Sunday afternoon, Randy drives up to Steven's house and doesn't say anything. He's just playing delivery man. He rings the doorbell and Kathy answers the door, and she says, "Oh yes, this is Allen Daviau's film." *Blam*—the door closes, and Randy goes off to a party. I flew back on Sunday. There was a TV movie I'd been up for that I didn't get, called *Whale for the Killing*, which I was going to see that night on television. So I came back home to Hollywood and I am sitting there, completely not knowing any of this is going on. I'm watching *Whale for the Killing* and the phone rings, "Hey Allen, it's Steven." I go "Hey Steven, how are you doing?" "Hey, I'm in reel three of *The Boy Who Drank Too Much*, looks great. How would you like to do my next movie?" Hurray for Hollywood! The next morning, he says, "I'll show you the script. I can't let you take the script home, but we're doing Automatic Dialogue Replacement (ADR) on *Raiders* over at Warner's Hollywood. Come by, and you can read the script there." I sat on the couch outside ADR 2 at Warner's Hollywood and read the script for *E.T. and Me*. One, you're the luckiest person in the world because there's so much in this script, it can be extraordinary, and two, totally terrifying—how do we do this—because I hadn't had any of the creature technology explained to me at all.

By this time, I was quite established in commercials. I could work on a day-to-day, week-to-week basis in commercials because initially when we signed, my deal on *E.T.* was for prep to start in May and shoot in June. As it turned out, we didn't shoot until September because Steven got all embroiled in *Poltergeist*. Kathy Kennedy would call and say, "We've got to postpone another month." I would go, "Fine," because I could just keep working in commercials. I could do day-to-day work and at the same time, whenever Carlo Rambaldi had a new improvement on the creature, I could run over, see it, and shoot a little test on it. I borrowed a friend's Arri 2C. The original art director had to leave because of all the postponements. Jim Bissell, a young guy who had won an Emmy for his work on *Palmerstown*

U.S.A., came on as production designer. It was just the most wonderful thing in the world, because I was there at the very beginning. That's why I have followed this practice ever since. The cinematographer has to be present at the start of discussions when you're getting into production design, picking locations, talking about where windows are going to be, what the effects are going to be, and all the rest. So I was there from the beginning and spent a lot of time. I was able to just show up whenever something was happening and that made a difference on how the look of *E.T.* evolved.

Steven had a beautiful screening room; we would go up to his house, eat Chinese takeout food and look at the work of Storaro, Deschanel, all classic cameramen from the past and the images that we most admired, like Ridley Scott and Derek Van Lint's work on *Alien*, trying to figure out what made something work. I've never had as long and satisfying a dialogue as I did with Steven, because it was this wonderful relationship with a guy I'd known from all of those years ago. He was coming through in a way which was so gratifying.

It was utterly fascinating the way we worked out how to light E.T. It was, less is more. Particularly at the beginning of the film, Steven said, "I don't want to see him, Allen." Then, one day I had a test where E.T. came back black, which was, "Well, I've got to see him a little!" You had to translate what Steven meant. You just barely wanted to see E.T., to identify him and know when he's there, but no more than is absolutely necessary or there's no magic to it. So, in the tests we were able find out what that level of magic was ahead of time. Our biggest problem was Steven was so enmeshed in *Poltergeist* we had to go stand on the set, wait, grab him as he was going by, and say, "What about this?" to get some decisions made up-front. We finally started to shoot *E.T.* in September.

E.T. was shot on 5247, the standard 100 ASA stock. Only one shot in the movie, E.T.'s finger lighting up, is pushed. I had to assure Steven it was the brightest that bright could possibly be—that we were getting everything possible out of that little bulb in the finger. Otherwise, everything on that film was straight-arrow, unpushed, normal 100 ASA. We shot *E.T.* in sixty-one days. Then we did two days of pick-ups the following February. There was one day on location. We did the overlook shot of the valley. It was a zoom dolly with Keys, played by Peter Coyote, coming in on the foreground. We did the nighttime shot of Keys's agents, because at one of the screenings Steven had for his friends, they didn't understand Keys and his relationship with the government. So we had them breaking into the house. We shot a lot of inserts like the flowers in those two days. Steven was just to the wall, not only did he have to do this miracle, he had to do it dead on that schedule and dead on that budget. The final total was $10.6 million, Universal somehow forgave him $600,000 in their heart. That was astounding! But it was brutal. I was going to Deluxe lab every morning at 6:30, seeing the dailies, and reprinting them if they weren't right because it was my chance. We shot *E.T.* at Culver City Studios. We wouldn't let Steven see dailies there because the projection booth was so bad, the brightness of the image would fluctuate in the projector. I'd go home with Steven after the wrap, see the dailies at his house, and then go home and try and sleep. Thank God it was only a five-day week in town. It was absolutely brutal because Steven was demanding about everything, and he was right to be demanding. We had a crew that was just worn to a frazzle, but the end of the film was just so difficult. Nothing came easily, and it all had to happen so fast. When you're dealing with kids you always have, "You're losing the kids in twenty minutes." The welfare worker is yanking them out of there. When you lost the kids, you were into E.T. close-ups or inserts or shots with the mother. You had to get that work in the course of the day, plus almost all of those interiors were smoked, the old oil-based smoke which looks beautiful but is brutal to breathe. In the morning, you'd fill the stage with smoke. It would stay nice and even and hang there, but in the afternoon the sun had hit the west wall of the stage and it started heating up. You'd come back from lunch, and all of the smoke would want to go in that direction. I can tell you every shot on *E.T.* that was shot in the afternoon. I could see that smoke moving around. We can't use that kind of smoke anymore—it's illegal, thank heavens—but the substitutes don't work and they're even harder to control. So in recent years, I've tried to stay away from smoke unless it's something where you need to have shards of light coming through windows.

There were three different endings for *E.T.* We kept shooting end sequences which were real good that didn't end up in the movie, but Steven knew when to quit when he was ahead. The only preview was in May, the film opened in June. It's absolutely the hardest picture *ever* for me, without question, because this was my opportunity. This was it. If I blew that one, that was it, off into some other land forever. You just don't get another chance like that. The pressure was incredible. What a great director does is inspire you, to say that you are going to achieve something that no one else could achieve. Nobody's ever tried to do this before, and you're acutely aware of that. We knew it was real, real good and real, real exciting, but the idea it became the phenomenon that it did was not what was in our heads. It was just to pull this film off and to make it happen.

Q: How did you work with Director George Miller on the *Nightmare at 20,000 Feet* segment in *Twilight Zone—The Movie*?

A: George wanted a lot of freedom to deal with the movement inside the airplane. Jim Bissell was the production designer. We took George around L.A. and showed him all the airplane mock-ups. They're *terrible*—just awful. Supposedly, they're for airline commercials. They're not even adequate for that. So we said, "You've got to talk to Warner's, they're going to want to shoot this on an existing airplane mock-up. It's going to look like *Airport*." He goes "No!" So we have to build it. I talked to him about using Garrett Brown and his Steadicam, and George was very enthusiastic, "Moving camera, moving camera—great!" He just liked the freedom to go all over the place. My gaffer went out and did a whole bunch of research on industrial, low-voltage lighting fixtures that are used in places where you have a very limited amount of space so they don't overheat. Then Jim Bissell designed places so these little high intensity lamps could be put right in the set. We hid fill light sources on dimmer switches on both sides of the overhead pods. We built all this lighting into the plane. We were not thinking in motion picture lighting terms, except for a few specific shots. I had John Lithgow, who is sheer magic. He can run the one hundred-yard dash, hit a mark within half an inch, and get into the light exactly where I need him. I am very prejudiced in favor of theater-trained actors because they have a sense of theater craft and tend to develop a sense of film craft. I can understand there are some types of scenes where actors cannot be burdened with a lot of technical considerations, but there are other times where technical considerations can be really important as to how the actor's performance comes off. The British actor, David Suchet, from the Royal Shakespeare Company who played the key KGB keeper to Sean Penn's character in *The Falcon and the Snowman*, was somebody with a theater background who had not done much film and wanting to know what he should do, "Now what lens did you say this is? And I'm where? I'm knee figure? Alright," and he'd live in that space. I had the same experience with Annette Benning on *Bugsy*. Annette Benning had ten years of big-time theater before she did a movie. This lady comes on the set—*pow!* take one—she's right there. She knows where everything is. I remember asking Annette, "Do you want me to mention where a light source might be?" She said, "No, just see how I do." She knows. You couldn't light her wrong. She's so beautiful and so aware of where she is in space—talk about just a complete mastery of film craft. I am so appreciative of working with people with that kind of background, it just spoils you. Lithgow spoiled me on *Nightmare at 20,000 Feet*; once I knew John could do this, it expanded a whole lot of other possibilities.

I had Garrett Brown on the Steadicam. I had John Toll handholding, he's the finest handheld operator ever. Some shots were better for the Steadicam and some were better for John Toll, each could do their own thing. There's only eight shots that were actually done on a dolly, everything else is either one form of handheld or the other, with the industrial lighting making all of this possible. We now had a high-speed film stock 5293 that had just been introduced. It was a different 5293 than the one used today. It was an experimental high-speed stock. Kodak didn't even know what it should be rated in terms of sensitivity. John Alonzo used it on *Blue Thunder*. Here we had this stock, which could be anywhere from 250 to 400 ASA. I had run tests of it. Knowing I had this speed capability, we built this set, put in these bulbs, but until we actually shot an exposure test on the set, I didn't know what it could do. So for *Nightmare at 20,000 Feet* we found out we could shoot at 2.5, which was dangerously open. Eric Engler, who's now a successful cinematographer in commercials, was the focus puller and did a marvelous job because there was so much moving camera, people running to camera, camera running to people, fights in the plane, and all the special mechanical effects which Mike Woods did, and the creature out on the wing. It was all a matter of using this high-speed stock and exploiting it as far as it could go. The beauty of George Miller was that everything stemmed from one mandate. He would say, "Be bold! Be bold! The worst thing is we'll have to reshoot it." We filmed *Nightmare at 20,000 Feet* in twelve days. The first scene we shot was one night at a little airport out in the valley. It was the end of the movie, when the people come off after the plane has landed. It's all one long Steadicam shot that then went into the ambulance, the rest was eleven days on-stage inside the airplane mock-up. It was a great chance to experiment. It's all a world of illusions. And we didn't reshoot anything!

Steven Spielberg's episode, *Kick the Can*, and George's *Nightmare at 20,000 Feet* were fun because they were short episodes and they wanted to be completely different from one another. In *Kick the Can*, I did a sunset over Scatman Crothers's speech. It starts yellow, orange and gets oranger. We did all the changes with dimmers, and it gets into red orange. It gets redder and redder, and then it fades away just as he's going up the stairs.

Q: What were the challenges in photographing *The Color Purple*?

A: On *The Color Purple*, Steven Spielberg said, "I want to see faces, I don't want to just see eyes and teeth." Michael Riva was the production designer. We got together and I said, "If we've got enough light on the faces, we've got to be able to have the sets dark enough." So it was keeping the walls, wallpaper, and all the decor down enough so I could pour light in through the windows and not have the sets overpowered by the light which was lighting the people. I could have a really good solid key light. I had Norm Harrison, a wonderful gaffer, on that picture. Norm had these plastic diffusers that looked like shower doors. He had them mounted on wood frames so we could put them outside and send two different directions of arcs through the window—these plastics would scatter the light around. By having darker walls and darker decor, we were able to make the faces stand out. It's actually a lot easier doing a movie with dark-complected actors if everybody's basically dark, but you wound up with the knowledge that it isn't all pigmentation—it's reflectivity. You can have people who have very dark pigmentation, but who have a wonderful reflectivity, the way that the planes of the face are set or the oil in the skin helps kick back light. Ernie Hudson in *Congo* was a snap to photograph because he's a strikingly hand-some man and his cheek bones and everything are on an angle where he re-flects the light so spectacularly. At the same time, you can have people that are lighter pigmentation, but that don't have the reflectivity. So when you have all of these different complexions walking through one scene in a movie, you really learn it's all about controlling the amount and the direc-tion of the light.

Q: Do you have a philosophy concerning lighting?

A: I am basically somebody who likes to shoot in soft light. I call it the "soft light, sharp lens," school of photography, but in the real world at any given moment there is soft diffused light, then there is hard direct light and they mix, rather than having a religion where you do everything with one or the other. I find it's just easy to develop a language where you can mix the sources as real life happens and then control them, because what you're do-ing when you're creating an illusion of light in an image is leading the eye to where you want it to fall. Whose face do we want you to be staring at during a given moment? When, in the same shot, do we want your eye to move across the screen to somebody else for a different beat? What are we doing to redirect your eye over there? This is all about composition. Composition is balance and placement. It's using light to emphasize some portions of the frame. This is one of the things you see people trying to accomplish from the very beginning of cinematography, because in the beginning they were only shooting in direct sunlight. Then the film got a little more sensitive and they were covering the sets with cheese cloth or muslin and still working with the sun as the source. It was the only thing powerful enough. The light-ing was general, but it could be quite attractive in that softness. As they got to adapt arc lamps and brighter specific sources, they experimented more and more with hard light. You watch Billy Bitzer's progress from the early Biograph films, to what he started doing in *Judith of Bethulia*, to what he wound up accomplishing on really sophisticated films in the later years. He was really learning as the process grew. Every generation of cinematographers relearns the same lessons, but with the advantage of newer technology, better film stocks with more latitude and a language of color. When three-strip Technicolor ceased to be the dominant force of color motion pictures, and the color negatives from Eastman, Agfa and later Fuji came in, we learned the language of these films. Just in the course of my career, we've gone from having arcs, which are still wonderful, but now we can work indoors with HMI sources that are daylight color temperature. I can use a practical light source and shoot a scene in available light, but I can also reproduce that look. I can make it look daylight at midnight if I have the right elements. I can make a shot intercut perfectly because I have the tools that can do it. It's learning the language and then personalizing it.

Q: What was it like to work on an epic production like *Empire of the Sun*?

A: I was very acutely aware during *Empire of the Sun* that they weren't going to make many more like this. You're not going to get to take all these people around the world and shoot this kind of film. We made it into Shanghai with little to spare, because another year and there would have been skyscrapers all over the place. So we got in and captured something. My parents had gone to Shanghai in 1939 on their around-the-world trip, which they did by freighter. Boy, did they see the old world at the last moment. So I had seen the pictures in their scrapbook. Norman Reynolds (*Star Wars, Raiders of the Lost Ark*), the wonderful production designer on that film, had all these pictures of what Shanghai looked like in 1940. The research department had dug out British Movietone newsreels of the same bridge where we were going to shoot a riot scene. They got the dailies—the British can research this material so well. They had the raw footage. This riot is going on, the police are beating the bejesus out of this crowd, and here is this sixteen-year-old clapper boy holding a slate saying, "Take five"—*bang* and he runs out of this shot. The camera tilts up and there is this mayhem going on. We screened this newsreel the night before we're going out to shoot the scene. So we had a chance to capture Shanghai just before it disappeared. We got to do so many things in that film.

Q: What was the concept behind how you photographed the flashbacks in *Avalon*, directed by Barry Levinson?

A: One of the things that really struck me right away when I read the script was that here you had a period film with period flashbacks. So you had period within period. You're dealing with something which starts in 1948, goes to 1952 with flashbacks to the teens and the twenties, then one in the thirties. How do you provide a visual identification for these time periods that distances them from this other period, because you had to have a look that said, "Yes, this is the late forties, early fifties." You also had to say,

"Yes, this is 1914, 1917, 1924." Those of us who weren't there remember those years as the silent film era, and what did the silent films look like? I had wanted to use stretch printing in a commercial ten years earlier. The commercial was for a bank, "In 1910, when we first opened our doors . . ." Silent films were shot at all kinds of speeds, but theoretically, sixteen frames per second was the mean. When you restore a silent film, you print every other frame twice to give you twenty-four frames per second, so you don't get this herky-jerky, speeded-up look. I said, "This is great. It doesn't look herky-jerky, but it has this strange little jutter in the movement and as people cross the camera. It has this look of a restored piece of film." They didn't understand it. It scared them. The guy at the optical house destroyed the whole project when he said, "If you stretch printed from sixteen to twenty-four frames, it's the same as if you shot it at twenty-four." "No, it's not. But if you're going to talk yourself out of the business, sir, you just did." So I didn't get to do it in the commercial, and it was right for *Avalon*. I didn't even say anything to Barry. I did a whole bunch of tests. I tried tricking the Eastman color emulsion by shooting through heavy color filtration and printing the color filtration out. The film is too good, I couldn't mess it up as much as I wanted to, but at the end of the day, my girlfriend was out at Panavision and I used her as a subject for the color tests. In the very late afternoon, I had her walk our dog from the street, up to the camera, turn, pick up the dog, and sit the dog down. I shot it at twenty-four frames per second and shot it again at sixteen frames per second. I'd gotten the agreement from Barry and the producer, Mark Johnson, to be able to process at DuArt lab in New York. They knew Don Donigi very well. DuArt has their own optical department. So DuArt could do the stretch printing and keep the color matched to the rest of dailies. I sent this back to Don and he printed the twenty-four frame shot. Then he took and stretch printed the sixteen-frame shot, matching the color to the twenty-four frame shot. One afternoon when we were down in Baltimore scouting locations, I took everybody into a downtown movie theater and showed Barry the color tests. Then I said, "Here's what I'm thinking about for the flashbacks of when Sam comes to America." He immediately saw what I was doing and said, "That's great! That looks familiar." I said, "Yes, you've seen it many times in restored silent films, newsreels, and documentaries, you've just never seen it in color before." And he said, "Right, we'll do it!" It's wonderful when you get the director to back you on an idea. Some people said, "Shouldn't we cover it both ways?" and Barry said, "No, that's great." We did one test to see how it worked with the fireworks. It worked great. As things crossed back and forth across the camera, you noticed it even more because it would have that jutter effect. One of the things Barry did that was very interesting was to place sync dialogue lines over the stretch-printed images. The young Sam looks at the guy with the big shoes and says something like, "What a country!" Barry sunk that line up with Armin Muller Stahl's voice and put it in the mouth of the young Sam. It wouldn't stay in sync for long. but you could do it line by line. The whole opening of the film, all the way through the wedding and the other flashbacks, just set *Avalon* in a different era. The opening flashback is a very theatrical moment, the fireworks are dying out in the sky, you see the glow of Sam's cigar, then the smoke comes out. On the puff of smoke, we started bringing up the whole room on dimmers—it pulls back, and Sam's telling this story to the grandchildren. So you have an opening of the film that really establishes you're going to do some traveling back and forth in time. That film is about memory and how we remember the past. There's a great line like, "If I knew things would disappear so fast I would have remembered better." It's just wonderful.

Q: What was your approach to the visual style in *Bugsy*?

A: I enjoyed my experience with Warren Beatty very much. It was a project he had wanted to do for some time. It was a challenge for everyone. We had a meeting with Warren, the director, Barry Levinson, and the producer, Mark Johnson. My theory about how to shoot Warren for this role was you could put the light on his look, shade around his forehead so that you really emphasized his eyes. He's a great-looking guy, plus he's a pro. He knew what we were going after. It was finding a look for him. Once that was done, I made the look work for everybody because it was a very forties style. I said, "We're taking modern-day film stock, lenses, and lighting equipment and then using them the way a cameraman would have used them in 1945." That was the visual concept of the picture. It worked for lighting all of the people. It was the look of the film. I switched from being a sharp lens, soft light cameraman to going to more of a hard light, soft lens. I used a greater diffusion base, put rear nets on all of the lenses, and used mild Tiffen Pro-Mist filters in front. It really gave me a chance to do some shots as they were done in the forties in terms of floating flags on people's foreheads and keeping the light chopped up, yet having a contemporary feel. I sometimes even got Warren to let me use soft light on him. He hadn't liked what soft light had done in the past. We did some scenes that were not all hard light, but I always like films to be naturally sourced. This is our school. This is how all my heros think—James Wong Howe, Haskell Wexler, Conrad Hall, Vilmos Zsigmond (*The Deer Hunter, Heaven's Gate*), Laszlo Kovacs (*Easy Rider, Shampoo*), Vittorio Storaro, and all of the people who formed the philosophy of contemporary film lighting. There's nothing new. There was soft lighting in the teens by using muslin. David Watkin's (*Chariots of Fire*, *Out of Africa*) work on *Help* in 1965 is a soft light movie. It's absolutely brilliant. David Watkin was doing his own thing then, but sophisticated soft lighting really had its rebirth in this country out of advertising photography of the fifties. In America, more soft light got into the movies because commercials were being directed by people who'd been illustrative still photographers. For still photos from the fifties into the sixties, they used Northern light, a single-source approach to lighting. Then, as they saw the big magazines starting to fade in the sixties, they made a transition into commercials. So you had these guys shooting commercials with interesting light quality. Directors in Hollywood would sit at home at night, look at commercials, come on the set and say, "I saw this commercial last night, now why can't we do that?" It was like, "You can't control soft light." But the new cinematographers came along and found a way to control it. They found different ways of working. So we got this look which defines most of contemporary cinematography. We go through phases. It's great to use hard light for a homage to a period. It also serves very practical purposes and it's easier to create certain kinds of moods. You always look to try something you haven't done. You've got to stir yourself up to change your ways when you get a chance on a project that really calls for it. Going from *Bugsy* to *Fearless* is a perfect example of shifting gears and doing something totally different to the look of the picture. It's great when you have a dialogue with a director you've worked with before, and he says, "Okay, what are we going to do this time? What's the look of it?" On *Avalon*, Barry Levinson and I looked at all kinds of movies, but I showed him a laser disc I had of Jam Handy industrial films from the forties and fifties. There was one from 1945, shot in Kodachrome about "Your advertising impact with color billboards." It was shot in Chicago in the winter. There were all these people walking around in black coats, black suits, black cars were parked everywhere, everything was grey, black, and a little bit of brown, and there were these color billboards screaming out. So I said, "Ahhh, old Kodachrome, Barry." "Yeah, old Kodachrome—that's it!" That literally was our point of departure for the majority of the look of *Avalon*. On *Bugsy*, I said, "I've been looking at a lot of 1940s films. We're just going to go with our general feeling of the mood of forties films and not overly film noir. Film noir is a term that's been used too much. I'd love to do a forties film in that genre and not light it anything like the film noir type of lighting.

　　Q: What are some of the challenges presented by shooting on location?

A: Sometimes you run into films where you're shooting in the tiniest rooms. The room in *Fearless*, for the scene where Jeff Bridges comes to visit Rosie Perez for the first time and she's sitting on the edge of the bed, was very small. I had to suspend a very large light pointing straight down outside the window between two apartment houses and that would bounce up from the floor. In *Bugsy*, Barry Levinson fell in love with this old crafts-man house out in Pasadena, a beautiful place where we shot the scene when Bugsy comes to visit Jack Dragna and Bugsy clips one of his thugs. That whole scene was shot in a tiny place because Barry had fallen in love with it. I just had no place to put anything in the room itself. Just on the edge of the frame, lights had to move during shots and flags had to come up, this light had to be covered over and a dimmer had to come up here. I had to change the f-stop as the fireplace came back into frame. Nobody notices all of this because they shouldn't. It's what you do, you develop equipment that will allow you to work in circumstances when it's impossible or impractical to build it. Sometimes you need to be able to shoot an interior scene in a neigh-borhood so that you don't have to shoot in a bad light in the middle of the day. Shooting in good light outside is about playing "Let's make a deal" with the production board, so you can find an interior or something that doesn't hurt to be shot in the middle of the day. So you can be there for the great light when she walks out onto the front porch at sunset and tells him the real secret of everything that has been going on. You say, "We've got to shoot this at 5:30. We've got to!" "Well, we'll have to move all of the trucks." Negotiating where the trucks park is one of the major things you do, particularly in New York. "Where can we shoot this scene in the morning? Can we shoot under the cover of these trees at midday? Can I come out in the late afternoon to shoot this?" This is all negotiated, and you've got to carry all of this in your mind. You're constantly asking yourself, "What is impor-tant?" Sometimes we're probably guilty of just wanting to make everything so perfect and so gorgeous, but sometimes you've got something in your mind you know is going to make an image work and it's really important to you. You have to listen to that and you have to fight for it. You don't always win. Somebody said to me, "Look, you walked away from a shot where you lost and you had to shoot it in bad light and it didn't work. The great take was out of focus and then the other take is just okay." It's just like the quarterback who's thrown an interception and been tackled on his own five-yard line and walked off the field with the crowd booing, but you've got to shake it off and come back for the next series and be up to marching down the field again. It's the same way. You can't let your losses get to you when you're on a film.

Q: What are some of the different ways a director covers a scene?

A: Steven Spielberg will walk away from a master shot of a scene without getting what I would consider a really good master, or a perfect one. He'll say, "Don't worry, we're going to be over here when that happens. I know we're going to cut to her listening and we are going to be able to use the beginning of take seven and the end of take nine—it's not going to be a concern." Even when he does a scene all in one shot, he always shoots what his editor, Michael Kahn, calls a hinge, which is somebody looking at what's going on. So if he doesn't get a perfect all-in-one take, in an emergency he can cut to that person just listening, then cut back into completion on another take and make the scene work that way. So Steven has that kind of assurance. Barry Levinson is very much more into what he has to take into the editing room, supplying himself with ammunition in terms of how he can create a scene. His major concern is getting the performances he wants while they're still fresh. That's why you wind up using two cameras with Barry. On *Avalon*, when we were working with kids, it's completely understandable. Kids will only do something a certain way one time and so you do work with two cameras. But multiple camera is a very mixed deal because you gain on one hand and lose on the other. For the cinematographer, it's just agony because you're always compromising the lighting in some way. Often times you wind up with two shots, neither of which is correct. If you put cameras side by side and one is just shooting closer, it's not going to be a good cut. You're going to need another cut yet to get you back. The two cameras jockey in position, and neither one is in the correct place. So there are times when it works. Steven Spielberg uses multiple cameras really well and sparingly. He always wants to carry the second camera, but he doesn't mind letting a week go by without using it for anything. In fact, working with Steven is where I started in the practice of having the B camera operator do some second-unit work on the film, because the production manager is always looking to throw the second camera crew off the picture because they're not doing anything. You always have to find something for them to do so that the B camera operator is there when you want to bring him in to get a shot. Every director is different, you find you bring different things to the party. The laser disc has been most wonderful to be able to investigate a whole filmography of a director before you start a film with him. So you can go to John Schlesinger and say, "Now John, in *Marathon Man*, what did you really . . ." It's amazing what the recall is like when you can ask the question from a filmmaking perspective as to why something was covered a certain way. Often times, you find out certain things were shot just to fix something that wouldn't work. You ask questions, and the solutions that are found aren't apparent from just looking at the film. Watching other people's movies with directors is always an inspiration. The night before we started *Empire of the Sun*, Steven and I were sitting in the Ting Yua Sheraton in Shanghai, watching Kubrick's *Paths of Glory*. We kept freeze-framing scenes of the men in the underground bunker—there's a light bulb burning and it's frying the faces of the people. We were saying, "In 1957, no one was allowed to get away with that." What a picture. There was a picture I saw in high school that really convinced me that there was a lot of good work to be done.

Q: What is your relationship to the technology of cinematography?

A: I love to harness a complex technology in the service of art. I love the technology, but it would be meaningless without a worthy creative goal. There's just something about the alchemy of taking all of these strange devices that form motion picture technology and putting them in the service of a vision. As a cinematographer, our toughest job is to find the dream inside the director's head. Some directors are extremely articulate at expressing some aspects of it and not of others. Some directors are not articulate at all, and it takes a real voyage of discovery to find out what their intentions are—that is what makes it fascinating. A lot of times, I find the most direct way of doing this is looking at films together; usually the best thing is somebody else's film, nothing that either of you were connected with. Also looking at art, looking at photography, looking at clippings, pop music videos—all these different things you can find and say, "Ahhh, something like that!" I remember Spielberg asking me one time, "Now, is that smoke or a filter or both?" And you go, "Hmmm, I think it's both." You do that kind of exploration and find ways of expressing something in a different way. Your knowledge of the technology is extremely important, but it is of small import, compared to your knowledge of human beings, your ability to communicate and influence others—to sell your ideas or a way of doing things to the director. Then you turn around and make your crew very enthusiastic about executing those ideas, even though that might be a formidable task. It's a neverending quest for the knowledge of how you're going to accomplish something new. The technology changes so rapidly, but certain things stay very much the same. It's the balance of loving the old and the new. You have to appreciate the past and anticipate the future, but you're always making movies in the present and knowing how they will resonate down the line. Films you are sure will be absolute deathless wonders are very dead even before they are in the theaters. Certain films you're wrong about, but the idea that you're willing to keep trying things is the most important aspect of it. I do really feel that a lot of beginning film people do not study the history of the medium enough. The history of the technology is for all the people who are going to be involved.

The artistic history of the medium is only a hundred years old—what could be easier to study? It's a piece of cake to seek it out. People say, "That's for art historians, not for artists." I don't think so. You see something, and it causes you to do something else. You may not realize that what is ringing in your head came from long, long ago.

13

Lisa Rinzler

Lisa Rinzler attended the Pratt Institute, where she first studied painting then switched to filmmaking. Rinzler made a transition to the New York University undergraduate film school, where she began to shoot many student films, knowing she wanted to be a cinematographer.

Rinzler shot two short films for Photographer Robert Mapplethorpe, and *Reverse Angle*, an art journal film for Director Wim Wenders. As an assistant, she worked with Cinematographers Nancy Schreiber (on many documentaries) and Fred Murphy (in feature films).

Rinzler began photographing documentaries, including *World's End*, *Kitty*, *No Sense of Crime*, *Hookers, Prostitutes, Pimps, and Their Johns*, and a film on the making of John Huston's last production, *The Dead*. In 1989, Rinzler photographed Nancy Savoca's directorial debut, *True Love*. She shot a series of music videos for Director Tamara Davis, which led to *Guncrazy*, a contemporary, color film noir starring Drew Barrymore. Davis showed Rinzler's reel to young filmmakers Allen and Albert Hughes, Rinzler screened *The Drive-By*, a Super 8mm film by the Hughes brothers, and this led to an impressive collaboration on *Menace II Society*.

Rinzler was director of photography on the Hughes brothers' second film, *Dead Presidents*, an ambitious production which gave the cinematographer the opportunity to expand her horizons of visual storytelling. She shot actor Steve Buscemi's directorial debut, *Trees Lounge*, and *Three Seasons*, the first American feature film to be filmed on location in Vietnam.

A socially conscious artist, Rinzler tries to vary narratives with smaller experimental projects. She shot *Black Kites* for Director Jo Andres, based on a Sarajevan woman's journals during wartime. Lisa Rinzler's documentary work informs her feature films, combining nonfiction reality with a heightened cinematic verisimilitude.

SELECTED FILMOGRAPHY

1987   *Forever Lulu*

1989   *True Love*

1992   *Guncrazy*
       Menace II Society

1995   *Dead Presidents*
       Lisbon Story

1996   *Trees Lounge*

1998   *Three Seasons*

Q: How did you come to study filmmaking?

A: I had read *Summerhill* by A. S. Neill, a book about a progressive school system in England, and thought, "There's got to be a more progressive way to educate people, including myself." I dropped out of high school, but wanted eventually to study drawing and painting. I went to Pratt Institute in Brooklyn as a nonmatriculated painting student. Then, just by fate or luck or both, New York State passed a law saying if you went to an accredited college, you could receive your high school diploma. So I matriculated. While I was at Pratt, I switched to film.

Q: What caused you to switch from painting to film?

A: I was painting a lot with motion, suddenly light wasn't the only issue—motion was involved. I couldn't quite get it all in painting. I must have had a dream, because one morning I woke up and said, "That's it, I'm switching to film!" It really came out of light, and drawing, and painting.

Q: There's a lot of movement in your cinematography.

A: The human eye and the human being are in constant motion, even when seemingly at rest. When focusing on someone, you are not only seeing them, but taking in, whether consciously or unconsciously, the background behind them and the foreground too.

Q: Was there any particular movie that captured your imagination as a child?

A: Madame X, with Lana Turner. I remember nothing of it, except for one shot of a blindfolded woman in a stark prison or hospital-like room that frightened me. That scene had hard light and hard cuts. The image was strong to me as a child. I bet if I saw this film today it would seem far less intimidating. That image may not even be accurate, but that is what shooting is about—perceiving and interpreting, not simply recording the shared common denominator.

Q: So what did you do at the point you had the revelation to study filmmaking?

A: I switched to New York University as an undergraduate because Pratt's film department was just so tiny. I did shoot a film there, but I wanted to shoot a lot, and at NYU you could. I shot a lot of terrible films there that were never completed, but it was very hands-on and I got to practice lighting and get comfortable with the camera. Operating a camera felt very natural, but syncing up the right balance of what you wanted the lighting to look like and pulling off the technical end of it was another story. While at NYU, I began working as a technician for free as a second assistant. I had a job once as a Production Assistant and quickly ended up in the camera department.

Q: When you first entered NYU as an undergraduate, was your goal to become a director?

A: No, I knew I wanted to become a cinematographer. Everything I did was directed towards cinematography. I never directed a film at NYU, I just shot a lot of films. It was great experience. You have to do it. You can read, you can watch, you can study, and one should do all those things—I do, to this day—but it's the physical reality of doing it that makes a difference. You need to make mistakes to really learn and move forward. When I see the films I shot for Robert Mapplethorpe, I am horrified. The lighting is dreadful and flat, and in one film almost every shot is a zoom—and it will live forever! I was still a student and had no experience. I was at the beginning of learning by doing.

Q: What did you learn from Robert Mapplethorpe?

A: Lessons about commitment. Be more into your subject than photographing it. Your subject comes first, photographing it comes naturally, organically, second. I was enamored with him because of his commitment.

Q: There was so much controversy over his work, but he also did a wonderful series of photographs of flowers.

A: The flowers were beautiful. He also did this amazing work with color. It was almost like a music video sense of color, it was very saturated. It was fashion, and never hyped to the public the way his celebrity portraits, his flowers, or his S&M male erotic work was, but it was amazing and it affected my cinematographic education. Now you see tons of oversaturated music videos, but he was doing that in stills and it was affecting my lighting style.

Q: What did you do after studying at NYU?

A: I assisted two people: Nancy Schreiber in documentaries, and Fred Murphy as a second assistant in features.

Q: What did you learn from working with Fred Murphy?

A: Fred was really my mentor. When I was beginning on my first job as a second assistant on a feature, Fred had me diagraming his lighting set-ups. I'm not as classical as Fred, but there was a great beauty in getting to diagram and study his work that closely. It made me look at every lighting unit. Why is that unit there? I worked for Fred for a long time as a second assistant. I was a much better second assistant than I was a first. First assistant is immensely technical, looking at the wrong end of the lens, figuring out focus. I wasn't too inclined towards that.

Fred taught me about being on the set. He is such a gentleman, a large part of being a director of photography is administrative. It's dealing with the production aspects, equipment coming and going—the politics of people and set etiquette. It's handling a lot that isn't the actual photography itself. It's dealing with time pressure and people leaning on you. I really observed his gentleness, but his steadfastness. How to ask for what you need. A lot of being a director of photography is having to fight for what you believe. In the beginning I had to fight more than I do now, although there's still a time in every day where I feel something might be better for a shot one way and a director feels it might be better another way. It's my job as a director of photography to persevere without hammering it to the point of infuriating them. When I prep a feature, I am astonished by how the last thing I get to do, which is to visualize and then write notes for a scene, is always the most single-handedly important thing. Production has so many questions in order to prepare for the location, special equipment, and additional day-players required, etc. Once the technical and logistical part is cleared, the final conceptual planning gets its final moment before jumping into the fire and committing that concept onto film.

I was also a first assistant on many documentaries, which was a great experience. That taught me a lot, not just technically and about working quickly, but also socially—it was invaluable. So I got some of each world because if I wasn't working on a feature with Fred, I was working on a documentary with Nancy Schreiber. It was very schizophrenic, but that was a great education.

Q: How did you know when to make the transition to director of photography?

A: A time came when I said, "I've got to shoot, I can't assist!" I was getting too old—there comes a time where you have to go for it. I really didn't like working as a first assistant. I got used up. I was literally falling asleep at night in the bathtub, looking at my Samcine calculator worrying about whether some hard dolly shot would be in focus the next day at dailies. It was so stressful, and I was just dying to shoot. I had a lot of my own opinions and ideas. I was constantly looking and just wanting to be doing it. I bought an Aaton camera with the money I made as an assistant. In those days, when you started shooting, you'd shoot for free. I remember saying, "Do I want this record or do I want to eat?" because there was just no money anymore, it had all gone into this camera. I got to a point where I said, "I can no longer assist because people are seeing me as an assistant, I have to shoot." In 1984, I was assisting Fred Murphy on *Key Exchange*, and two weeks before the end of the film I got an offer to do a very low-budget 16mm feature. Fred said, "Go ahead, go do it."

Q: You shot *Guncrazy*, which was Tamara Davis's directorial debut. What is the responsibility of the director of photography on a director's first feature?

A: To help them put onto film what they see in their mind's eye. Some directors are highly visual, and others are more inclined towards the actors. Some are both. It's our job as a director of photography to help them know a little bit more about cinematography as part of the language, part of the expression in telling the story. To show them that visually, cinematography can help to express an emotion, a mood, an idea, a concept. There's a lot of, "What do you think of trying this?" A lot of, "Is this the way you want it to feel? If it is, why don't we work with this type of light, this type of camera movement." It is the director of photography's job to enhance the director's vision.

Q: What films did you and Tamara Davis screen prior to shooting *Guncrazy*, which is a contemporary film noir?

A: We screened the original *Gun Crazy* (1949, directed by Joseph H. Lewis). Tamara's film wasn't a remake, just a name in homage only, but there were some really amazing sequences shot in cars in the original. We screened a lot of James Cagney films like *White Heat*, and expressive black-and-white films like *The Night of the Hunter*. We were influenced by a modern French New Wave film, Godard's *Breathless*. When you shoot a feature in twenty-four days, you can't afford to have a lot of coverage. You have to plan your shots. You commit it to film, it has a life of its own. You don't get to second guess. In editing, you can at least change something if it doesn't work. I haven't had the luxury to light something one way and then have a change of mind and start over entirely after seeing it. There's just not that kind of time. I'm in many situations where we light something, look at it, don't like it, and we start turning lights off. It almost invariably gets better. So that teaches you to commit, to work fast. You have to read the script, think about the feeling, the emotion and psychology of each scene, break it down, come up with an approach beforehand, agree upon it with the director, do it, and move on to the next one.

Q: You use the technique of rack focus in *Guncrazy*, where the camera switches from one point of focus to another within a shot. What is the purpose of a rack focus shot?

A: It means directing the viewer's attention exactly where the director and the director of photography think it should be. Pulling focus for the most part is and should be unnoticeable, but a real specific rack focus is to rack attention from one thing to another. Racking between lines isn't so psychological. If you can't hold your depth of field, you're forced into racking between lines. It still happens to me at some point on every film. I don't much care for it. I do like a specific psychological focus shift, it's like saying, "Look here, look there."

Q: Nancy Savoca's directorial debut, *True Love*, captures a sense of truth about the Italian American community in New York. What research did you do on this project?

A: That's a compliment to Nancy Savoca. I went up to the Bronx and asked her to really take me through the whole script, really tell me how do *you* see it—take me into this world. Then, once we started location scouting, I was so taken with the visuals, with the homes of people. What a person has in their homes, the colors they paint their walls, the objects, really says a lot about their character. The Italian American homes in the Bronx were really exciting for me. They are dark and rich, the light was trying to come in from the outside, but was controlled by dense curtains. Locations have history and vibration, they speak loudly in a very quiet way.

Q: True Love is a dialogue-driven film. How did you and Nancy Savoca bring visual storytelling to it?

A: Through working with backgrounds. What's behind a person is telling you something consciously or it's affecting you subconsciously. These real-life backgrounds were crammed full of exciting information. They weren't moving, but they were speaking. So, since there was an immense amount of dialogue, I thought, "That's a way we can get a visual sense into this film!"

Q: How do you photograph someone in their environment and make the background part of the scene?

A: Choices are at hand every step of the way. In a feature, you're working with the production designer to create the backgrounds. What color? What fabric? What texture? Is it wool? Is it cotton? Is it shiny? Is it satin? Does it have a pattern? What color is the wall? What hue of that color? In a feature, you work with a background by creating every millimeter of it, every inch of every space.

Q: In the pizzeria sequence, you achieved a good balance between the exterior light coming through the window and the interior light. How did you approach this?

A: Balancing exterior and interior light is something directors of photography do every day. Realistically, a pizza place is lit with fluorescent light. We took artistic license in turning the fluorescents off. The characters are close enough to the window that it would be daylight. We wanted to see through the window, we did not want a whited-out background. The film is about people in their neighborhood, so you want to see life going on in that neighborhood. So the exterior can be two stops hot, but it can't be five stops hot. It's building up your interior light to hold the balance to the exterior light and keeping it a natural feeling.

Q: How did you first meet the Hughes brothers and come to photograph their first feature, *Menace II Society*?

A: I had shot a lot of black-and-white rap videos for Tamara Davis, D.O.C., and MC Lite. The Hughes brothers had seen those, and an Elizabeth Taylor commercial for White Diamonds which I had shot in Mexico. I saw a Super 8mm film they made, called *The Drive-By*. I just loved the roughness, the economy, and the cleverness with which it was shot. I liked the visual style. Working on a lot of rap videos, I was around young black culture, so my eyes and ears were open to that subject matter. I was staying at Tamara's house in Los Angeles on some project, and I met the Hughes brothers there by chance. I said, "Look, if you ever want to do a Super 8mm film, I'll shoot it for you. I love your work." Within six months, suddenly *Menace II Society* was on the burner and going to happen. I said, "Great, I want to do it, I'll be there." It was a low-budget film, around $2.7 million. It was a thirty-five-day schedule, and off we went.

Q: Both Allen and Albert Hughes direct their films. How did they work with you on *Menace II Society* and *Dead Presidents*?

A: Allen Hughes worked with the actors and Albert Hughes worked with me in terms of the camera and the lighting. Albert is very interested in camera style. They confer and agree. Albert and I spent a lot of time in preparation shotlisting and storyboarding, more so on *Dead Presidents* in terms of storyboarding, but on *Menace II Society* we made an entire shot list, mine was maybe six scenes. They are a team. They agree or disagree and they work it out until they agree. Their areas are pretty specific. They both overlap in terms of having say, but at one point they make a commitment to a vision. Allen went to a lot of acting rehearsals while I was sitting with Albert doing shot lists and shot design. People always think it's hard to work with two directors; for me it isn't. They are *both* directors. In *Menace II Society*, I wanted to do a lot of handheld. I said, "Look, it's raw, it's urgent, there's a beauty to it." I was thinking about John Cassavetes's films, or more recently Nick Gomez's film, *Laws of Gravity*. Having come from handheld out of so much necessity, the Hughes brothers wanted to try the tools of the trade. There were times it was completely appropriate to use Steadicam and at times it wasn't.

Q: Menace II Society really captures an aspect of the black community in the seventies. How did you and the Hughes brothers approach the period in this film?

A: The Hughes brothers lived in Pomona, California at that time. I drove out to their house, and they pulled out a scrapbook from the seventies of their father sitting in chairs in different outfits, in different cities. That was the bible reference book. It told me the color sense. There was a lot of ochre, brown, orange, yellow, and lot of purple in the seventies. That photo album from their father was the key to the film.

Q: How did you light the apartments in the seventies sequences?

A: They're very saturated. We directed a lot of hard light and then flagged it to control it and create contrast. It was a very standard lighting package of tungsten and HMI, and it was fairly direct lighting. There was a trend for a while where moonlight and street light was very blue. I was moving away from that, towards streetlights being warmer. Color takes on cold and warm psychology and emotion. It felt right to have a blue tone as the cold interior tone and a warmer tone for the outside world existing as a hot, vibrating world.

Q: How did you utilize smoke?

A: Sometimes we used smoke for an effect, like in the party scenes, and other times we used it ideally just for more atmosphere. It wasn't a world that was meant to feel particularly clear, it was a night world, a hazy world, a stoned world.

Q: What kind of smoke is available for filmmakers?

A: There's Mole Foggers, now outlawed because of toxicity, smoke cookies, there's fire, oil crackers. There's a new kind of oil cracker which is safer and diffuses and hangs in the air a lot better. The trick in smoke is in getting the same level in every shot. Also, you have more to the eye than you see on film, so it's becoming familiar with how much that amount truly is. A Mole Fogger looks like an oil can with the bellows. An oil cracker is a larger machine you turn on and off. It makes a noise. If you want exterior smoke, a bazooka is a long, thin bullet-like shape which makes a huge, loud sound. Which type of smoke you use depends on the size of the space. Smoke is very hard on the crew and on actors. We used much less smoke on *Dead Presidents*, almost none. Smoke also has a tendency to give away where the light is coming from—it rises towards the source. So it's a real telltale lighting diagram for the viewer. On a good film, you shouldn't be watching the lighting.

Q: The party scene in *Menace II Society*, where the camera moves from one end of the house to another, was a good use of the Steadicam. Was lighting this shot complicated?

A: The lighting was tricky because the shot covered a lot of territory, moving from the front of the house, through it, then out into the backyard. The ceilings inside were low. It was not as hard as if it had been daylight outside. You want that balance between stylized yet natural. You want the viewer to feel like they are walking into the party. They may never have been at a party like that. So you have to plant a seed for what it would feel like and then you have to hide all the lights because you're moving through an immense amount of space. You're putting lights at the edge of the frame and if you're operating yourself, which I often do, you're missing them by millimeters. You're doing a retake because you hit a light. We didn't do many takes on that shot. You don't usually get to light until lunch, which is six hours from your call, but we had agreed we would light until lunch and then shoot because there were two scenes that night. We had to be out of there early because of the neighborhood.

Q: Were there exposure changes in that Steadicam shot?

A: No, it was night, so we could control it. If it was day, we might have to do an aperture pull from the outside to the inside. We were able to control that more easily than had it been f2.8 outside and we had to light inside the house to f2.8. Then you need to have aperture pulls and a way to camouflage them.

Q: The interrogation sequence was very effective. What was the concept behind the repeated 360-degree passes of the camera?

A: We wanted it to feel like his head was starting to spin, that sense of vertigo. He was getting a big finger pointed at him, and it was beginning to affect his ability to keep clear.

Q: How did you move the camera during that shot?

A: The grips laid down a big dance floor around the table. I was operating. We went around and around on a dolly. We would start in one direction and then go in the opposite direction to create that off-balance, trying to catch your breath, out of control feeling.

On *Dead Presidents*, we did a 360-degree shot which was more straightforward and less psychological. There was a group of men sitting in a circle. So to show what each character was doing, we used a track and went around the circle once. It was much more precise and specific. Not working on a track is less precise, but it has a beauty to it.

Q: Did you and the Hughes brothers screen films prior to production on their second feature, *Dead Presidents*?

A: We screened *Superfly*, *The Mack*, *Shaft*, *Taxi Driver*, and *GoodFellas* are big influences for them. *GoodFellas* in terms of Steadicam, that shot through the Copa. A lot of their references are to films because they love films. I was really excited to find out they had seen and loved *Midnight Cowboy* because to me it was a visual and emotional, synchronous experience. It was so perfect, even the imperfections were perfect. There were two years between *Menace II Society* and *Dead Presidents*. Albert and I kept up a big fax relationship, "Look at this, look at that." For *Dead Presidents*, it was Martin Scorsese and Sergio Leone, they love the framing in those two. For *Menace II Society*, there was a lot of Scorsese referencing. One of the first films I brought to them was Stanley Kubrick's *The Killing*. There's a scene in Sterling Hayden's apartment where the walls were removed and the camera moves across the apartment. I was really intrigued with that, and I remember saying, "Can we do this?" Albert loved it. When we did that shot moving across the removed wall in *Menace II Society*, there were so many negative voices, "This isn't going to work! This is going to be cut out of the movie," but we wanted to do it. There's a scene in which a fight breaks out in an apartment and at the very end of it, the camera tracks across from the living room to the kitchen to other rooms with the walls removed. You come out on the other side into someone's bedroom, so it looks like a seamless cut. I was operating the camera. After we lit it, set it up, and got to the end of the track, I remember seeing scowling faces still not wanting us to do it. The Hughes brothers wanted to do it.

Q: Did you bring the Hughes brothers any references from painting or still photography?

A: Yes, because I love still photography so much. I showed them photographers I like, such as Robert Frank; it makes it very quick to see the lighting.

Q: What was the visual approach to *Dead Presidents*?

A: The film was about a young, middle-class black man who doesn't want to go to college and instead goes off to Vietnam. It's set between 1968 to 1972. He goes to Vietnam, he has some experiences, it affects him, he comes back, and America is not waiting with open arms. We wanted it to quietly feel like there were different looks. In terms of color and lighting, we tried to play the film like a three-act experience: before Vietnam, brighter, more saturated, more hopeful, more sun; Vietnam, it's own world, hot, somewhat drab, frenetic, urgent, confusing. There was a lot of handheld camera and handheld on a dolly. Then, coming back from Vietnam was colder, drabber, less known, more dangerous, more mysterious, more darkness.

Q: What preproduction was done on *Dead Presidents*?

A: Albert and I shotlisted. We had two storyboard artists, one did the rough sketches, then the second did extensive sketches. There weren't too many conceptual conversations on the set of *Dead Presidents* because it had happened in preproduction. The discussions on the set had to do with minute nip-and-tucks in terms of lighting and operating. The prep time between a director of photography and a director develops rapport, references, guidelines, and a shorthand to be used on the set. The shotlists are a blueprint and sometimes a jumping-off point. Once the scene is rehearsed with actors, a new life is brought to it in a way that imagining it couldn't. Changes and adjustments are frequently made, and rightly so. Still, I cherish the time of talking through the script with the director and listening to them describe how they imagine it. I have also worked without shotlisting or storyboarding—more wild-style, or designing completely on the set after rehearsal. This is more European. We worked this way on *Lisbon Story*, a film by Wim Wenders. Wim is such a visualist and has such a strong sense of where to put the camera. It is a pleasure to work with someone so embracing of the visual aspect of storytelling.

Q: What was your overall approach to lighting *Dead Presidents*?

A: In the past, I worked with a lot of hard light. On *Dead Presidents*, I wanted to work with much softer, bounce light, but made sure to maintain contrast. We wanted the film to feel natural, but somewhat dark. We wanted always to be appropriate. We agreed to shoot the master shot of one of the scenes in the church in silhouette. There was no light on the faces in this shot. In the close-ups I agreed by the directors' request to have enough light to see the faces when we lit for the close-ups. A preacher was being asked to come in on a heist, so it was appropriate to play that scene in silhouette. Another time we were able to do a silhouette, when Anthony is walking forlornly down a cold winter street.

There was a scene in which the characters are planning the heist at a table, and they lean in and out of light. The Hughes brothers had seen *The*

Asphalt Jungle. They said, "We want people to lean in and out of sharp cuts of light." So we worked with a raw 2K bulb, which is very rough on faces, not beauty light. There was no diffusion on the bulb, no diffusion on the lens. People had eye sockets, depending on how steeply overhead the light was placed. It was not meant to be pretty. The character Delilah was in that scene, played by N'Bushe Wright. She's a beautiful woman, that was not a flattering light, but it was agreed upon and it was appropriate to that scene.

There was a character called Skip who dies of an overdose, and as I read that scene, I thought, "Green is a good color for death by overdose." I asked the production designer, David Brisbin, "Could you give me a green lamp?" so I could motivate the light, and he did. It was a light shade of green, so people spent a lot of time gelling that oval shade darker and so you didn't see the gel.

We used a lot of strip lights on *Dead Presidents*, which are multiple bulbs. We used a lot of incandescent bulbs, a lot of dimming. Sometimes we used ring lights, bulbs in a circle, and a couple of times we had to throw up some cuts or diffusion for Keith Gardner, the boom man, because multiple bulbs can make multiple shadows. Albert got into shooting with two cameras. We had made a handshake deal at the outset there would be no 45-degree or 180-degree opposite, double-camera set-ups. There would be different lenses on axis so that lighting wouldn't be compromised—we tried to stick pretty close to that.

Q: How did you employ camera movement in *Dead Presidents*?

A: Handheld camera was used for Vietnam. Even in the earlier parts of the film, there was some handheld. We did a shot in the pool hall scene handheld on this little speed rail cart dolly made by the key grip, Dennis Gamiello. It was a fairly big shot, and I thought if it was all handheld it might be too rocky in this location. The operator handheld the camera in the cart. So it's a combination of both feelings. There was always a lot of movement in the film. You're dealing with a young character. He was meant to be eighteen, and the character moves a lot. The Hughes brothers were twenty-three, so there's a lot of energy going on. There were some static shots and a lot of close-ups in the film. It's hard to move on a big close-up, you really need a reason, but there was a lot of camera movement. We used the Steadicam more judiciously and sparingly on *Dead Presidents*. We didn't use one Steadicam shot in the Vietnam sequence—we used it in other parts of the film when appropriate.

Q: What film stock did you use on *Dead Presidents*?

A: I used 5293 for exteriors. I had toyed with using 5245 for the more bright, cheerful, saturated sequences because it's fine grain and lovely, but daylight was fleeting. It was fall, and 7:30 to 4:00—Bam!—the light was done. So it was 5293, which is contrasty, and 5298. *Dead Presidents* was shot in Super 35mm, and I didn't want to use 5298 for the interiors. I started with 5293, but because of the 200 ASA, we would have needed more lights and more people, so we went to 5298 because we could use a little bit less light and have a little bit more f-stop. I considered 5287 for Vietnam, but 5293 is a much more contrasty stock.

Q: There must be a lot of homework to do when new film stocks come out.

A: Yes—intense homework. We tested a lot of filtration, which I threw in the garbage. We used the lightest, lightest, black ProMist. *Dead Presidents* is almost a nonfiltered film.

Q: What camera and lenses did you use on *Dead Presidents*?

A: Panavision. The Primos are nice sharp lenses. They're very flare free. For a Super 35mm blow-up, you don't want flare and you don't want soft focus. Shooting *Dead Presidents* in Super 35mm, I found a little bit longer lenses were better. A 35mm lens became the normal. If you use wide-angle lenses, the backgrounds become far away in a hurry, so a little bit longer lens is good. A 75mm is great for a close-up.

Q: How did you work with the production designer, David Brisbin, on *Dead Presidents*?

A: David presented a color palette and worked with me beautifully in terms of the lighting and colors. We enjoyed an active collaboration. Around eight sets were built, but the tour de force was the Kirby's Pool Hall set. It felt old and lived-in. It was a russet orange with checkered linoleum. David was very attached to wanting a tin-patterned ceiling, and I felt we needed ducts to hide the occasional lights placed up in the ceiling. David had worked very hard on the tin ceiling and had never seen ducts in any of his research of pool halls. But in order to accommodate the cinematography, he found a real existent pool hall that had a tin-patterned ceiling with ducts. We were always trying to motivate the light through windows or existent practical sources. Occasionally, we had to rig from over top. We also tried to work with bounce lighting whenever possible and maintain contrast by flagging.

Rochelle Edleson, the camera scenic, could age down a wall within seconds if something was too white or too new—Bam!—she'd spray it down. If something was too bright for me, David would find every way to accommodate it for lighting and make changes without compromising what felt right to him. He was very concerned about wardrobe because those patterns and colors also function within the set.

Q: What shot in *Dead Presidents* was particularly challenging?

A: We ended the movie with a reflection shot that was outside of a bus window. Anthony is being taken off to jail in a prison bus. We meant to make a series of shots of shackled feet up to faces. We're driving back from the location scout, and Dennis Gamiello said, "Why don't we just do it as an overhead shot?" It was a joke. Albert's ears perked up, "Yeah, that would look great!" I was actually really attached to some of the other shots—they were simple and beautiful. You'd see how forlorn the character was, but the reflection is the moment.

The bus was parked in a studio and the top was cut off, as if with a can opener. We shot the reflection shot first, saw the dailies, and picked which lighting we had to match. Bill O'Leary, the gaffer, set up a bank of 10Ks on one side and nine lights on the other. Two electricians ran through the 10Ks with wooden, jerry-rigged items simulating trees so that a moving reflection would go by. A truss bridge was built over the top of the bus that dollied down over the top and to the side at the same time. It was a costly shot. It took a big rig and time, but everyone was pleased with it.

Q: What does the director of photography contribute to an actor's performance?

A: It's a multifaceted process, where you have to support the director and how they're approaching the character and the subject. There are some directors who don't want to ask the actors to do so much and some that are more willing. Sometimes hitting marks gets in the way of the acting. It depends on the experience of the actor, if they're more or less willing to have those demands put on them. Sometimes it's not comfortable to say to a young actor, "This is your key light, favor this way. Lift your chin up," because it's too much information for them. They're trying to stay in character. Other times, with a more veteran actor, I'd say, "This is where your light is. You don't have to lock to that light, but know it's there—hit it." They embrace it as a tool that is going to make them come across. Some directors like actors to come to dailies and some don't. A young actor may need to see what a close-up means, to see what light does on their face.

As cinematographers, we have our own perspective, our own feelings, our own opinions. I try not to take scripts I can't relate to on some level. I have my own feelings about the characters. I try to listen to that, but also moderate and try to remain true to what I feel the scene and that character is meant to be portraying at that moment in the script. Characters change a lot, there might be a moment where someone's angry. There might be a moment where they're making love, and you have to light it and photograph to support that mood. So directors of photography do contribute to expressing those moods. It's especially tricky with women because often there are powers-that-be that want the actors to look beautiful, and there are times when it's not appropriate to look beautiful. There are more actors now that are willing to not look beautiful if it's not appropriate.

Camera blocking is an important way to work with actors because the actors are working with the camera as a tool, as a character. At times it is aggressive, at other times it's more subtle. Moving actors within a frame in relation to a camera is a form of manipulating—not in a negative way—but as a tool in storytelling language. It might be more quiet. It might not be shooting and violence, but by moving actors within a frame in relation to the camera, there's a psychology of movement that's not conscious. It's all part of the language. If an actor walks into a close-up, it affects you one way. If the camera moves toward the actor, then the camera is doing something the opposite way—it's all affecting the viewer. You feel it viscerally and it affects your perception of the story.

Q: In the past, you have operated the camera yourself. How do you work with a camera operator?

A: Not operating is hard for me because I can see it more clearly through the camera. I like lighting through the lens, so the operator has to step aside during the lighting process. I give the operator the camera to practice the move as soon as I can, but in terms of lighting, I really need to see it through the frame. I'm not comfortable working through a video monitor. A lot of times during the actual take I stand at the camera, not at the monitor. I watch a take or two on the monitor to see the operating, and I'm very specific about the operating. So if on one take there is just the wall framed behind someone's head, where if you move over literally three inches you see the depth of a corridor or the narrow depth of a bar in the background, it makes all the difference.

Video assist is a very important tool you have to have. When I shot *Lisbon Story*, a very low-budget film, in Portugal, Wim Wenders didn't want video assist. I operated because that's the European style. Sometimes you just have to see to know, particularly on a close-up. That's how I can best see the lighting and the emotion on their face. I grew to love having an operator. Sometimes there are shots the operator can do a lot better than I can. I embrace that, and it gives me more time to light. They can rehearse a tricky move, they can perfect it, do it over and over. I can really just work on the lighting with the gaffer.

Q: What is your involvement in working with the laboratory?

A: Working with the labs in terms of dailies is crucial. I've worked with Don Donigi and Steve Blakely of DuArt. Don Donigi is really an unsung hero. All the directors of photography who work with him know what a brilliant man he is. He oversees the timing. The man is a great synthesis of technique and knowing what people want. He also keeps up with current style. From seeing lighting, contrast, and filter tests, he gets a sense of what I am after. The man is able to aesthetically be an ally. If you're pleased with your dailies, basically you want your answer print to look like a good set of dailies. The answer print is a crucial part of the process. You deal with the density, the lightness and darkness, the color and the saturation, whether you lean towards blue or red. It's an utterly controlled, focused process. You have to work very closely with the laboratory and the timer who's doing the answer print.

Q: Three Seasons was the first American feature film to be filmed on location in Vietnam. What is the film about and what challenges did it present?

A: Three Seasons is three stories set in contemporary Vietnam. To connect the stories, the characters from one season/story appear in the others. The first season is the Dry Season, the story of a cyclo driver and a prostitute. The second story is the Wet Season, which takes place all at night in the rain, starring a ten-year-old and a four-year-old street urchin. The third story is the Growth Season, about a teacher and lotus picker and takes place on a lake with a temple built in the middle of it. The film was shot on an extremely low budget and was also extremely ambitious. The script was poetic and lyrical, and demanded a technical sophistication beyond our monetary means. The struggle to achieve a seamless and elegant image was simultaneously invigorating and frustrating. Ultimately, it was well worth it. The struggle itself was enticing and became part of the challenge.

The Dry Season took place predominately on a moving cyclo. In Vietnam, there was no such thing as a Shotmaker—a Jeep with bad shocks or seemingly no shocks at all was used as a camera car at the time we filmed. The streets of Ho Chi Minh city can be potholed and bumpy. A cyclo is approximately eight feet long, and the camera lens from a Jeep was approximately twelve feet from the subjects. This forced us into using a 75mm or 100mm lens for close-ups—too long of a lens to use on unsteady moving vehicle shots with dialogue. Bumpy footage would be distracting from concentrating on the story. We brought in Will Arnot on Steadicam. This minimized the bumpiness of the roads. Another time, we used Steadicam to make a poor person's crane, as the only crane available to us was unsafe, ancient, and too heavy to move onto location. With the use of the Steadicam, we created a rig where the operator walked down a ladder, creating a crane-like effect.

For the Wet Season, we worked with rather antiquated rain towers. A special effects expert came in from Los Angeles and trained the Vietnamese in placement and operation of the nozzles. There was a learning curve involved in this, and a beauty in collaboration of skills and countries. The Vietnamese and the American crews enjoyed one another.

While our camera package was generously donated to us by Panavision, our lighting package was a bit too small and basic. We were hurting for large units, our biggest unit was a 12K. When units went down, we found ourselves making due with Pars and 10Ks, as it took ten days getting gear back into the country.

In the Growth Season, working on a temple in the middle of a lake brought with it serious lighting limitations due to the distance of the land banks to the temple and the smallness of the units and rigging possibilities.

Other unforeseen challenges had to do with weather. We had postponed production until the end of the rainy season and began shooting with the dry season, but the end of the rainy season was stubborn. For the first week of exteriors, we had bright sun every morning until lunch, then overcast clouds for the remainder of the day. This made matching light with a scene a real struggle and at times forced us into splitting scenes between days.

It was fascinating working in a foreign tongue. As I read the scenes each night before shooting, I could not follow the dialogue literally. As multiple takes progressed, I found myself noticing the changes in the actors and thereby felt the emotion within the scene without knowing the language.

Q: Editors often talk about invisible cuts. Is there such a thing as invisible photography?

A: In film, you have to not just record, but express the mood of the scene and the story. Some of the most beautiful paintings, still photography, and movies speak in a very quiet way. It's not necessarily the loud stripes of light, it is if it's appropriate, but often it's not. So quiet photography is something to work towards. Not to say as a cinematographer, "Look at me, I did this. I can use this type of light or crane or type of smoke," but to serve the emotion of the story. *Trees Lounge* is an actor's vehicle. All emphasis was on the characters. The nuance and subtlety of the acting was in itself powerful. This film was shot in twenty-four days on a low budget. The exercise of understatement in the cinematography, good lighting without fanciness, fit the limitations of the production and created a style for the film.

Q: What films do you consider to be landmarks in cinematography?

A: In American films, *Midnight Cowboy* for its perfect execution of technique, style, form, and content. It's a great story. *Raging Bull* is a favorite. Also, *Dr. Strangelove*, *The Last Picture Show*, *The Misfits*, and of course

Citizen Kane for its immense deep focus and ground-breaking expressive style. *Mean Streets* and *The French Connection* for their urgency and marriage of style and story. *The Godfather, Part I* and *The Godfather, Part II*, *Broadway Danny Rose*, *The Deer Hunter*, and *McCabe and Mrs. Miller* all represent great cinematography and are repeated studies. In European films, I adore *Stroszek* by Werner Herzog. There are some single images, such as the bank repossessing this man's mobile home and leaving his Midwestern plot empty, that are sheer and powerful poetry. *Wings of Desire* and *The American Friend* by Wim Wenders are repeatedly watched favorites. Also, *Time Stands Still* by Hungarian director Peter Gothar.

Q: In what direction do you see your career headed at this point? Do you want to concentrate on features or do you want to continue to shoot documentaries, music videos, and commercials?

A: It's a real goal of mine to continue in features, but I want to be connected to the material. When I first began shooting, I was more interested in stylized cinematography, leaning toward expressionistic rather than realistic. As time has progressed, I have grown more inclined to a naturalistic, heightened realism. The end result may appear less flashy. The goal is always first and foremost to aid in telling the story. I love lighting and shooting. I hope to continue shooting feature films, but I want to feel committed to the subject matter. I want to feel that whatever the story I am part of telling—I stand behind the material and am proud to have my name on it.

Glossary

A camera: Camera shooting the main action in a scene.

anamorphic: Wide-screen format. A camera lens which squeezes the horizontal plane of an image to approximately half size so it can fit into the width of 35mm film. A deanamorphizing projection lens restores the image to full size.

animatic: An animation technique, whereby a storyboard or drawings are shot and edited to be used as a reference guide in the work print for special-effect sequences that are not yet filmed.

answer print: A sound and picture composite print struck off the cut negative with track used to judge timing and color. When the final answer print is approved, an internegative is made from which release prints are made.

arc light: High intensity lighting instrument which employs two burning carbon rods. A standard Hollywood lighting source during the classic studio era. *HMI* lights have largely replaced them.

Arriflex: Brand name of German manufactured motion picture cameras widely used in film production. Also known as *Arri*.

ASA: A numerical rating system determined by the American Standards Association given to the speed of motion picture stock which relates to light sensitivity. Also known as *EI*, for exposure index.

ASC: American Society of Cinematographers. Honorary society for cinematographers located in Hollywood. Membership is by invitation only. The society maintains a clubhouse, publishes *American Cinematographer* magazine, hosts a website and educational services.

aspect ratio: A measurement of the camera film frame or the projected image, stated as ratio of horizontal to vertical. A 1.85:1 (normal *wide-screen*) and 2.35:1 (*anamorphic*) are the most common ratios.

available light: Natural light available when shooting. Can be daylight, night street light, or fluorescents or the existing lights on location.

B camera: Camera shooting main action from additional or complementary angle to the *A camera*.

back light: Light coming from behind a subject and directed towards camera lens.

base: Shiny side of the film which is opposite the *emulsion* side.

bead board: A kind of reflective board used to bounce light on a set.

camera operator: The person who physically operates the camera during a shot under the supervision of the *director of photography*. Also called the *gaffer*.

changing bag: Light-proof bag used to load the camera *magazines*.

chief lighting technician: Person in charge of setting the lighting instruments on the set under the supervision of the *director of photography*.

clapper: Also called *slate*. Board with a hinged stick clapped by hand onto the base so that later the picture and sound can be synchronized. The clapper contains written information concerning the scene, take numbers, filtration, exposure, etc.

close-up: Tight shot which focuses on specific information.

composition: Art of designing and positioning the subject being photographed into the film frame.

computer-generated imagery: Also known as *CGI*. Images created directly on a computer, often combined with live action photography.

coverage: Additional camera angles which complement a *master shot* of a scene.

crane: Device used to raise the camera and operator high above a scene while shooting. The movement of a camera crane is similar to a cherry picker. Many current cranes are operated remotely, from video console.

cutters: Pieces of hard black material of various shapes held by hand or on Century stands to block or control light on the set.

dailies: Processed film direct from the lab which contains all of the material shot and printed on the preceding day. Also called *rushes*.

desaturation: Process employed either before, during, or after shooting which drains some color out of the image.

diffusion: Plastic or paper material placed on lights to soften the light source.

diffusion filters: Glass or plastic materials placed on the lens to lower contrast and soften the image.

director of photography: Also known as *dp*. Person responsible for the photography of a film. The director of photography is in charge of the camera crew and utilizes cameras, lights, and technical equipment to interpret and realize the screenplay on film.

dolly: Freewheeling camera cart used to move the camera and operator during a shot. The dolly is operated by the *dolly grip*.

dupe: Copy made from a positive print. A *dupe* negative is a copy made from another negative.

emulsion: Dull side of the film stock where the photo chemicals are layered.

exposure: The act of light being focused to the emulsion of the film stock.

exteriors: Outdoor locations.

eyeline: Direction in which a character is looking.

fill light: Light added to the *key light* of a scene to fill in shadows or highlight an area.

filters: A treated transparent piece of glass or gelatin put over the lens to reduce light, control color, or create optical effects.

fine grain: A film stock which produces a sharp image with a small and tight grain pattern.

first assistant cameraman: Works directly under the *director of photography*. Maintains the camera and follows focus. Known as *focus puller* in British system.

flicker: Repetitive pattern of light and dark produced on a screen by the projector. Not seen by the naked eye because of persistence of vision.

focus: The process of turning the lens ring until the image is clear and sharp.

footcandle: A measurement of the intensity of light. One footcandle is the intensity of the incident brightness of a surface one foot in radius from the source of one standard candle.

format: Size and dimensions of the film frame.

gaffer: Person on the set responsible for electrical work. Reports directly to the *director of photography*.

graduates: Neutral density filters graded from top to bottom to control exposure in specific areas, such as the sky. Called *graders* in British system.

grip: Person who works with and under the supervision of the *director of photography* and the *gaffer* to control, cut, and modulate the light. Grips also construct camera platforms and rigs and pull set walls.

handheld: Technique where the camera is held and operated by the operator without a tripod or dolly.

HMI: Stands for hydrargyrum (mercury), medium arc length, and iodide. Lighting instruments color balanced for daylight.

IATSE: International Alliance of Theatrical and Stage Employees. Union which includes cameraman, editing, sound, and production design guilds.

interiors: Scenes shot inside a studio or location.

interlock: When a separate picture and track are projected together in sync.

Kelvin: A scale for measuring color temperature of a light source.

key light: The main light used to illuminate a shot, the nominal source.

keystone: A distortion of an image caused by a camera or projection lens not being at a right angle to what it is photographing or the intended surface. The image then appears in the shape of a keystone.

lens: Optical device made of glass which collects light. Lenses are manufactured in various focal lengths and, when attached to the camera, they carry the image to the film's emulsion.

letterbox: Process which allows a wide-screen film to be presented on videotape in its original *format*. When a videotape is letterboxed, black bars appear on the top and bottom of the image.

loader: Person who loads the film into the camera magazine, often the *second assistant cameraman*.

lo-mode: An extremely low camera angle. The camera is shooting from very close to ground level, usually from a *Steadicam*.

low con: Low contrast filter.

magazine: Casing which houses film stock as it moves through the camera. Also called *mag*.

master shot: Full shot which contains all of the action in a scene.

multiple cameras: Two or more cameras positioned in contrasting or complementary angles to simultaneously photograph a scene.

negative space: Parts of a composition, usually black or neutral in color, adjacent to the principal element of a shot.

net: A netting material placed over the lens to soften or diffuse a shot. Tulle or women's stockings are used frequently.

original negative: The camera negative exposed during the shooting of a film used to make *dupe* negatives and positive prints.

overexposure: More than normal amount of light strikes the film emulsion, causing an overbright image. Overexposure can be utilized as a creative tool to produce hot, desaturated images for aesthetic, atmospheric, or psychological purposes.

pan: Horizontal camera movement, right to left or left to right, from a fixed camera position.

pan and scan: Electronic process applied to a *wide-screen* film transferred to video, so the entire image can be presented in what simulates a camera pan or in a readjusted composition.

Panavision: Popular brand of movie camera which employs both a spherical and *anamorphic* lens system.

Par light: A powerful directional lighting unit on which various lenses can be put on sealed beams, such as car headlights.

practical light: Light emanating from a working fixture on-set, such as a table, ceiling, or floor lamp seen on-camera.

principal photography: The main body of the film photographed during the production process. Does not include reshoots, special-effect shots, or other photographic elements which are produced and added during the postproduction of a film.

rack focus: When the point of camera focus is deliberately shifted from one person or object to another. Used as a storytelling device to direct the viewers' attention.

reflectors: Silvered, reflective material used to bounce or control light.

registration: The placement of each frame in exactly the same position at the film plane to maintain steadiness of the image.

saturation: The degree of density or purity of color.

second assistant cameraman: Person who works under direct supervision of the *director of photography*. Responsibilities include keeping camera reports and operating the *clapper*. Known as *clapper boy* in British system.

slate: See *clapper*.

sprockets: Small, mechanically produced holes on the edge of film used to transport it through the camera, editing equipment, and projector.

Steadicam: Stabilizing camera device invented by Garrett Brown which allows the camera to move smoothly and freely in any direction, simulating dolly or crane moves.

Technicolor: Color process developed by the Technicolor company in 1915. Later, a three-strip process, the color standard from the late thirties to early fifties. Also, a laboratory of the same name.

telephoto lens: A lens of a long focal length which compresses perspective.

time-lapse photography: Frame-by-frame exposure of film in the camera over a period of time to present an action (such as the opening of a flower, or the rise or setting of the sun) in a few seconds of screen time.

underexposure: When insufficient light strikes the film emulsion, causing a darkened image. Underexposure can be utilized as a creative tool to produce moody and dark images for aesthetic, atmospheric, or psychological purposes.

VistaVision: A 35mm *wide-screen* process developed by Paramount in the 1950s. It was unique in that the film traveled horizontally through the camera because the frame is larger than conventional 35mm. The format is still often utilized for special-effect compositing.

wide-screen: Any film format where the image is more rectangular than the standard Academy ratio of 1.33:1.

zoom lens: A lens which produces a range of focal lengths giving the ability to move from far to close or close to far within a shot, or to offer an array of frame sizes without moving the camera. Sometimes called a *varifocal lens*.

Bibliography

PERIODICALS

American Cinematographer. Magazine published by the American Society of
    Cinematographers (ASC), dedicated to the art and craft of cinematogra-
    phy and filmmaking: 1782 N. Orange Dr., Hollywood, California 90028.
    From the 1960s to present, this publication has covered all of the cine-
    matographers interviewed in *Principal Photography* (and countless oth-
    ers) in articles pertaining to films they have photographed.

International Photographer Film and Video Techniques Magazine. Published by
    the International Photographers Guild Local 600 IATSE: 7715 Sunset
    Boulevard, Suite 300, Hollywood, California 90046. This publication
    presents articles on cinematographers and their work. The careers of
    those interviewed in *Principal Photography* have been covered through-
    out the magazine's history.

Operating Cameraman, The. Magazine published by the Society of Operating
    Cameramen (SOC), dedicated to the art and contributions of the camera
    operator and the field of film and video photography: P.O. Box 2006,
    Toluca Lake, California 91610.

Steadicam Letter. A publication of the Steadicam Operators Association: 780
    Parkway, Broomall, Pennsylvania 19008.

BOOKS

Filmographies

Each of the following books covers a variety of cinematographers and time
periods.

Brenner, Debbie, and Gary Hill. *Credits*. Vol. 1 compiled by film title, vol. 2 by production category, vol. 3 by individual. Wallington, NJ: Magpie Press, 1985.

Film Review. New York: St. Martin's Press (published annually).

Monaco, James. *Who's Who in American Film Now*. New York: New York Zoetrope, 1981. Updated Edition, 1988.

Stockly, Ed. *Cinematographers, Production Designers, Costume Designers, and Film Editors Guide*. Fifth Edition. Beverly Hills, CA: Lone Eagle, 1996.

Technical

Alton, John. *Painting with Light*. Berkeley, Los Angeles, London: University of California Press, 1995.

Belton, John. *Widescreen Cinema*. Cambridge, MA, London: Harvard University Press, 1992.

Box, Harry C. *Set Lighting Technician's Handbook: Film Lighting Equipment, Practice, and Electrial Distribution*. Second Edition. Boston: Focal Press 1997.

Carlson, Verne, and Sylvia Carlson. *Professional 16/35mm Cameraman's Handbook*. New York: Amphoto, 1981.

Clarke, Charles G. *Professional Cinematography*. Hollywood, CA: American Society of Cinematographers (ASC), 1962. Second Edition, 1968.

Cox, Arthur. *Photographic Optics*. New York: Focal Press, 1971.

Elkins, David E. *The Camera Assistant's Manual*. Boston, London: Focal Press, 1991.

Fielding, Raymond. *A Technological History of Motion Pictures and Television*. Berkeley, Los Angeles, London: University of California Press, 1967.

Hart, Douglas C. *The Camera Assistant*. Boston: Focal Press, 1996.

Hines, William E. *Operating Cinematography*. Hollywood, CA: Ed Venture Films/Books, 1997.

Katz, Steven D. *Film Directing Shot by Shot*. Studio City, CA: Michael Wiese Productions in conjunction with Focal Press, 1991.

Lipton, Lenny. *Independent Filmmaking*. San Francisco: Straight Arrow Books, 1972.

Lowell, Ross. *Matters of Light & Depth*. Philadelphia: Broad Street Books Publishing, 1992. Second Edition, 1994.

Malkiewicz, Kris. *Cinematography*. Second Edition. New York: Prentice Hall Press, 1989.

———. *Film Lighting*. New York: Prentice Hall, 1986.

Neale, Steve. *Cinema and Technology: Image, Sound, Colour*. Bloomington: Indiana University Press, 1985.

Pincus, Edward. *Guide to Filmmaking*. New York: New American Library, 1969.

Rabiger, Michael. *Directing: Film Techniques and Aesthetics*. London: Focal Press, 1989.

————. *Directing the Documentary*. London: Focal Press, 1987.

Roberts, Kenneth H., and Win Sharples, Jr. *A Primer for Filmmaking*. New York: Bobbs-Merrill, 1971.

Ryan, Dr. Rod, ed. *American Cinematographer Manual*. Seventh Edition. Hollywood: The ASC Press, 1993.

Samuelson, David W. *Panaflex User's Manual*. Boston, London: Focal Press, 1990.

Schmidt, Rick. *'Hands-On' Manual for Cinematographers*. Oxford: Focal Press, 1994.

————. *Feature Filmmaking at Used-Car Prices*. Revised Edition. New York: Penguin Books. 1995.

Uva, Michael G., and Sabina Uva. *The Grip Book*, Boston, Oxford: Focal Press, 1997.

Wheeler, Leslie J. *Principles of Cinematography*. London: Fountain Press, 1971.

Wilson, Anton. *Anton Wilson's Cinema Workshop*. Second Edition. Hollywood: American Society of Cinematographers, 1997.

Wysotsky, Michael Z. *Wide Screen Processes and Stereophonic Sound*. New York: Hastings House, 1971.

Theory

Barthes, Roland. *Camera Lucida: Reflections on Photography*. New York: Hill and Wang, 1981.

Brakhage, Stan. *A Moving Picture Giving and Taking Book*. West Newbury, MA: Frontier Press, 1971.

Bresson, Robert. *Notes on Cinematography*. New York: Urizen Books, 1977.

Frampton, Hollis. *Circles of Confusion: Film, Photography, Video: Texts 1968–1980*. New York: Visual Studies Workshop Press, 1983.

Sontag, Susan. *On Photography*. New York: Farrar, Straus, and Giroux, 1977.

Reference

Almendros, Nestor. *A Man with a Camera*. New York: Farrar, Straus and Giroux, 1984.

Bitzer, Billy. *Billy Bitzer: His Story*. New York: Farrar, Straus and Giroux, 1973.

Boorstin, Jon. *The Hollywood Style: What Makes Movies Work*. New York: Cornelia & Michael Bessie Books, an imprint of HarperCollins Publishers, 1990.

Bordwell, David, Janet Staiger, and Kristin Thompson. *The Classical Hollywood Cinema*. New York: Columbia University Press, 1985.

Brouwer, Alexandra, and Thomas Lee Wright. *Working in Hollywood*. New York: Crown Publishing, 1990. Contains interviews with Key Grip Tom Ramsey, Gaffer Steve Mathis, Director of Photography Laszlo Kovacs, and Camera Operator Walt Lloyd.

Brownlow, Kevin. *The Parade's Gone By* . . . New York: Alfred A. Knopf, 1968.

Cardiff, Jack. *Magic Hour*. London, Boston: Faber and Faber, 1996.

Carringer, Robert L. *The Making of Citizen Kane*. Berkeley, Los Angeles, London: University of California Press, 1985.

Chell, David. *Moviemakers at Work*. Redmond, WA: Microsoft Press, 1987. Contains interviews with Cinematographers Allen Daviau and Chris Menges.

Eyman, Scott. *Five American Cinematographers: Interviews with Karl Struss, Joseph Ruttenberg, James Wong Howe, Linwood Dunn, and William H. Clothier*. Metuchen, NJ, London: The Scarecrow Press, 1987.

Gallagher, John Andrew. *Film Directors on Directing*. New York, Westport, CT, London: Praeger, 1989.

Higham, Charles. *Hollywood Cameramen: Sources of Light*. Bloomington, London: Indiana University Press, 1970.

Higham, Charles, and Joel Greenberg. *The Celluloid Muse: Hollywood Directors Speak*. Chicago: Henry Regnery Company, 1969.

Knight, Arthur. *The Liveliest Art*. New York: Mentor Books, 1957.

Krasilovsky, Alexis. *Women Behind the Camera: Conversations with Camerawomen*. Westport, CT: Greenwood Publishing Group, 1997.

Laskin, Emily, ed. *Getting Started in Film*. New York: Prentice Hall, 1992. Contains interviews with Cinematographers Haskell Wexler, Caleb Deschanel, and Allen Daviau.

Lassally, Walter. *Itinerant Cameraman*. London: John Murray, 1987.

Lewis, Jerry. *The Total Film-Maker*. New York: Warner Paperback Library, 1973.

LoBrutto, Vincent. *Stanley Kubrick: A Biography*. New York: Donald I. Fine Books, 1997.

——— . *By Design: Interviews with Film Production Designers*. Westport, CT, London: Praeger, 1992.

Madsen, Roy Paul. *Working Cinema*. Belmont, CA: Wadsworth Publishing Company, 1990. Contains section on cinematography with Vilmos Zsigmond.

Maltin, Leonard. *Behind the Camera: The Cinematographer's Art*. New York: New American Library, 1971. Contains interviews with Hal Mohr, Conrad Hall, Hal Rosson, Lucien Ballard, and Arthur C. Miller.

McDonough, Tom. *Light Years: Confessions of a Cinematographer*. New York: Grove Press, 1987.

Miller, Pat P. *Script Supervising and Film Continuity*. Boston, London: Focal Press, 1986.

Oumano, Ellen. *Film Forum*. New York: St. Martin's Press, 1985. Contains section with film directors discussing cinematography.

Rainsberger, Todd. *James Wong Howe: Cinematographer*. San Diego, CA, New York: A. S. Barnes & Company, Inc. London: The Tantivy Press, 1981.

Rebello, Stephen. *Alfred Hitchcock and the Making of Psycho*. New York: Dembner Books, 1990.

Rogers, Pauline. *Contemporary Cinematographers on Their Art*. Boston, London: Focal Press, 1998.

Russo, John. *Making Movies: The Inside Guide to Independent Movie Production*. New York: Dell Publishing, 1989.

Samuels, Charles Thomas. *Encountering Directors*. New York: G. P Putnam's Sons, 1972.

Sayles, John. *Thinking in Pictures—The Making of the Movie* Matewan. Boston: Houghton Mifflin Company, 1987.

Schaefer, Dennis, and Larry Salvato. *Masters of Light: Conversations with Contemporary Cinematographers*. Berkeley, Los Angeles, London: University of California Press, 1984.

Sherman, Eric, for the American Film Institute. *Directing the Film*. Boston: Little, Brown and Company, 1976. Los Angeles: Acrobat Books, 1988.

Sterling, Anna Kate, ed. *Cinematographers on the Art and Craft of Cinematography*. Metuchen, NJ, London: The Scarecrow Press, Inc., 1987.

Taub, Eric. *Gaffers, Grips, and Best Boys*. New York: St. Martin's Press, 1987. Contains section on director of photography with Haskell Wexler and gaffer, grip, electrician, best boy, and rigger with Gary Holt.

Truffaut, Francois, with the collaboration of Helen G. Scott. *Hitchcock*. New York: Simon and Schuster, 1967. Revised Edition, 1985, Touchstone/Simon & Schuster. Second Touchstone Edition, 1997.

Vidor, King. *King Vidor On Film Making*. New York: David McKay Company, Inc., 1972.

Walker, Joseph, and Juanita Walker. *The Light On Her Face*. Hollywood: ASC Press, 1984.

Wiley, Mason, and Damien Bona. *Inside Oscar*. Tenth Anniversary Edition. New York: Ballantine Books, 1996. Contains nominations and winners of the Academy Award for cinematography from 1927 to 1994.

FILMS ON CINEMATOGRAPHY

Visions of Light: The Art of Cinematography. An American Film Institute/NHK Jan Broadcasting coproduction, 1992. Contains interviews with John Bailey, Michael Ballhaus, Allen Daviau, Conrad Hall, Lisa Rinzler, Sandi Sissel, Gordon Willis, and many other cinematographers.

For further interest, there are many instructional videos on cinematography featuring noted cinematographers, as well as a myriad array of Web sites concerning cinematography and filmmaking too numerous to list here. The reader is encouraged to read, search, and browse.

Index

About the Author

VINCENT LoBRUTTO is the author of *Selected Takes: Film Editors On Editing* (Praeger, 1991), *By Design: Interviews With Film Production Designers* (Praeger, 1992) and *Sound-On-Film: Interviews With Creators Of Film Sound* (Praeger, 1994). He has a bachelor of fine arts in filmmaking from the School of Visual Arts and has worked as a postproduction coordinator for the ABC television network and as a film editor for the Fox and HBO networks. Vincent LoBrutto is an editing and production design instructor for the School of Visual Arts Department of Film, Video and Animation where he is a thesis advisor and member of the thesis committee. LoBrutto is also the author of *Stanley Kubrick: A Biography* (Donald I. Fine, 1997). He is a contributing writer for *American Cinematographer* and *Films In Review* and has appeared on *Entertainment Tonight* and National Public Radio's *All Things Considered*.